☆ do not Bend ☆

LOS ANGELES / HOLLYWOOD CA
9 A
900
14 NOV
2005

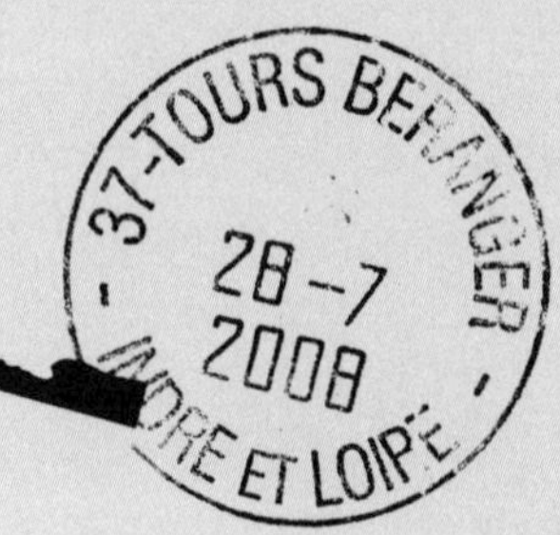
37-TOURS BERANGER
28-7
2008

PHILADELPHIA, PA 191
5

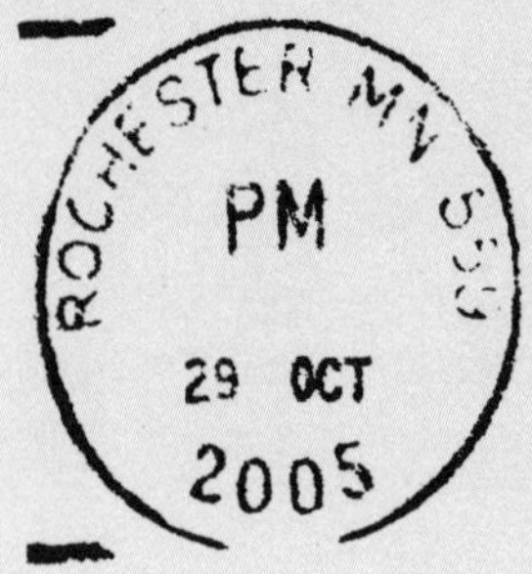
ROCHESTER MN 559
PM
29 OCT
2005

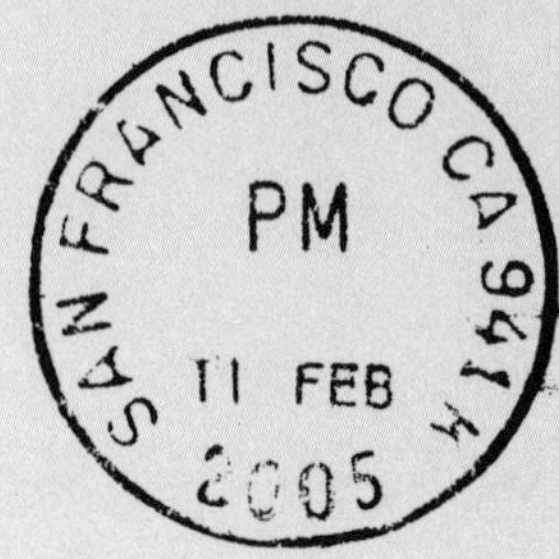
SAN FRANCISCO CA 941
PM
11 FEB
2005

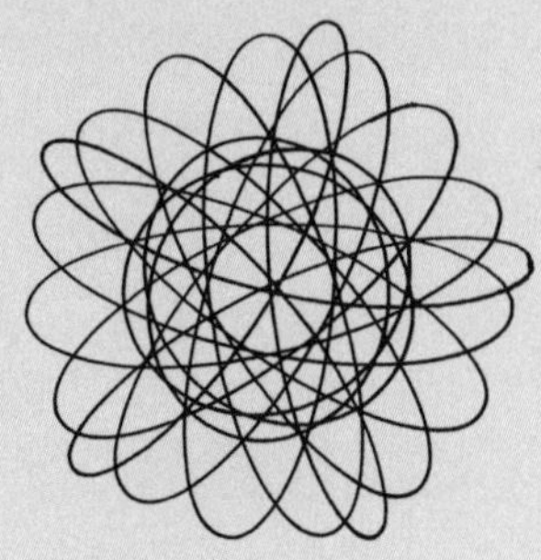

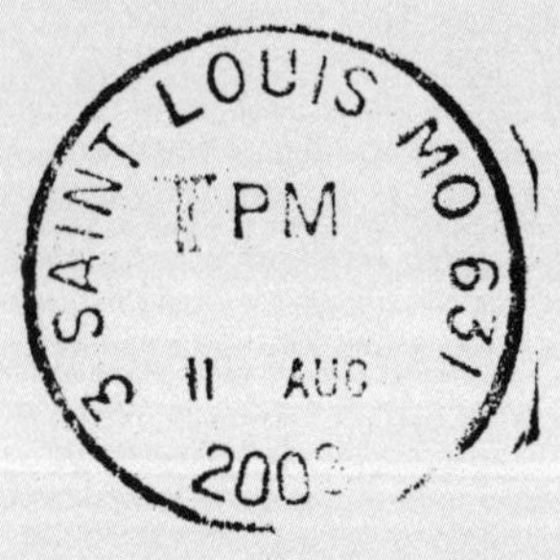
SAINT LOUIS MO 631
PM
11 AUG

BROOKLYN P&DC 11256
PM
28 JUN
2004

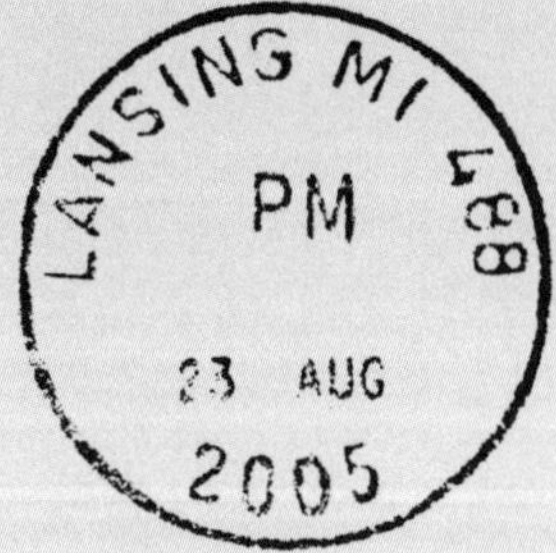
LANSING MI 488
PM
23 AUG
2005

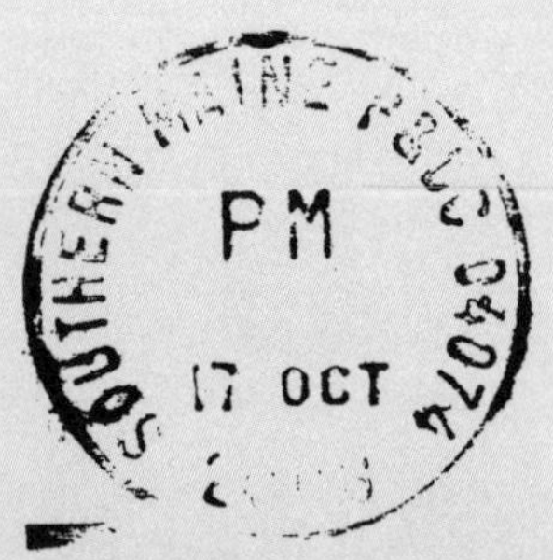
SOUTHERN MAINE P&DC 04074
PM
17 OCT

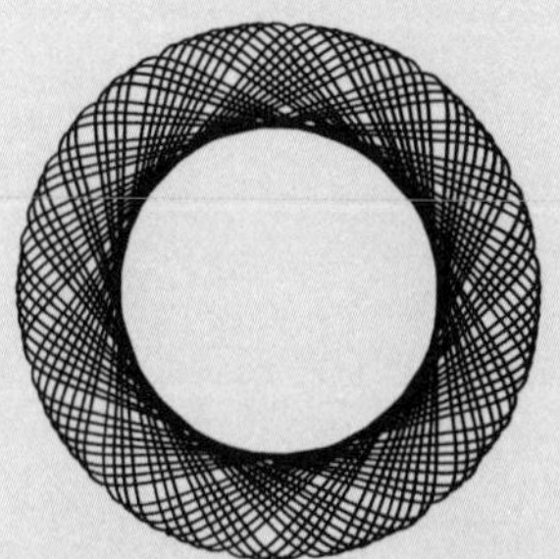

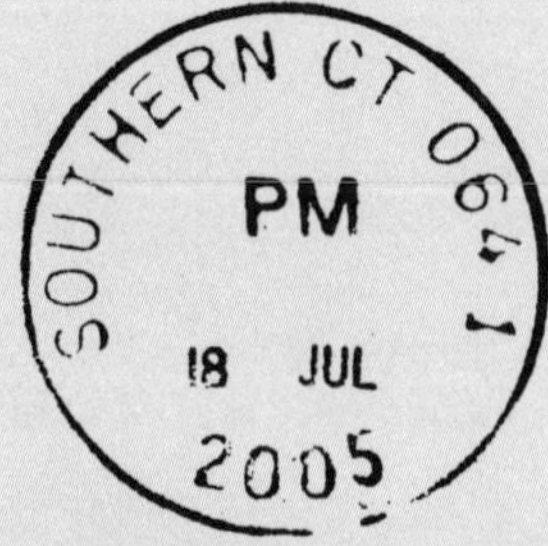
SOUTHERN CT 064
PM
18 JUL
2005

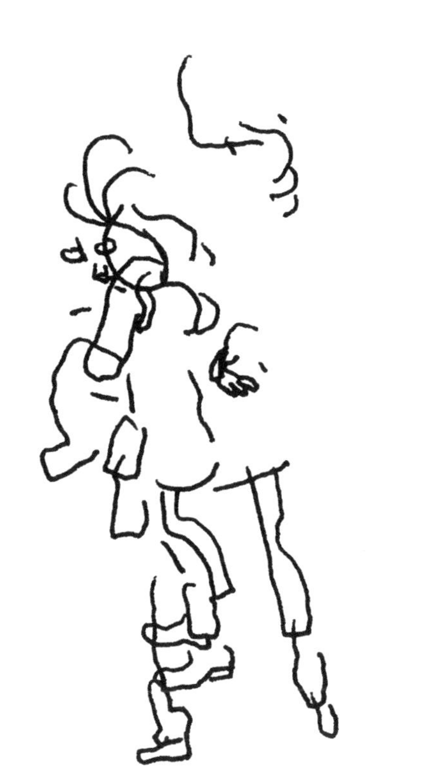

WOMAN
AT POST
OFFICE
ON CANAL
2·18·2017

Jason Polan: The Post Office
Edited and designed by Jason Fulford
Published by Printed Matter, Inc., 2025

First edition of 4000 copies
ISBN: 978-0-89439-103-3

Printed by Narayana Press, Denmark
Paper: 120g Munken Kristall Rough and 290g Custom Kote
Typeset in Trade Gothic

For information about trade distribution for this title please visit D.A.P. / Distributed Art Publishers

Printed Matter, Inc.

Printed Matter
231 11th Avenue
New York, NY 10001
printedmatter.org

Printed Matter, Inc. is an independent 501(c)(3) non-profit organization founded in 1976 by artists and art workers with the mission to foster the distribution, understanding and appreciation of artists' books and related artists' publications.

JASON POLAN

THE POST OFFICE

Edited by Jason Fulford

Printed Matter, Inc.

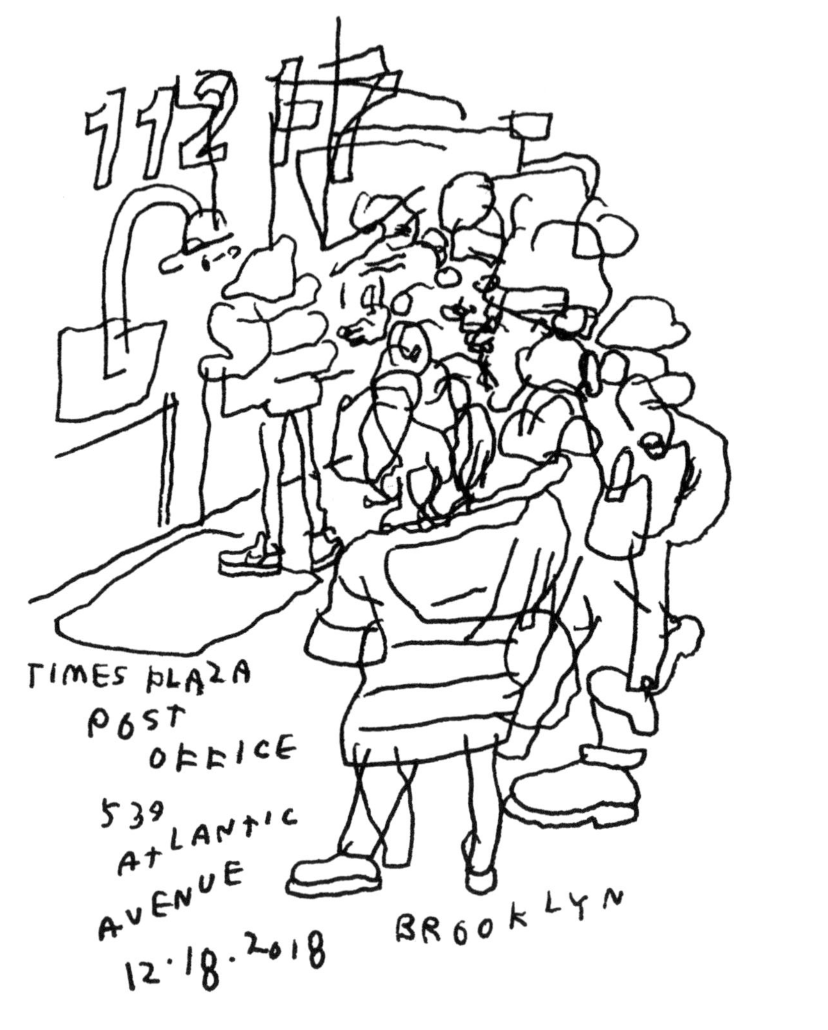
TIMES PLAZA
POST
OFFICE
539
ATLANTIC
AVENUE
BROOKLYN
12.18.2018

CONTENTS of this book include:

* deep cuts w/ Celebs
pp. 89-112

ADVERTISEMENT

DOESN'T IT FEEL NICE
TO WRITE SOMEONE A LETTER?
DOESN'T IT FEEL NICE TO
RECEIVE A LETTER FROM SOMEONE?
THIS IS AN ADVERTISEMENT BY ME
FOR THE POST OFFICE.

Dear Jason (P),

I remember the first thing you sent me in the mail. It was a drawing you'd made on an old junk store photograph. I replied to the return address, and that was the beginning of our friendship.

I wonder how many people you met this way?

Alongside your routine activities - wandering the streets of New York (sometimes Tokyo), book-store browsing, going to art openings & lectures, organizing group drawing sessions at Taco Bell, writing in wet cement, eating w/ friends, enjoying the serendipity of everything in person - you also had a robust mail correspondence in the background. You reached out to living artists you admired. You mailed drawings to people you met on social media. You got a P.O. Box address downtown and published it so that strangers from around the world could write to you. And you even created a bootleg ad for the post office & paid to run it in The New Yorker.

Your mom told me that you'd send boxes of mail back to Michigan when your NYC apartment filled up. I went to Ann Arbor to see for myself. It was the same weekend as the annual "World's Longest Yard Sale" (Alabama to Michigan), so I made it a road trip, driving up through the Midwest. When I got to the storage unit, your friends had already organized everything. There were boxes of drawings, newspaper clippings, books (including an entire box of Catcher in the Rye, various editions), artworks by your friends, and more... But I was drawn to the correspondence. I love the post office too, and this collection of printed matter seemed like a kind of portrait of you as well as a manifesto for finding happiness in the small details of life.

Curious about what else you sent out in the mail, we started asking around. You might be happy to know that a lot of your friends have a "Jason Polan box" somewhere in their house, full of your drawings, letters, notes, and ephemera.

So, here is a book about it all. I hope that by sharing this with people, it will serve as an inspiration - an encouragement, like your ad, to connect w/ others through the exchange of paper.

Your friend,

Jason (F)

JASON FULFORD

P.S. - I've made a selection of your correspondence, arranged more like an art book than an academic study. The BLUE paper has mail that you RECEIVED. The OFF-WHITE has mail that you SENT.

Dear Jason,

DEAR JASON,

Dear Jason.

Dear Jason,

Dear Jason,

Dear Jason,

Dear Jason,

Dear jason,

TO= mr Jason

Dear Jason

Dear Jason,

Dear Jason,

Dear Jason,

Dear Jason –

Dear Jason,

dear jason!

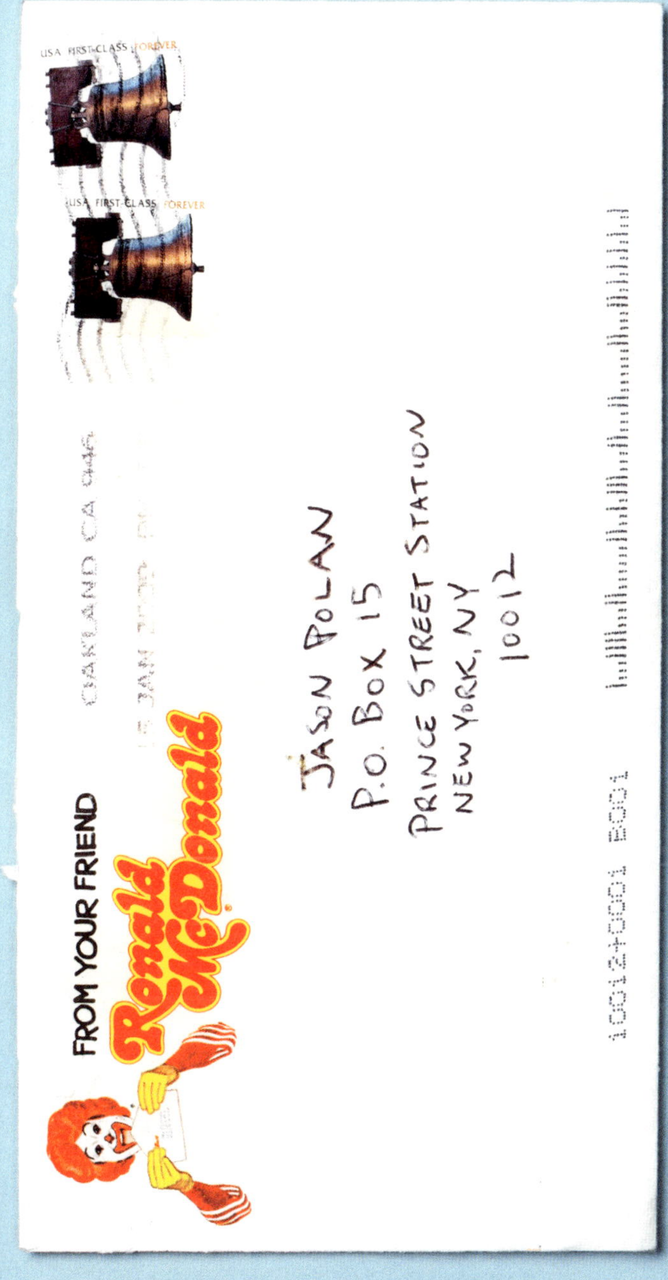
USA FIRST-CLASS FOREVER
USA FIRST-CLASS FOREVER
OAKLAND CA
FROM YOUR FRIEND
Ronald McDonald
JASON POLAN
P.O. BOX 15
PRINCE STREET STATION
NEW YORK, NY
10012

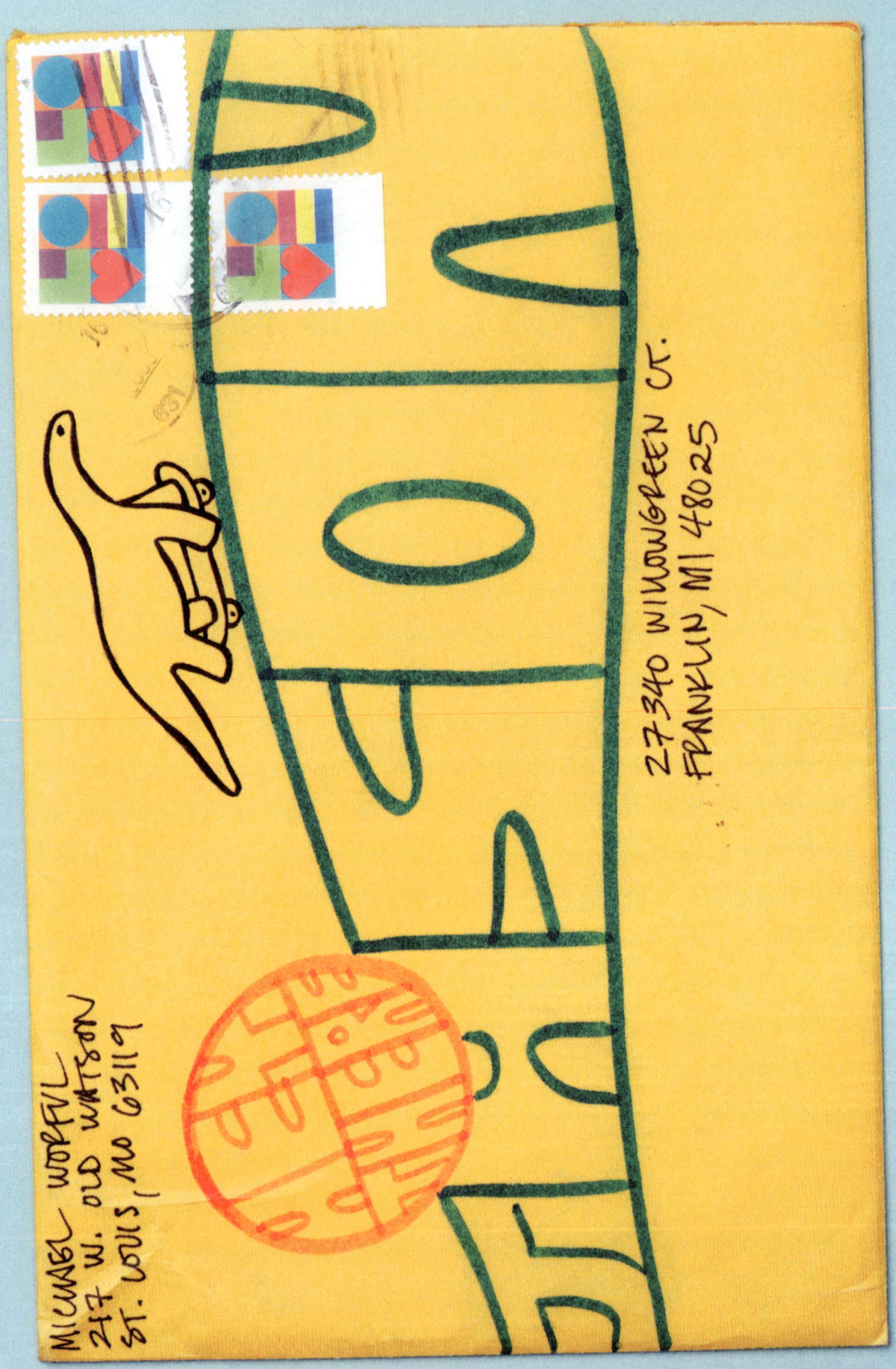

14 • Michael Worful to JP

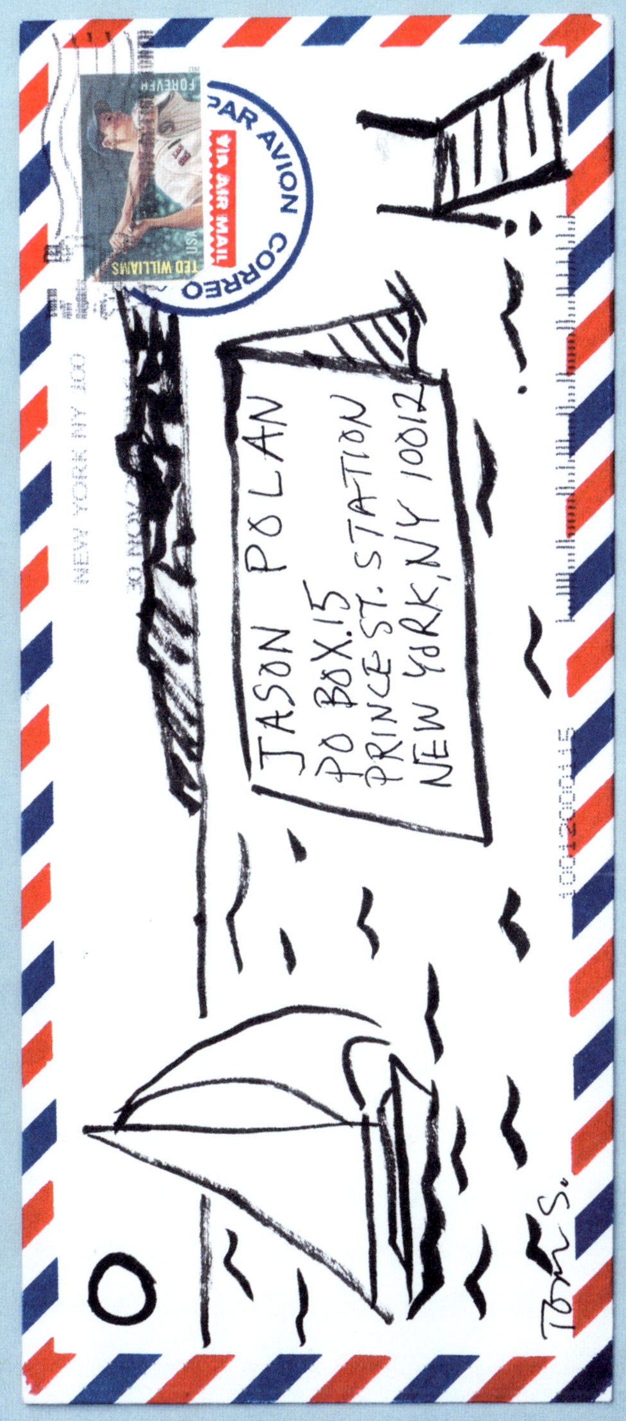

PAR AVION
VIA AIR MAIL
CORREO
TED WILLIAMS
USA
FOREVER
NEW YORK NY 100
30 NOV
JASON POLAN
PO BOX.15
PRINCE ST. STATION
NEW YORK, NY 10012
Tom S.

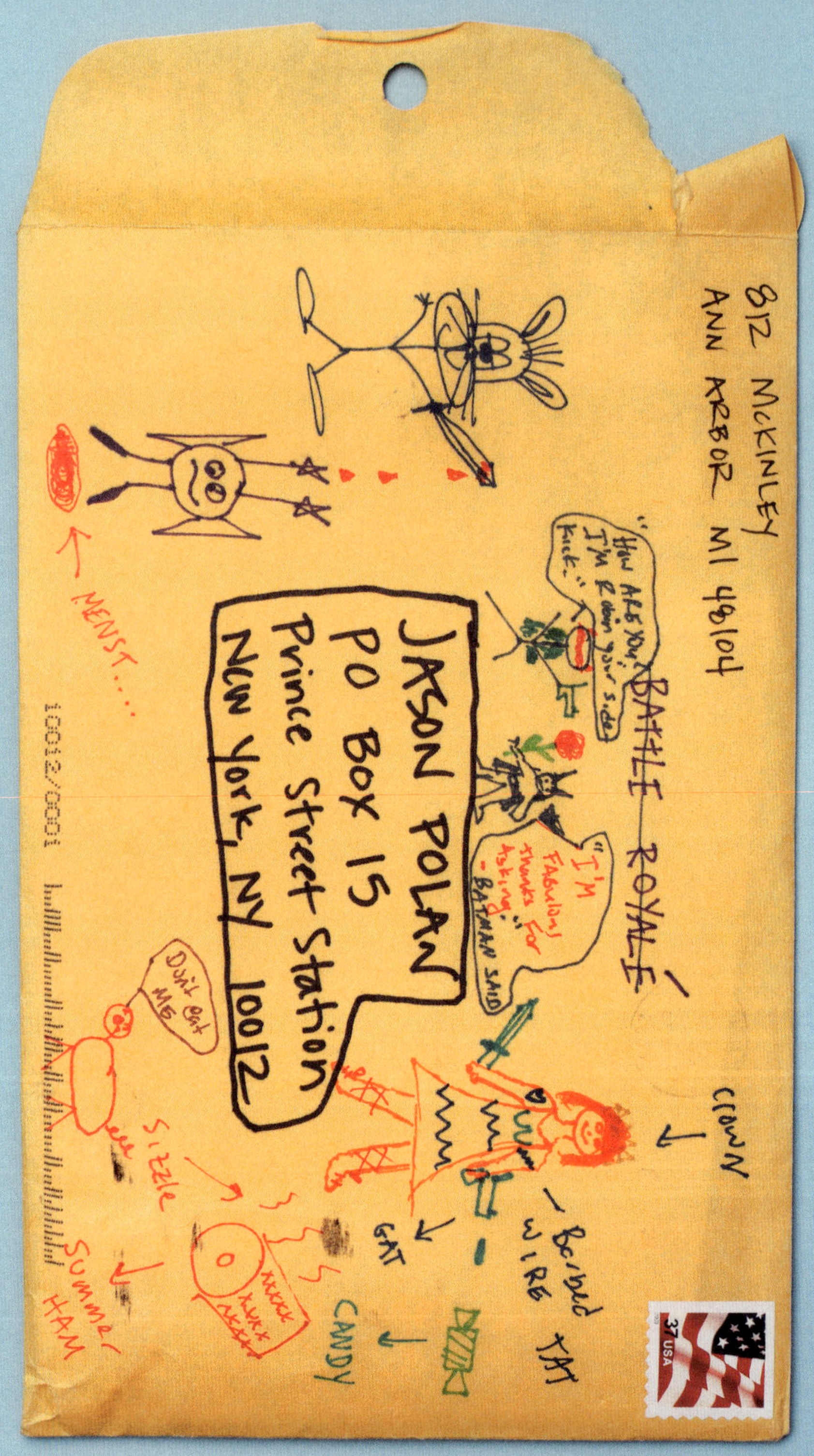

812 McKINLEY
ANN ARBOR MI 48104
JASON POLAN
PO BOX 15
Prince Street Station
New York, NY 10012
BATTLE ROYALE
CROWN
Barbed WIRE TAT
GAT
CANDY
sizzle
Summer HAM
MENST....
Don't eat ME
10012/0001

JASON POLAN
P.O. BOX 15
PRINCE STREET STATION
NEW YORK. NY
10012
NANCY FORD
1663 N. FRANCISCO AVENUE
#1F
CHICAGO. IL 60647
FRAGILE
DO NOT BEND OR FOLD
USPS TRACKING NUMBER
9534 6110 6443 4335 4107 45
U.S. POSTAGE
PAID
$9.92

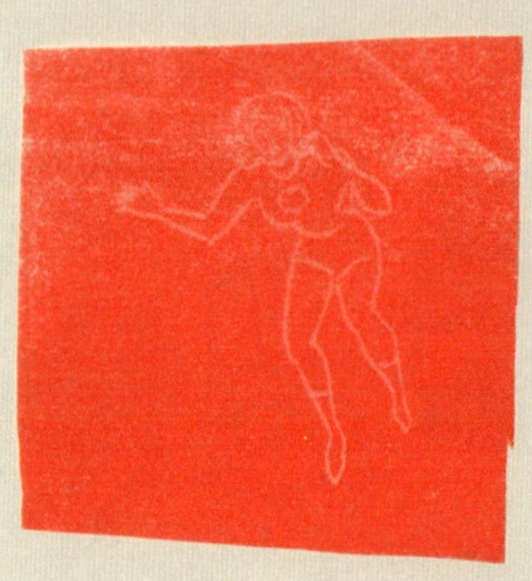

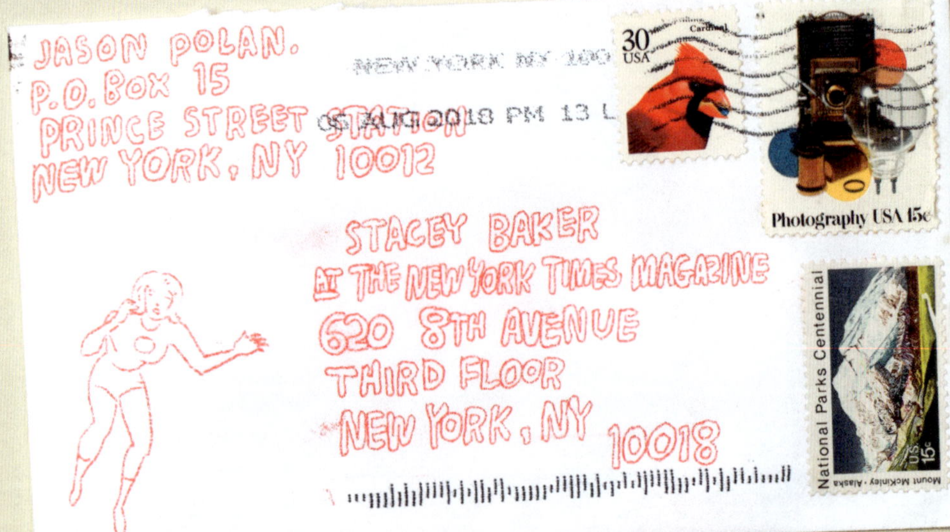
JASON POLAN.
P.O. Box 15
PRINCE STREET STATION
NEW YORK, NY 10012
NEW YORK NY 100
30 USA
Cardinal
Photography USA 15c
National Parks Centennial
Mount McKinley · Alaska
US 15c
STACEY BAKER
AT THE NEW YORK TIMES MAGAZINE
620 8TH AVENUE
THIRD FLOOR
NEW YORK, NY 10018

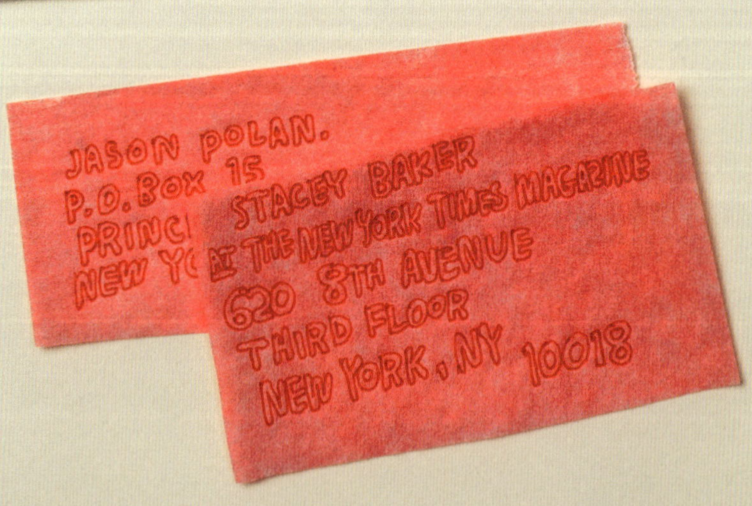
JASON POLAN.
P.O. Box 15
PRINC
NEW Y
STACEY BAKER
AT THE NEW YORK TIMES MAGAZINE
620 8TH AVENUE
THIRD FLOOR
NEW YORK, NY 10018

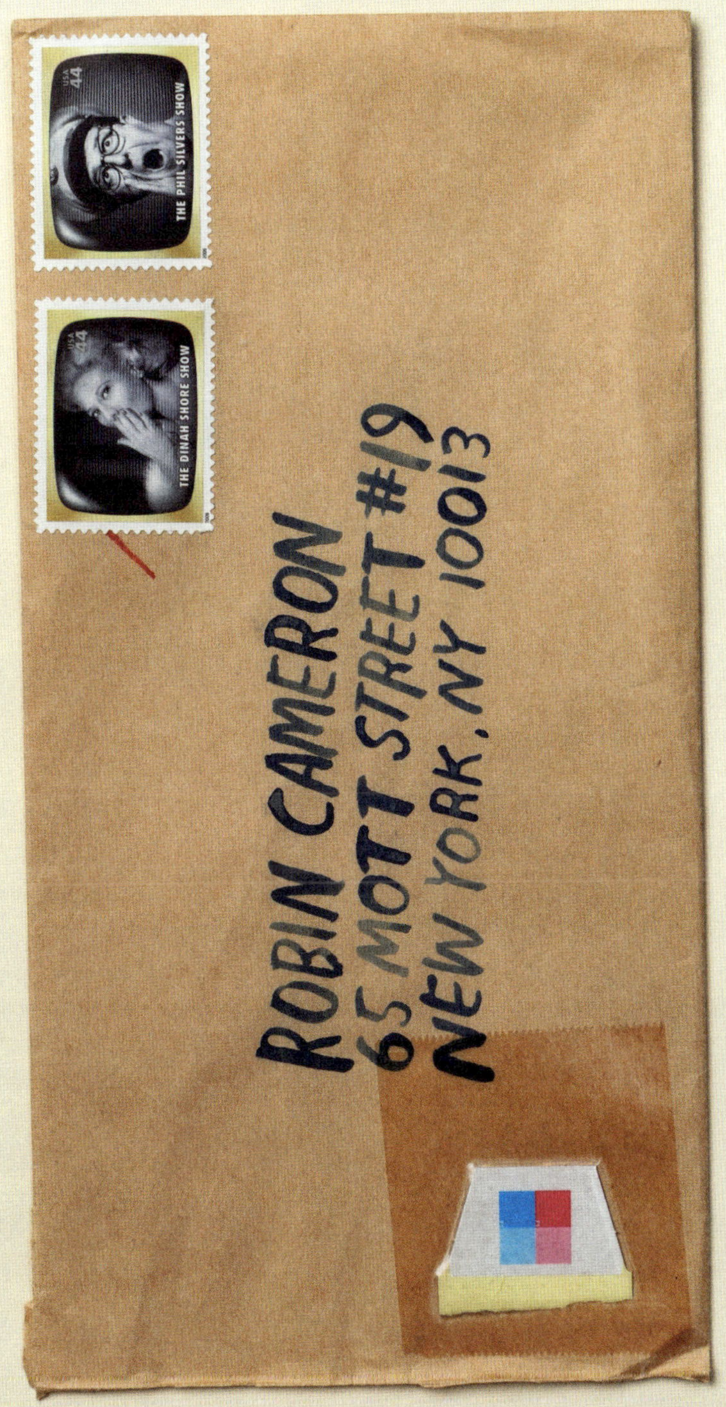
USA 44
THE PHIL SILVERS SHOW
USA 44
THE DINAH SHORE SHOW
ROBIN CAMERON
65 MOTT STREET #19
NEW YORK, NY 10013

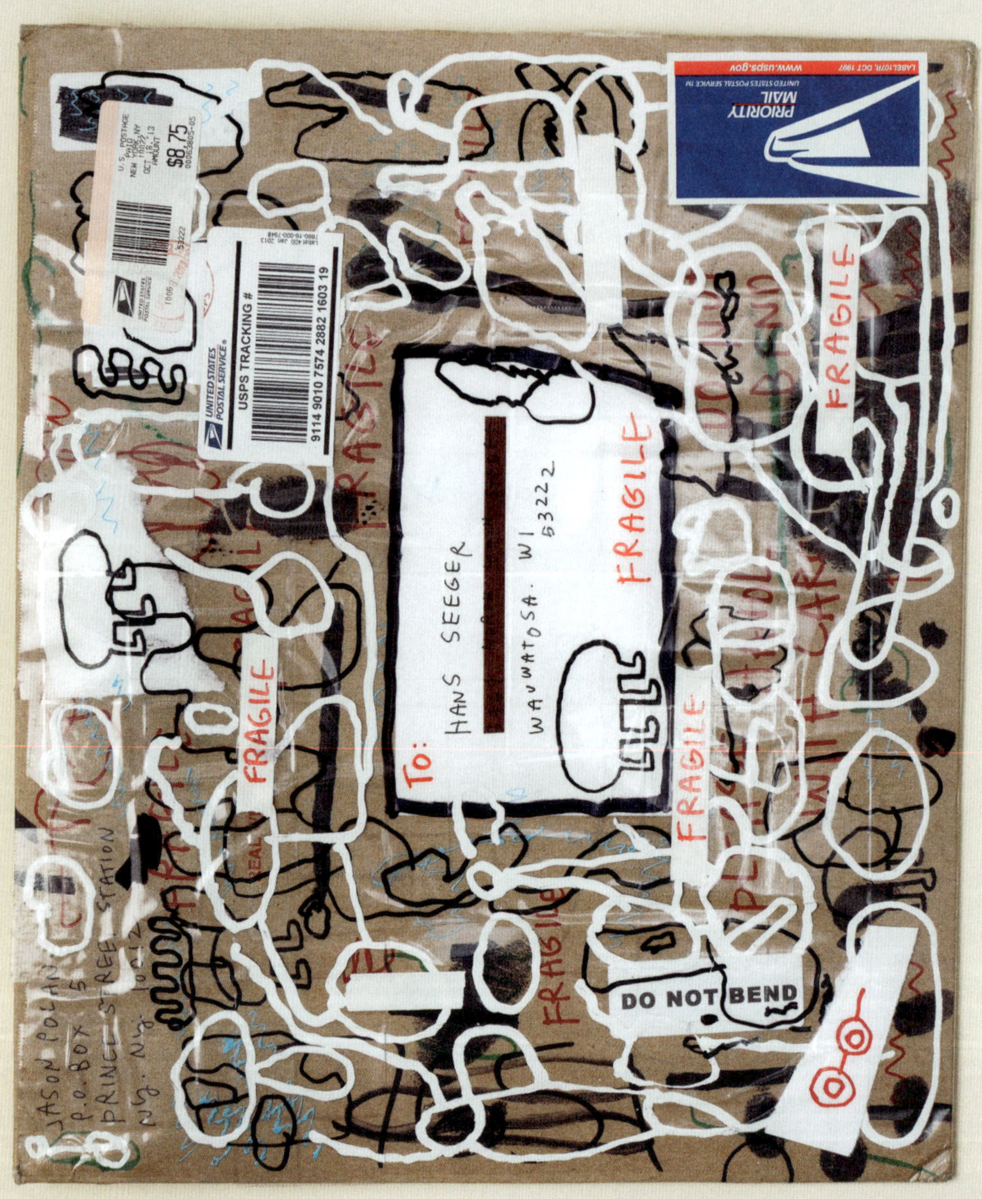

20 • JP to Hans Seeger

I DON'T KNOW IF "HEY" WAS AN INVITATION TO WRITE BACK, BUT I'M GOING TO PRETEND IT WAS.

HEY!

I AM JUST ON MY
LIVING ROOM FLOOR
WRITING TO YOU

I packed a snowball for you as a souvenier but it melted.

24 • Elaine Bleakney to JP

REMEMBER WHEN
THAT LITTLE DUDE
SMUSHED MY DRAWINGS
AND ACCIDENTALLY
SPIT PEAR IN YOUR
NOTEPAD?

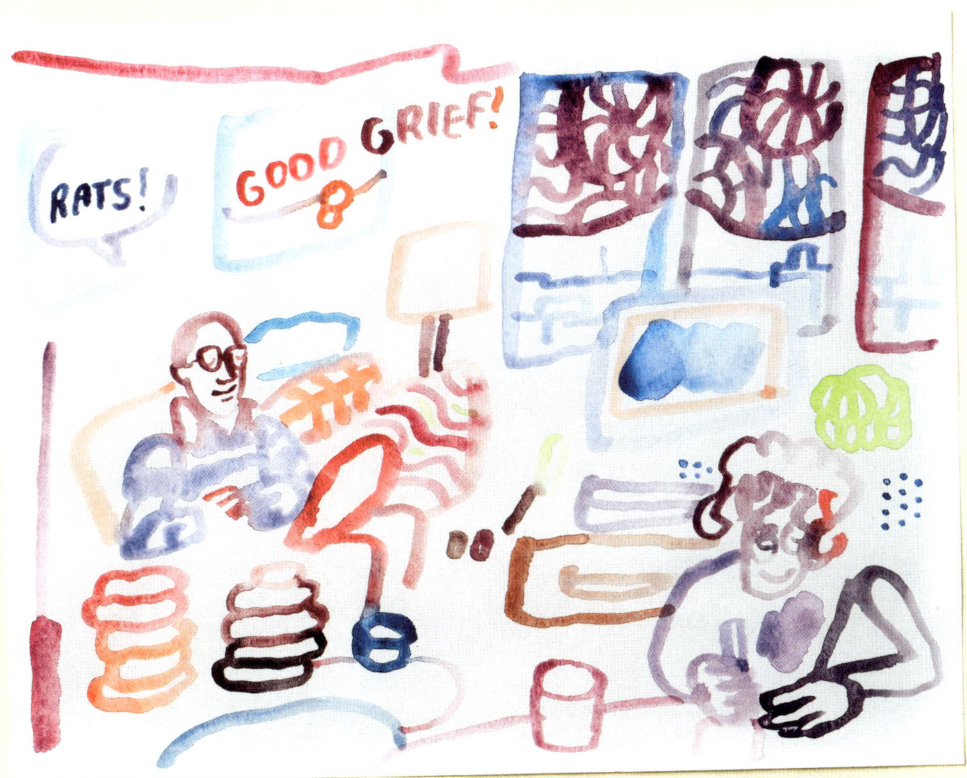
RATS!
GOOD GRIEF!

SHARPIE·

I HAVE BEEN A SHARPIE USER FOR A LONG TIME. I GO THROUGH 3 OR 4 FINE TIP SHARPIES A WEEK. I AM AN ARTIST AND YOUR MARKER IS MY TOOL OF CHOICE WHEN I DRAW.

I AM WRITING TO ASK IF YOU ARE INTERESTED IN SPONSORING ME – WITH YOUR MARKERS. I HAVE HAD NUMEROUS ART SHOWS IN ANN ARBOR WHERE I AM A STUDENT AT THE UNIVERSITY OF MICHIGAN. DURING MY SHOWS PEOPLE TEND TO ASK THE MEDIUM OF THE ART – THE ANSWER IS SHARPIE.

THANK YOU – AND I LOOK FORWARD TO FURTHER CONTACT. JASON POLAN ADDRESS

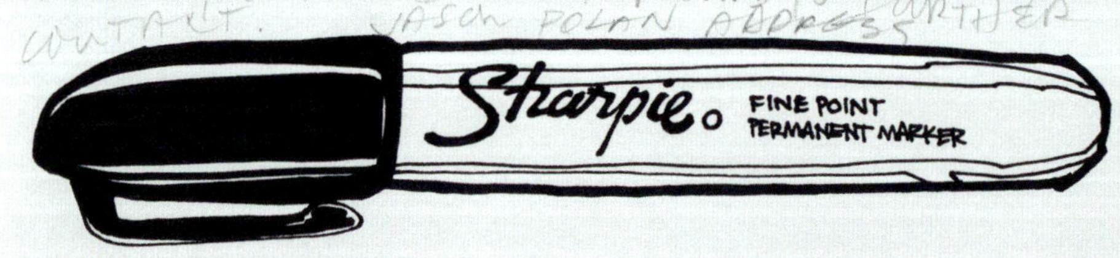

Yesterday I had to fasten a 17 foot two seater canoe to a trailblazer with a ball of twine. I hope that is a metaphor for something in your life.

Intuitive Counseling

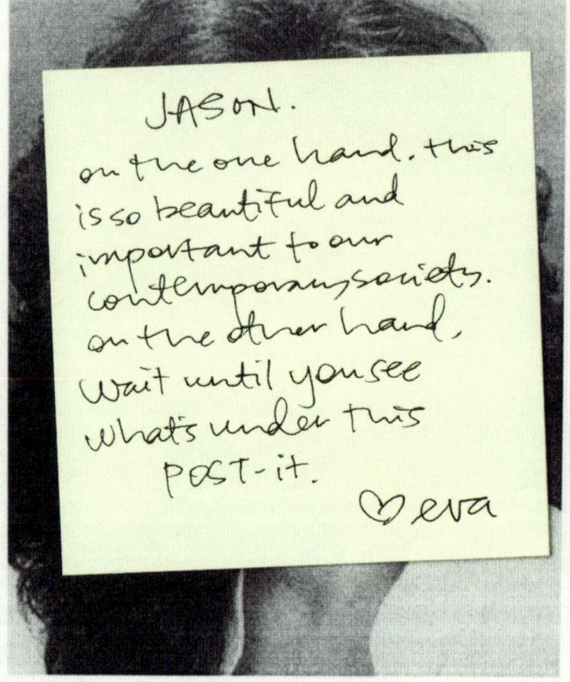

Barbara Van Diest

NOW MAKES HER PRIVATE SESSIONS AVAILABLE TO YOU!

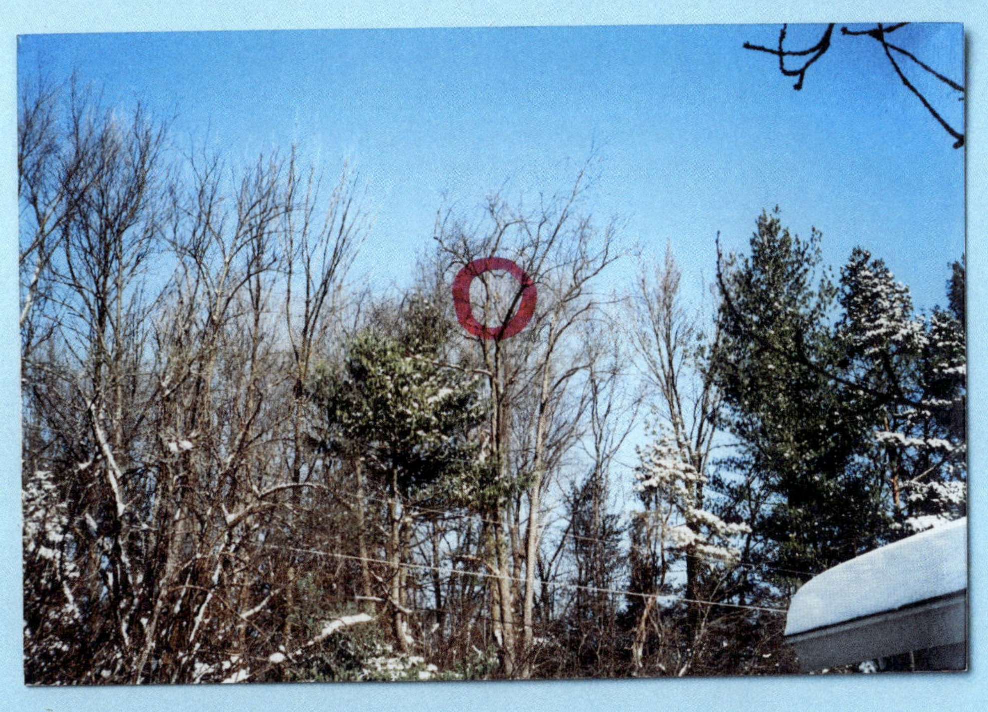

It's pretty hard to see, but there was a big hawk in the trees behind the house.

I'm writing this next to a small drawing of yours that sits on my kitchen table. It's a street scene you gave me, I enjoy seeing it every day over breakfast.

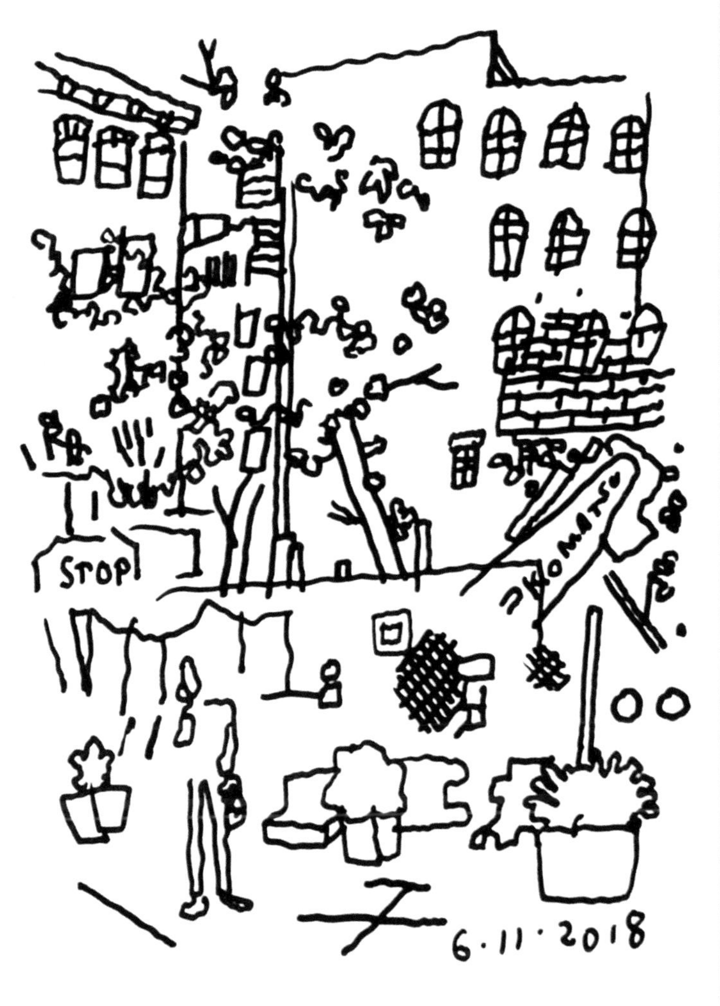
STOP
6.11.2018

THANK YOU
FOR THE SWISS
ARMY KNIFE
TOM!

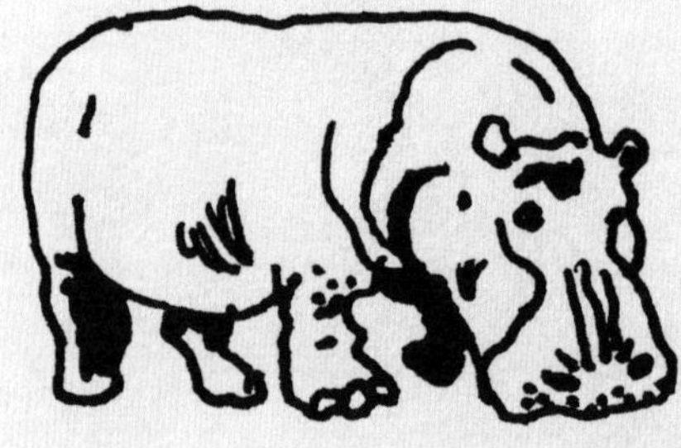

HERE IS A HIPPO
FOR YOU.

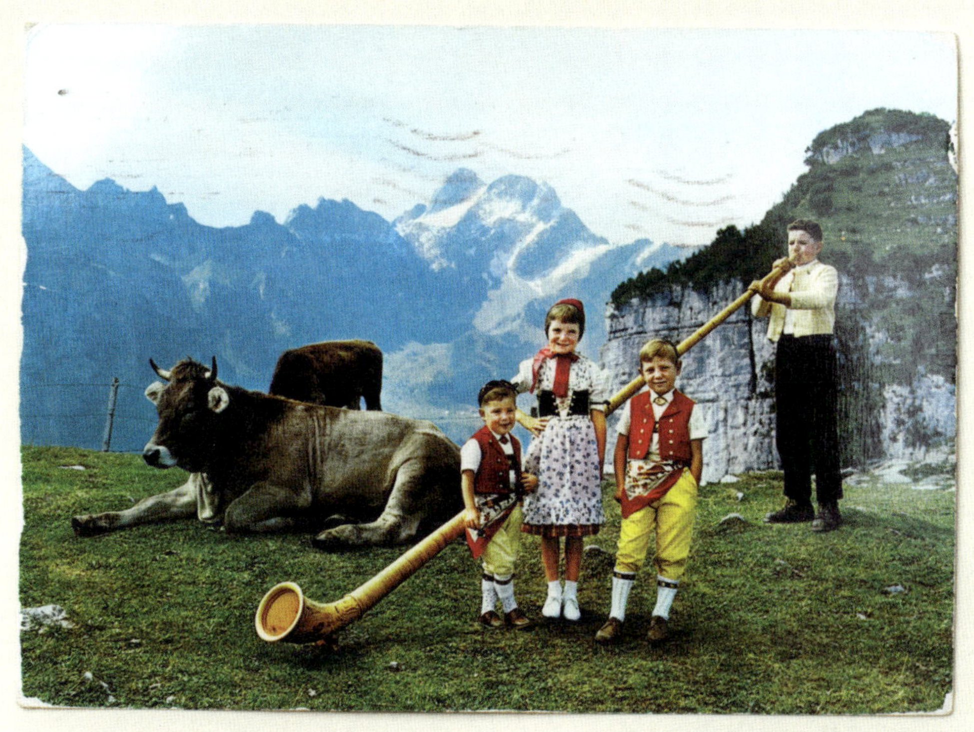

HOW ARE THINGS. THIS IS WHAT I PICTURE YOU AND MIKE + I LOOKING LIKE... IF WE KNEW EACHOTHER WHEN WE WERE 5, 9, AND 7 RESPECTIVELY. MIKE IS ON THE RIGHT, YOU ARE IN THE MIDDLE, AND I AM ON THE LEFT. I DON'T KNOW WHO THAT GUY BLOWING THE HORN IS - POSSIBLY A LOCAL.

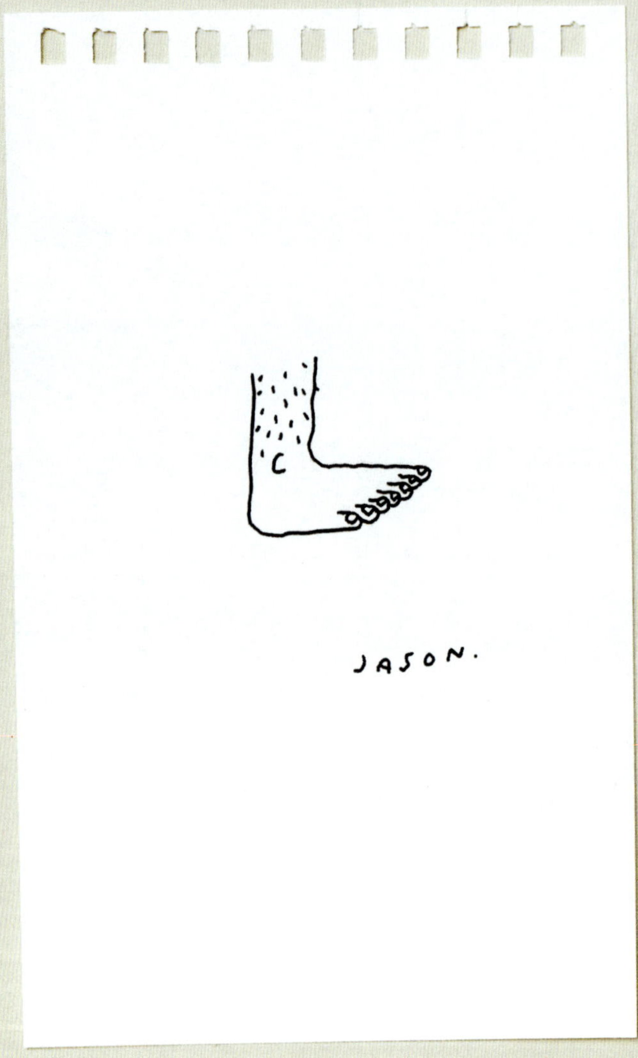
C
JASON.

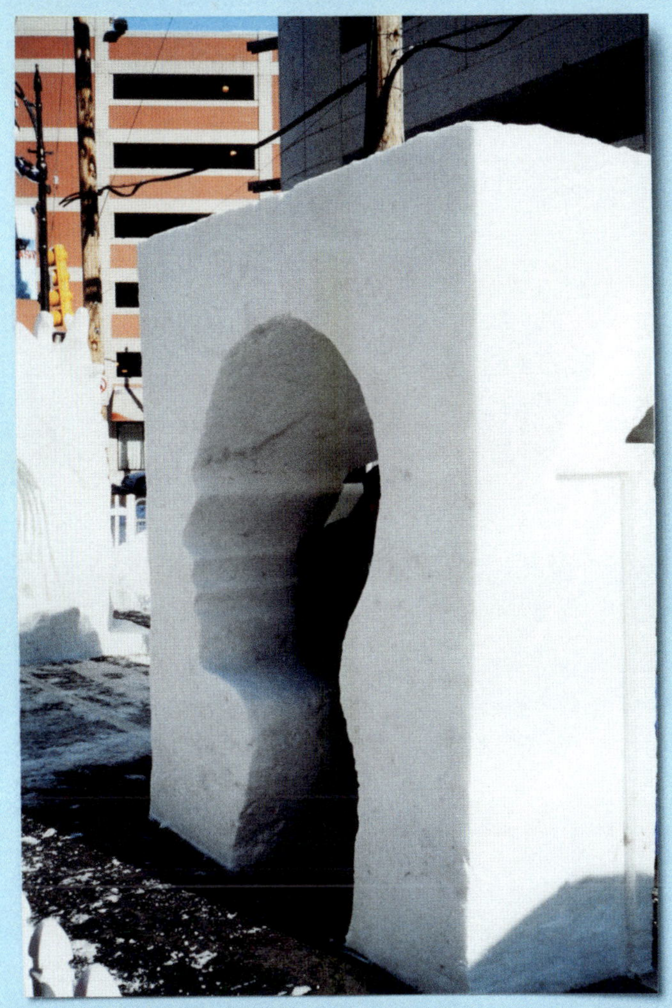

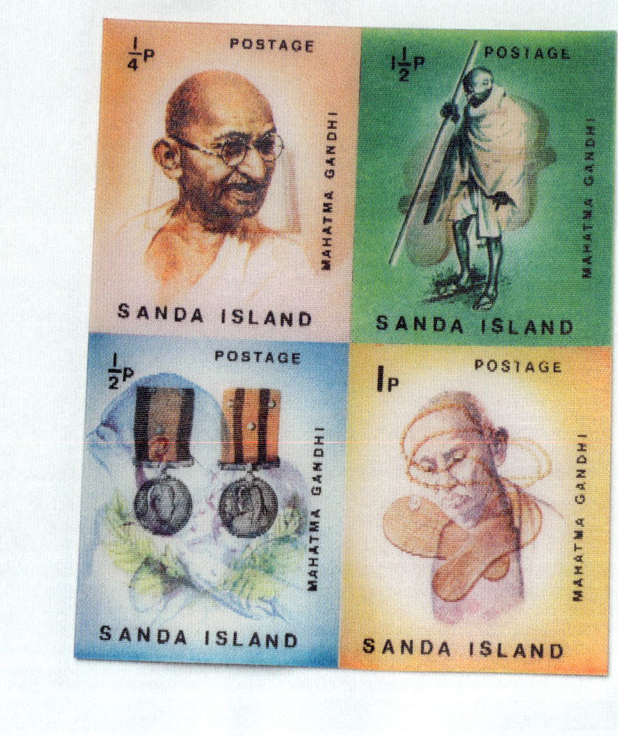
2D GANDHI
1/4 P
POSTAGE
MAHATMA GANDHI
SANDA ISLAND
1 1/2 P
POSTAGE
MAHATMA GANDHI
SANDA ISLAND
1/2 P
POSTAGE
MAHATMA GANDHI
SANDA ISLAND
1 P
POSTAGE
MAHATMA GANDHI
SANDA ISLAND

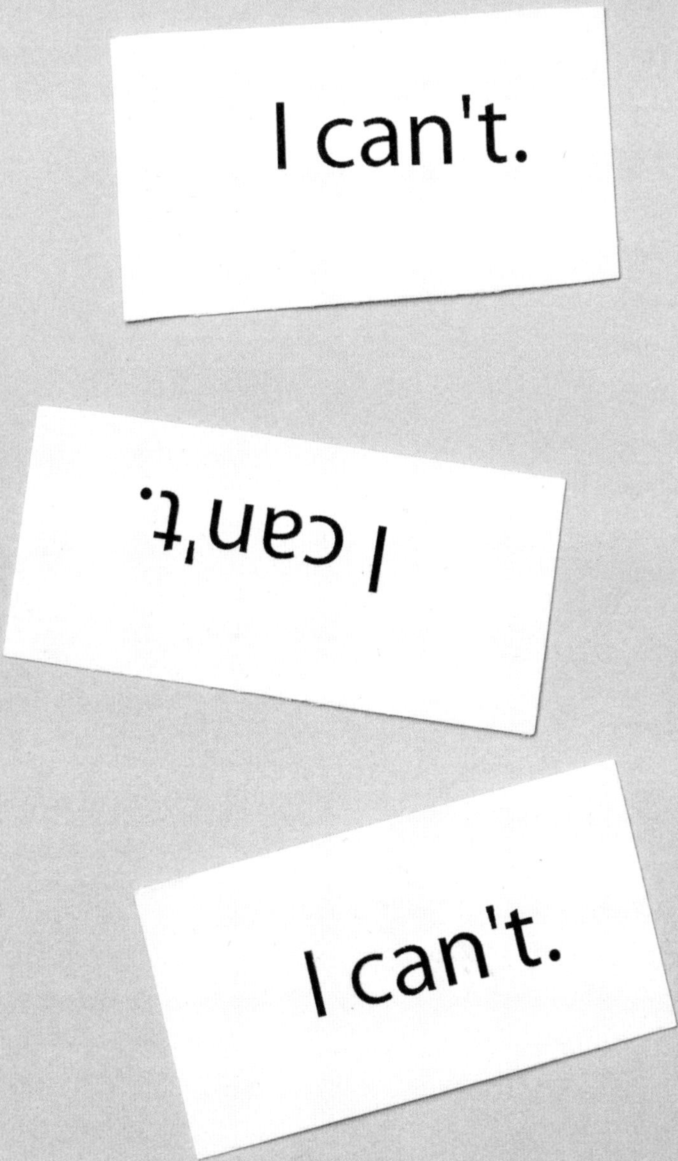
I can't.
I can't.
I can't.

Jason Polan
Jason Polan
Jason Polan
Jason Polan
Jason Polan
Jason Polan
Jason Polan
Jason Polan
Jason Polan
Jason Polan
Jason Polan
Jason Polan
Jason Polan
Jason Polan
Jason Polan
Jason Polan
Jason Polan
Jason Polan
Jason Polan
Jason Polan
Jason Polan
Jason Polan
Jason Polan
Jason Polan
Jason Polan

Jason Polan
Jason Polan
Jason Polan
Jason Polan
Jason Polan
Jason Polan
Jason Polan
Jason Polan
Jason Polan
Jason Polan
Jason Polan
Jason Polan
Jason Polan
Jason Polan
Jason Polan
Jason Polan
Jason Polan
Jason Polan
Jason Polan
Jason Polan
Jason Polan
Jason Polan
Jason Polan
Jason Polan
Jason Polan

SSSSSShey Stacey

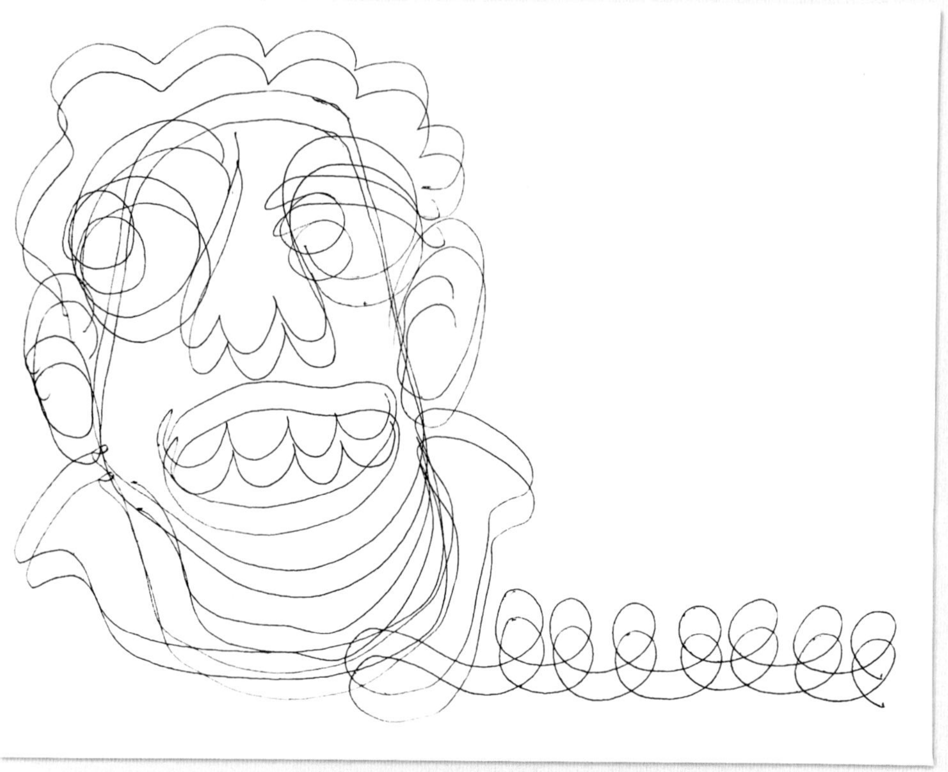

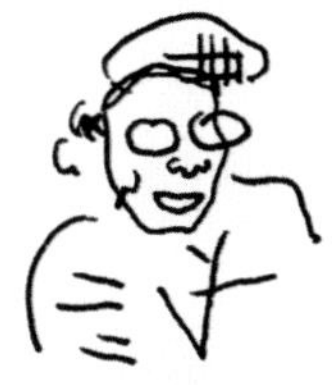

DAVID
HOCKNEY
AT PACE
GALLERY
4.5.2018

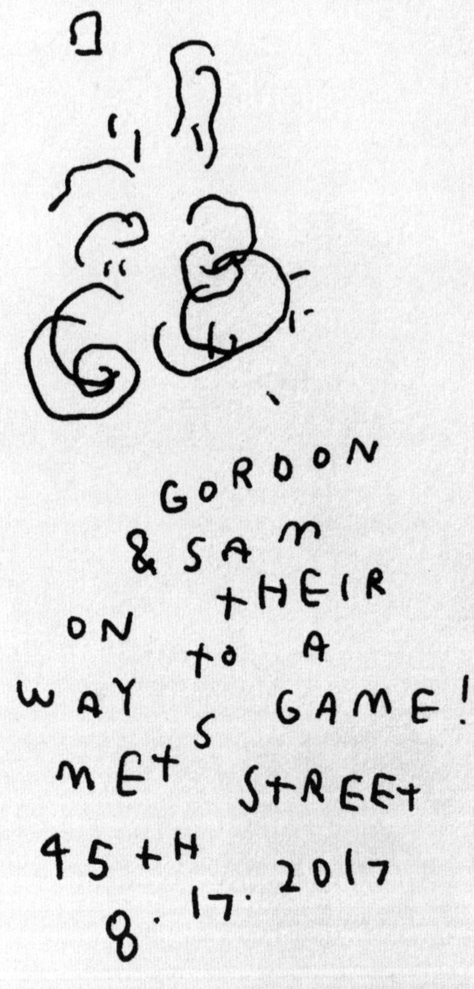

GORDON
& SAM
ON THEIR
WAY TO A
METS GAME!
STREET
45TH
8.17.2017

44 • JP to Gordon Stevenson (aka BVF) and Samantha Stoecker (aka Sami Kitty)

I was just remembering all the times I've spent in New York city, which didn't take long, as I have only been the one time. Please do watch out for the bad guys from Home Alone 2. As far as I know, they are still in your city.

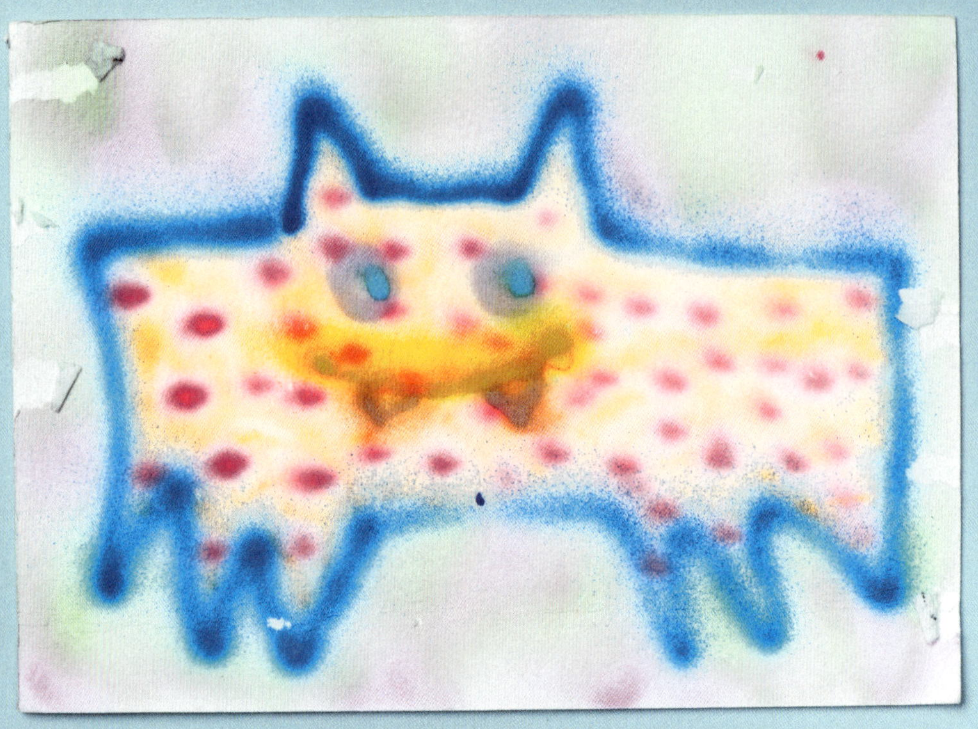

 Gordon Stevenson (aka BVF) and Samantha Stoecker (aka Sami Kitty) to JP new york can be a cold, cold woman... but that's why we love her. right?

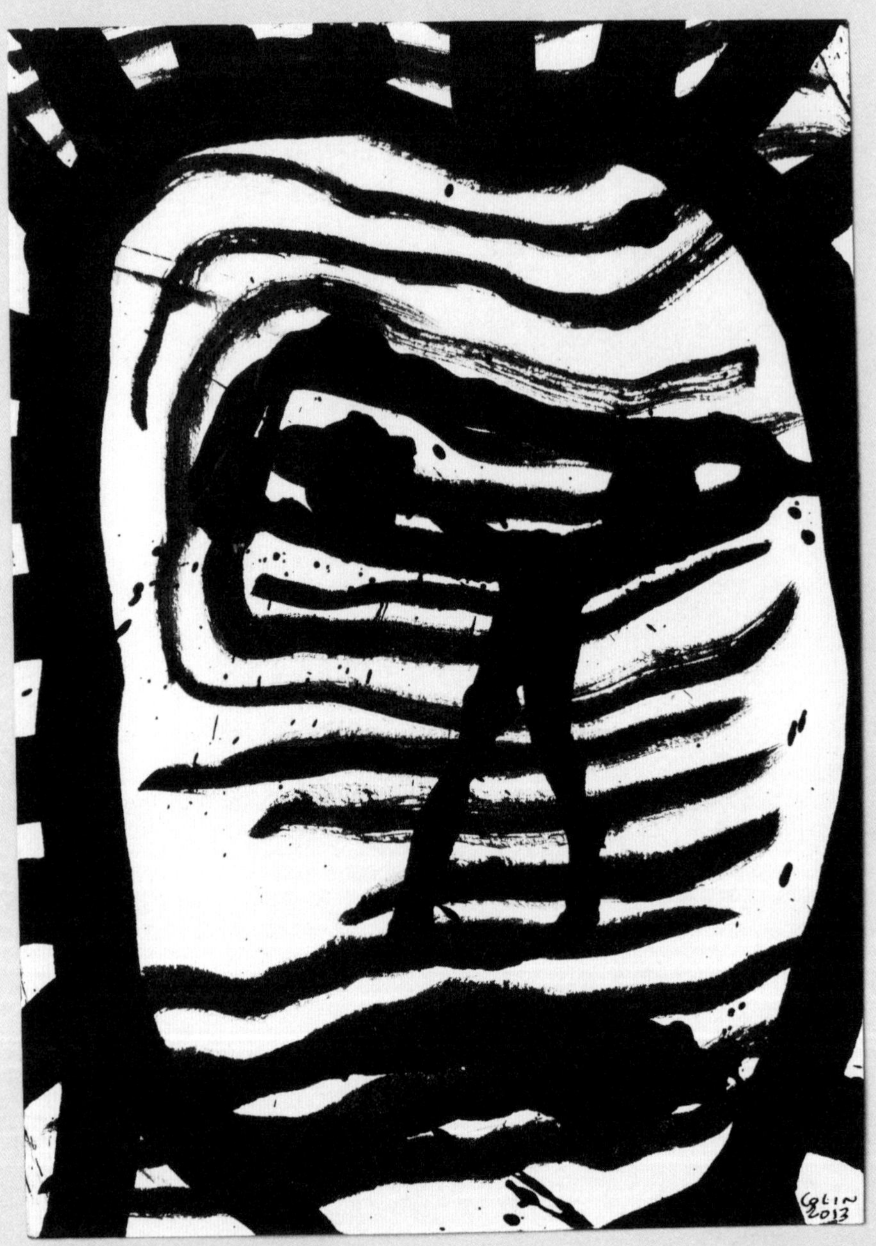
COLIN
2013

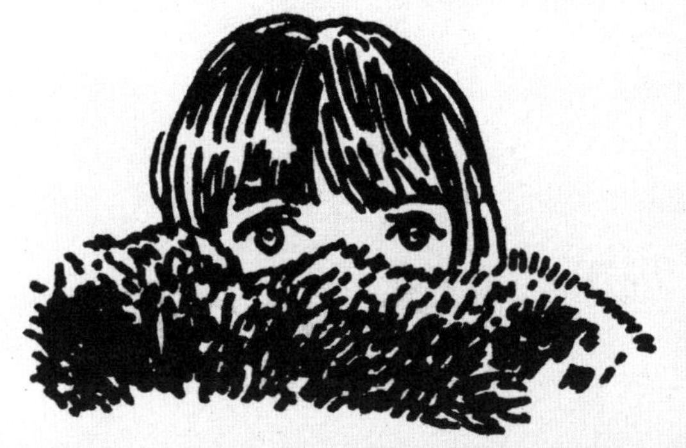

CHRISSY LEAVELL

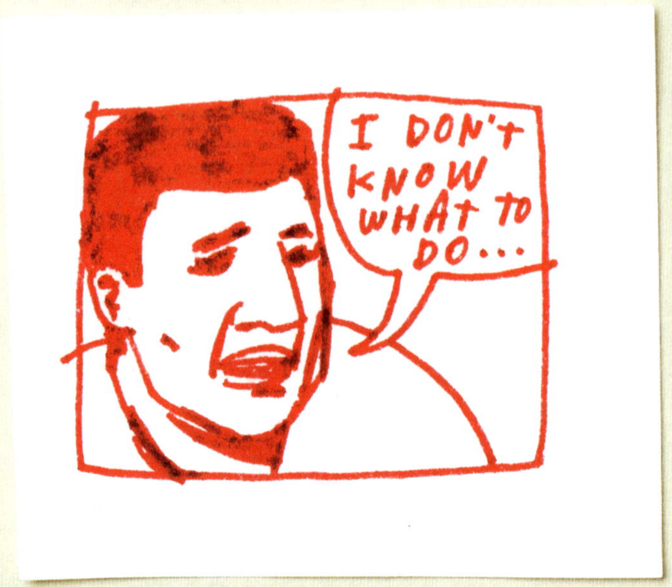
I DON'T KNOW WHAT TO DO...

We sell fun

GUS!

(have some)

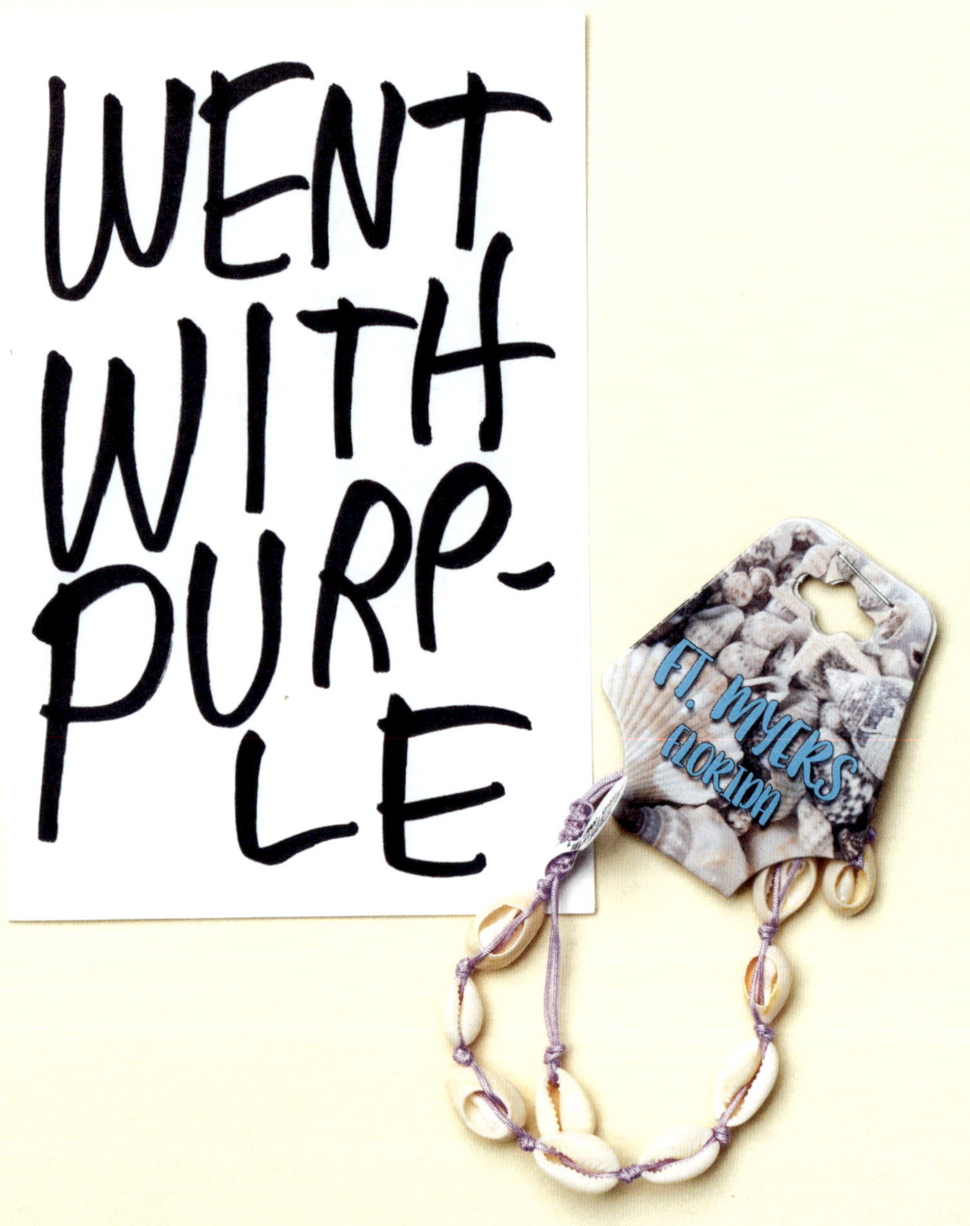
WENT
WITH
PURP-
LE
FT. MYERS
FLORIDA

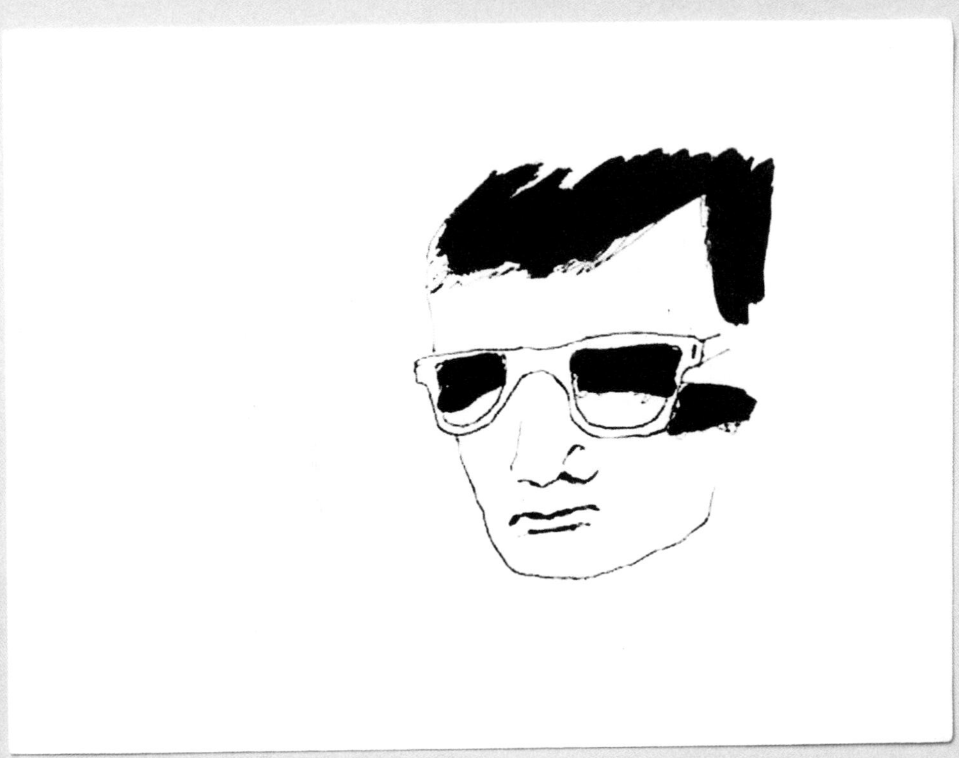

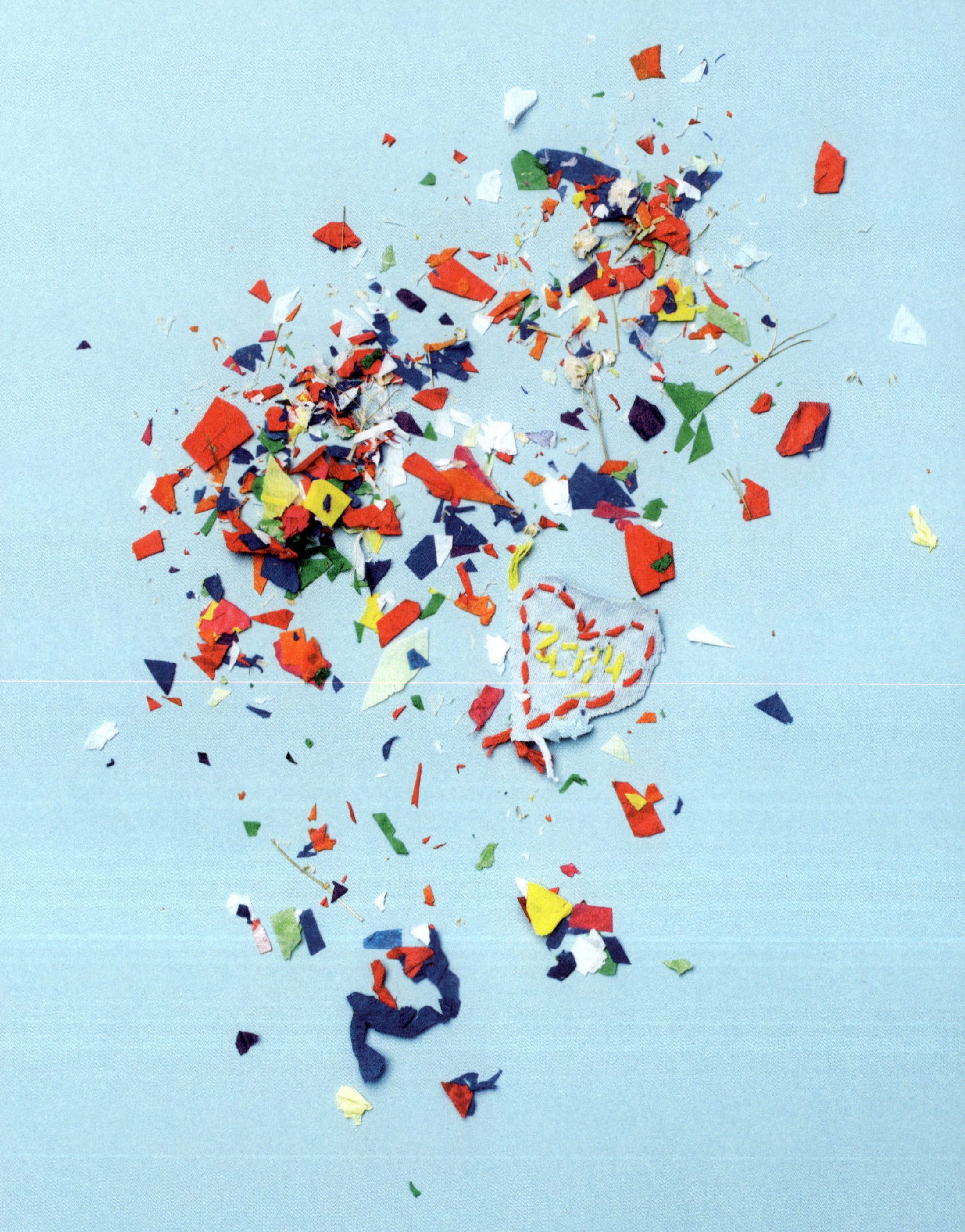

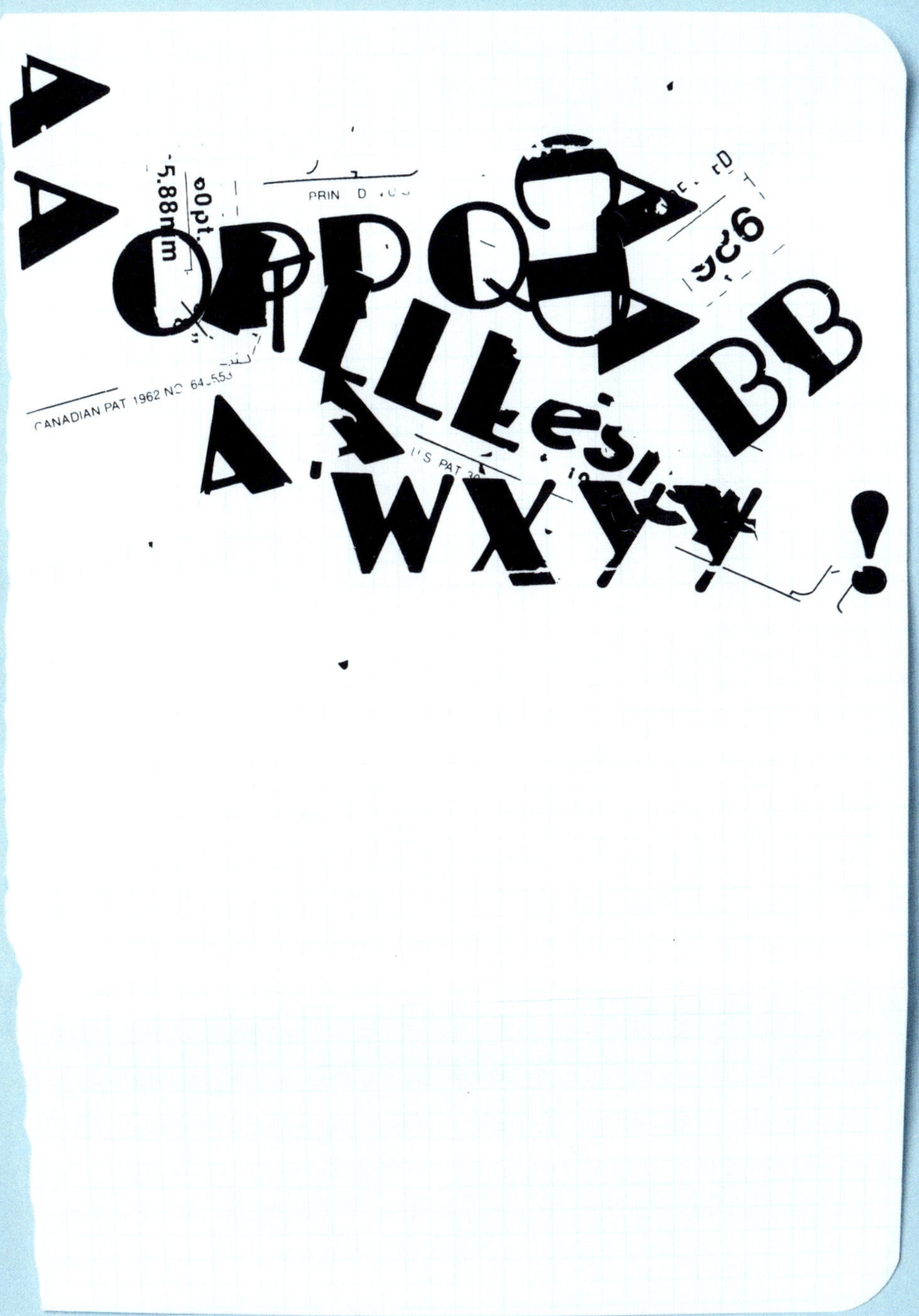

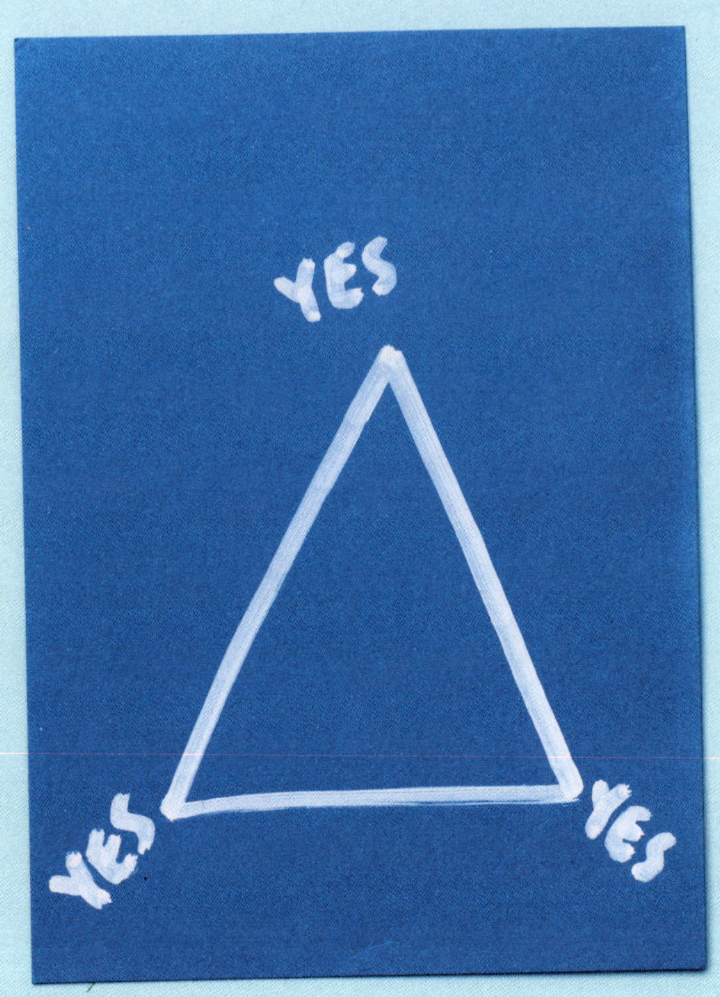
YES
YES
YES

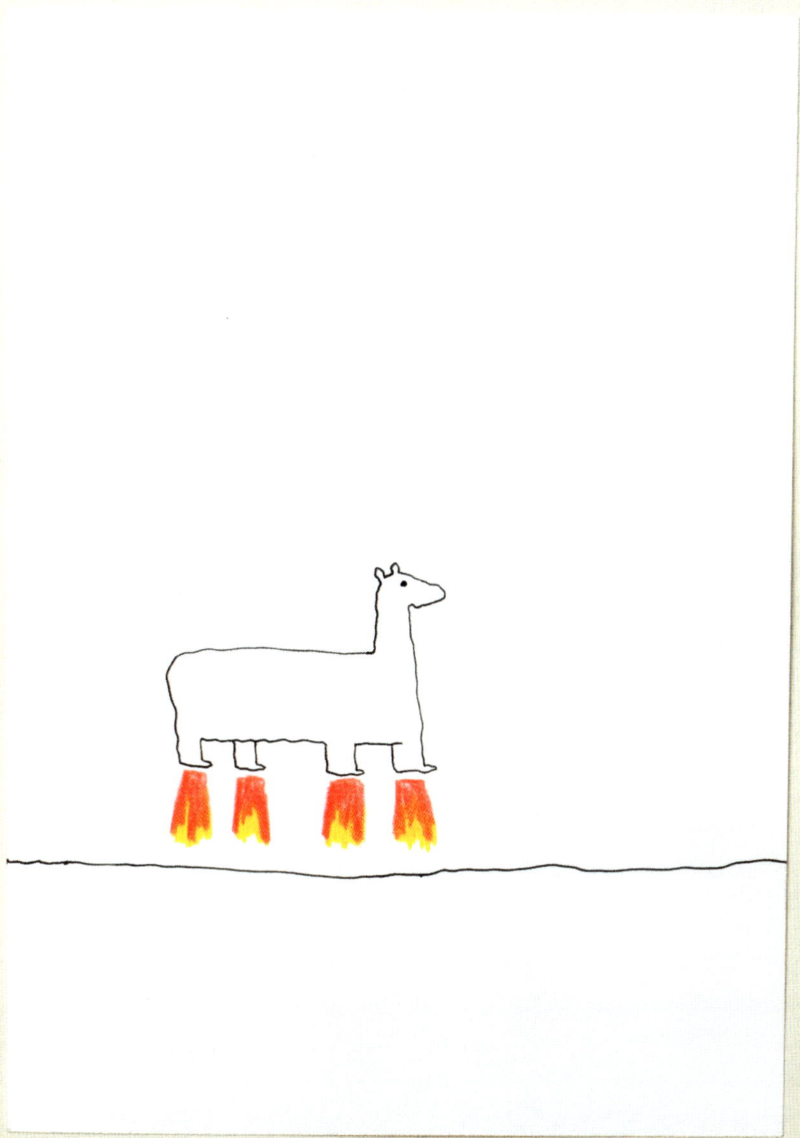

ROBERT ADAMS

DARREN ALMOND

NAYLAND BLAKE

PETER CAIN

THOMAS DEMAND

VINCENT FECTEAU

PETER FISCHLI DAVID WEISS

JASON POLAN

LUCIAN FREUD

KATHARINA FRITSCH

ROBERT GOBER

NAN GOLDIN

ANDREAS GURSKY

MARTIN HONERT

PETER HUJAR

GARY HUME

JASPER JOHNS

ELLSWORTH KELLY

INEZ VAN LAMSWEERDE

BRICE MARDEN

ROY McMAKIN

KEN PRICE

CHARLES RAY

PAUL SIETSEMA

TONY SMITH

ANNE TRUITT

REBECCA WARREN

TERRY WINTERS

MARY & MATT

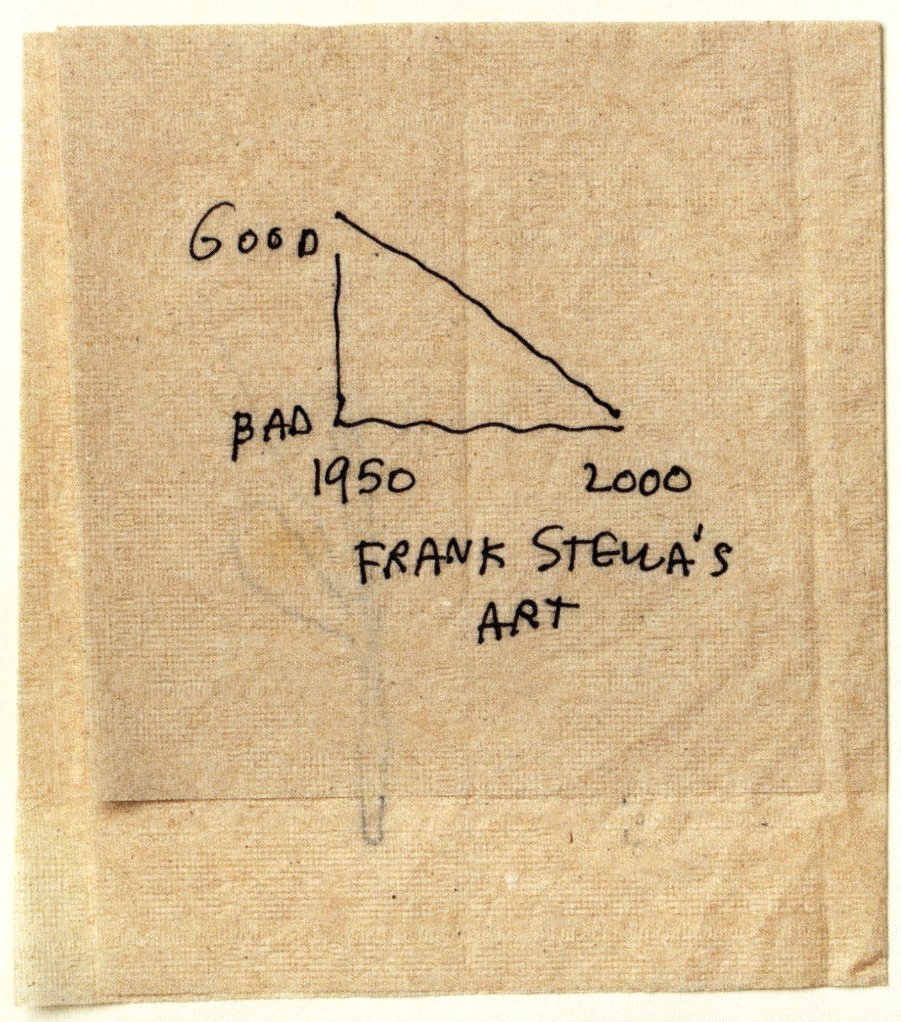
GOOD
BAD
1950
2000
FRANK STELLA'S
ART

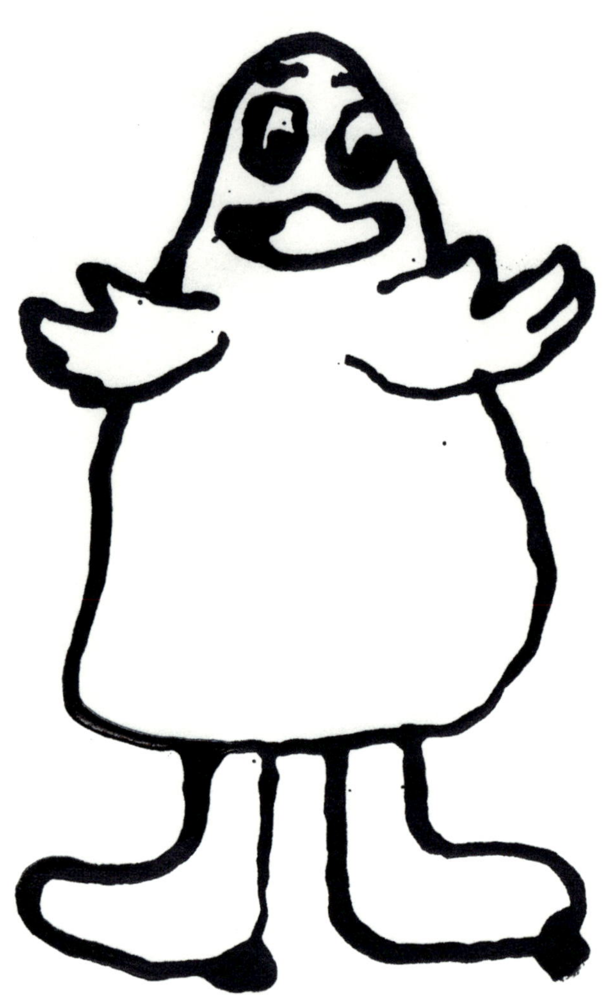

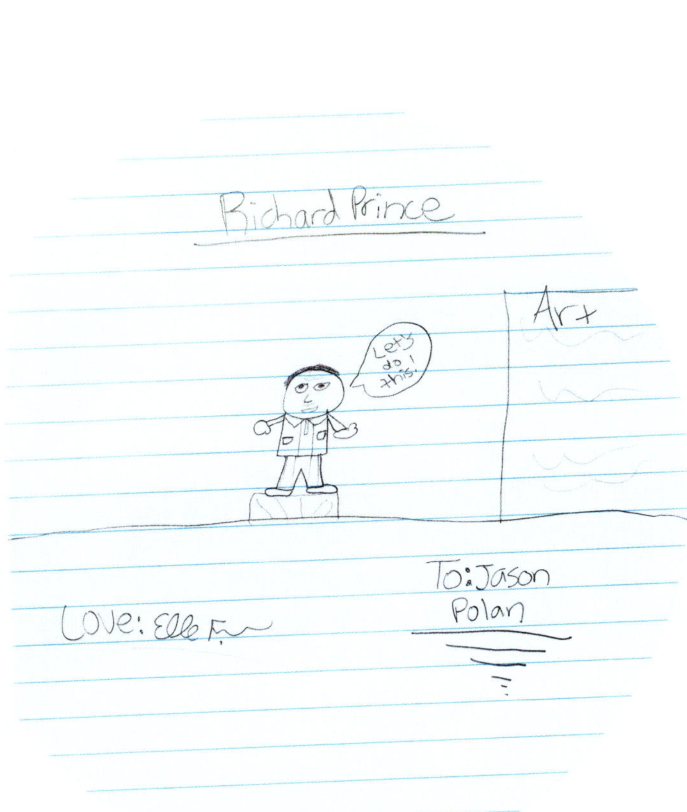
Richard Prince
Let's do this!
Art
To: Jason Polan
Love: Elle F.

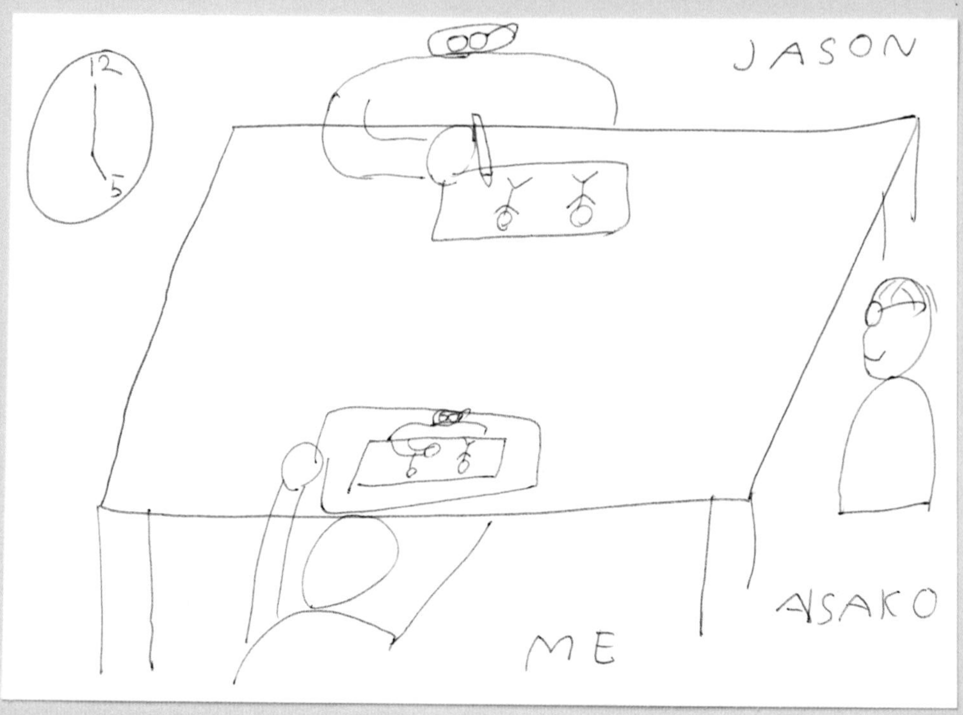
12
5
JASON
ASAKO
ME

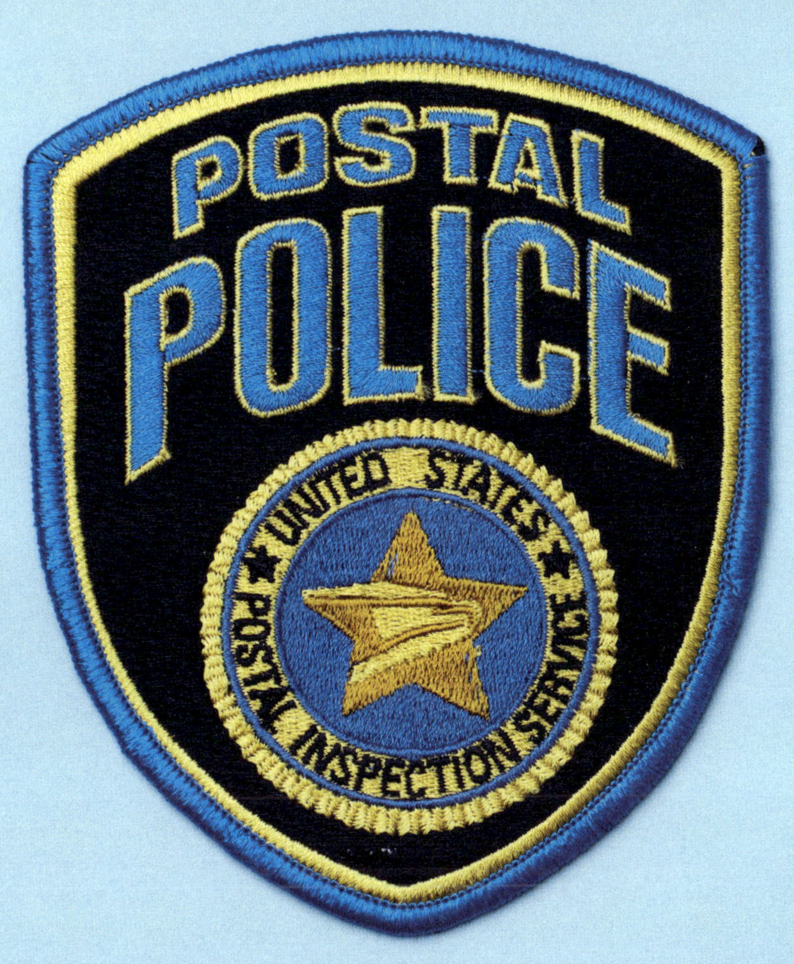
POSTAL
POLICE
UNITED STATES
POSTAL INSPECTION SERVICE

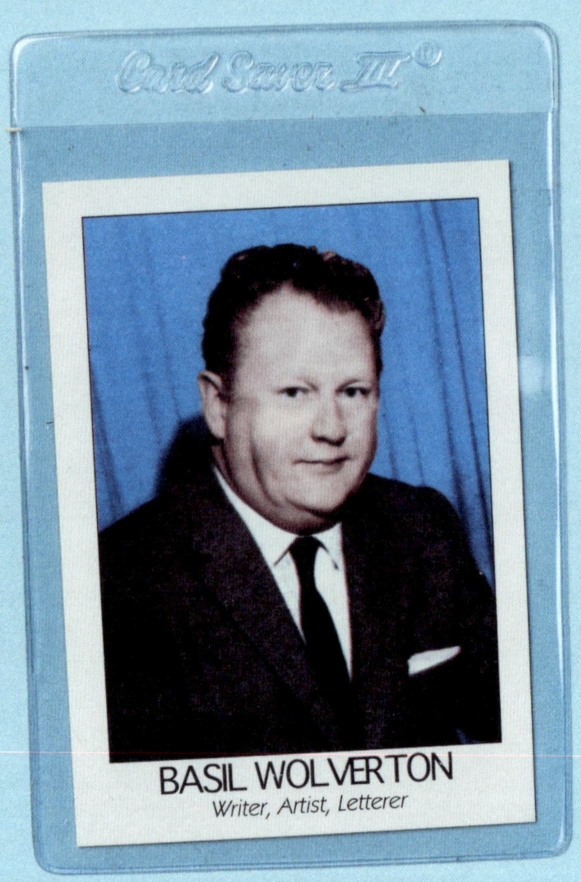
Card Saver III
BASIL WOLVERTON
Writer, Artist, Letterer

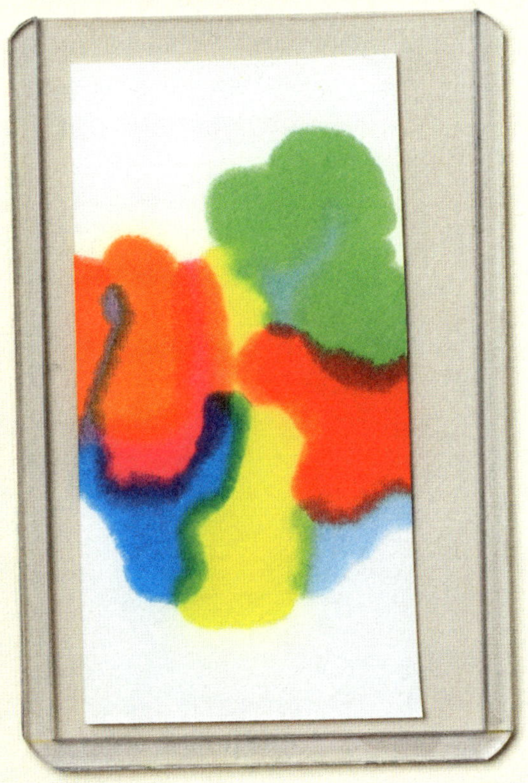

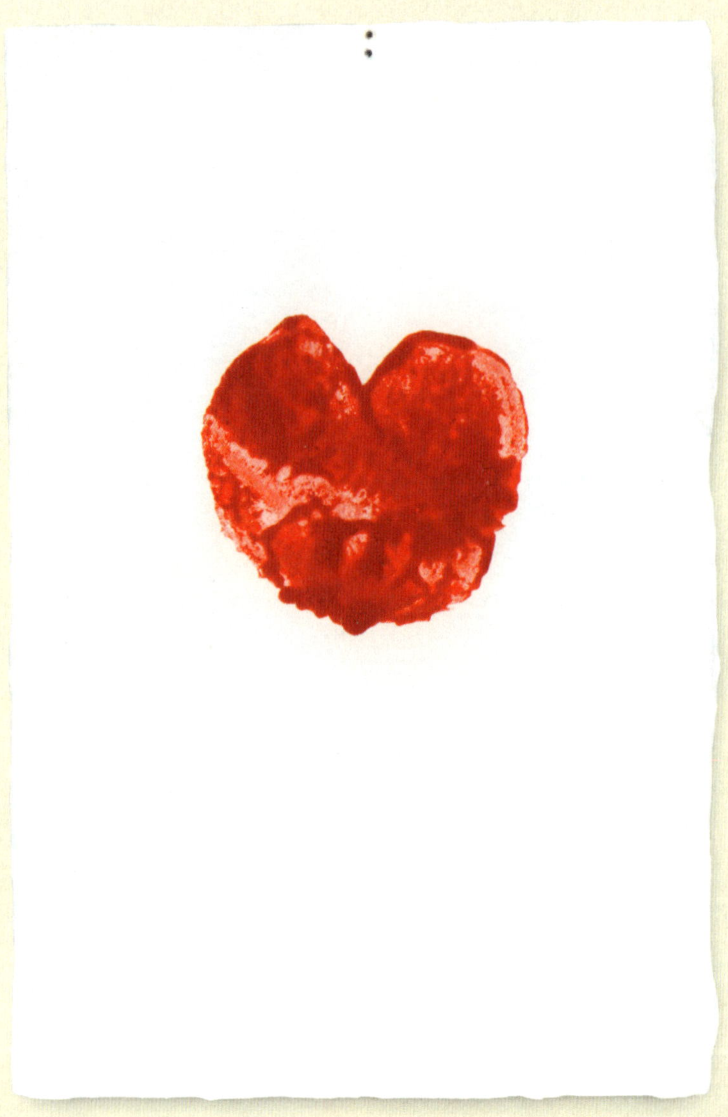

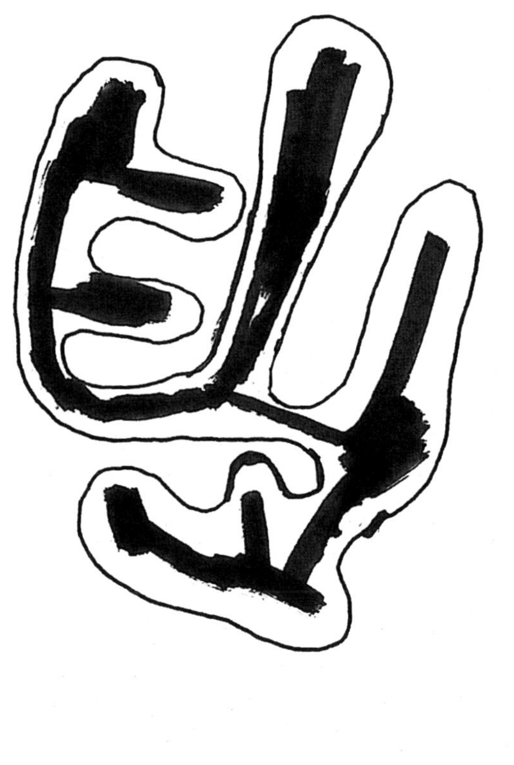

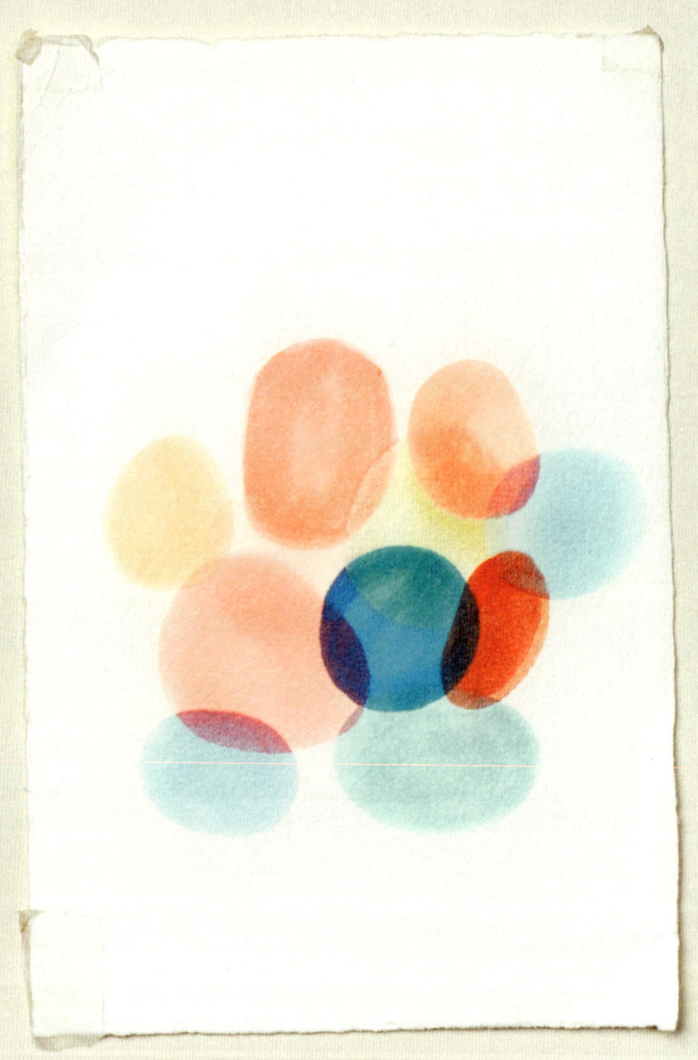

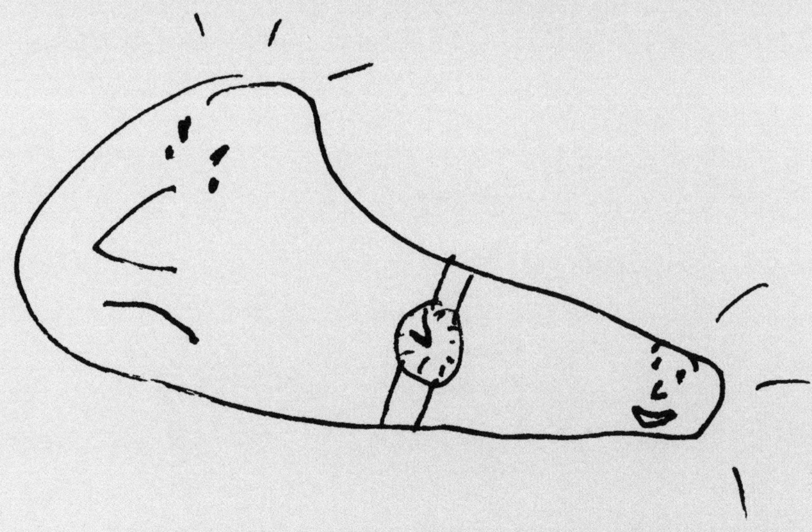

POLAN IS KING

SEA ANEMONE SEA ANEMONE

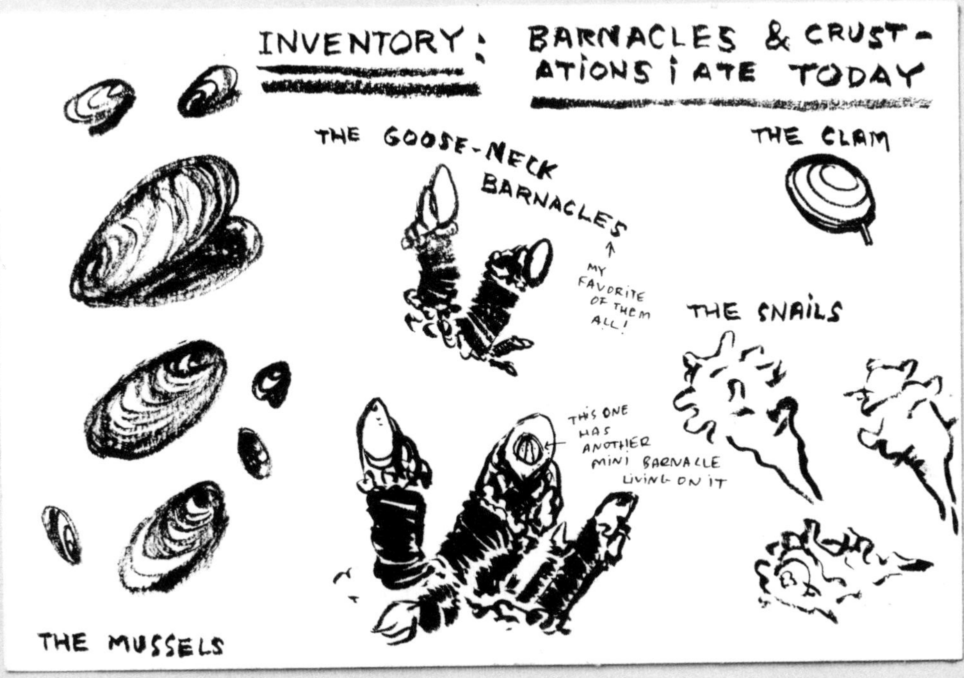
INVENTORY: BARNACLES & CRUST-ATIONS I ATE TODAY
THE GOOSE-NECK BARNACLES
MY FAVORITE OF THEM ALL!
THE CLAM
THE SNAILS
THIS ONE HAS ANOTHER MINI BARNACLE LIVING ON IT
THE MUSSELS

I found large mushrooms
in Greenwood Cemetery
that were shaped like
funnel cakes.
They even had extra
spores on top that
looked like powdered
sugar.

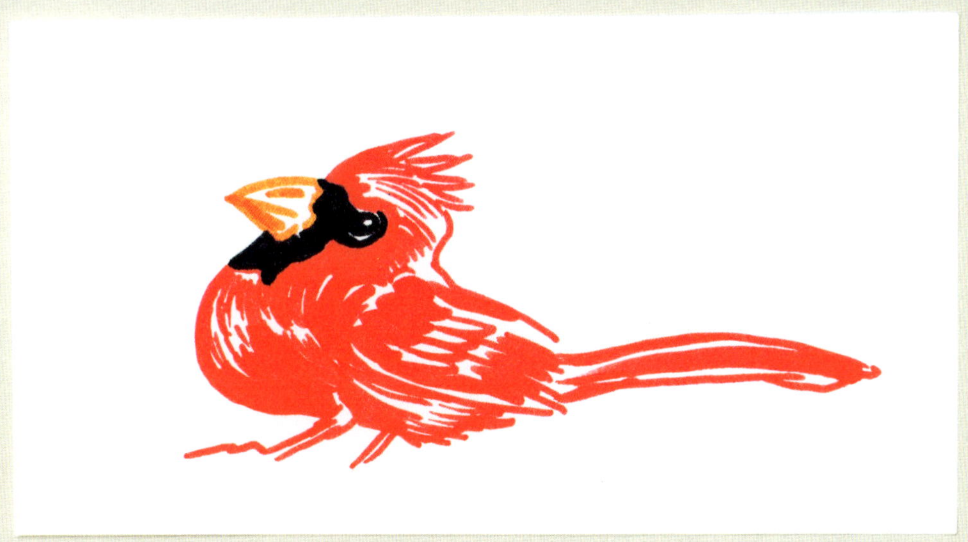

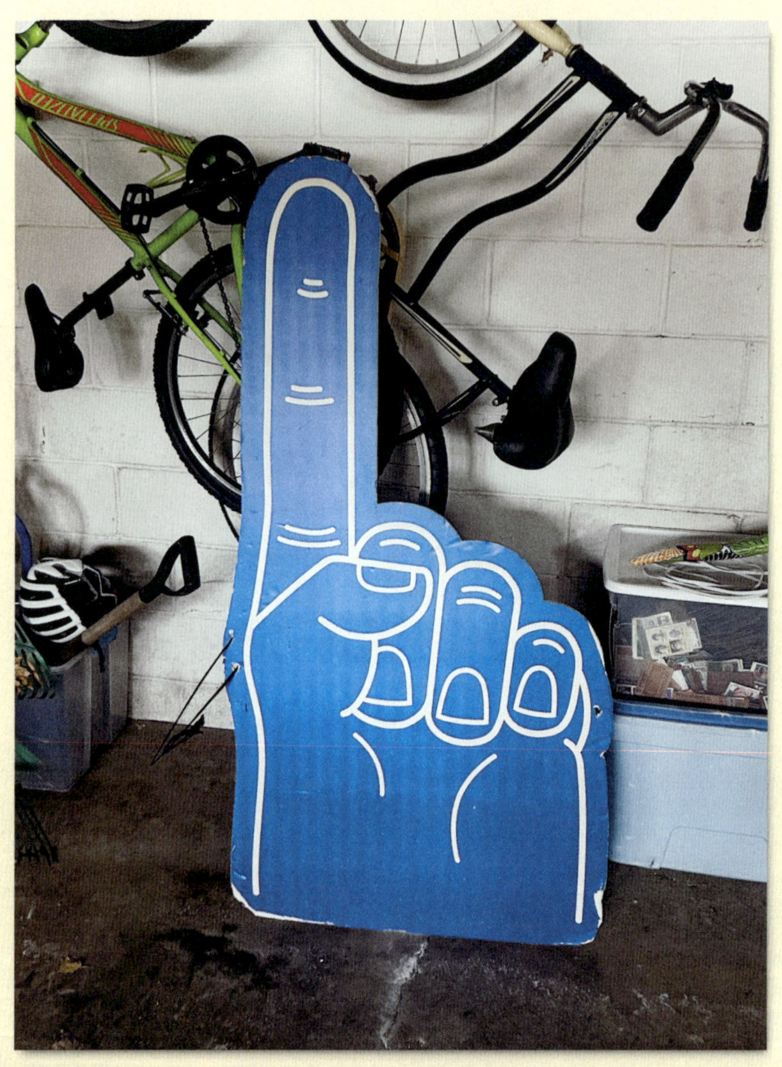

JASON POLAN.

TURBULENCES

LOUIS VUITTON

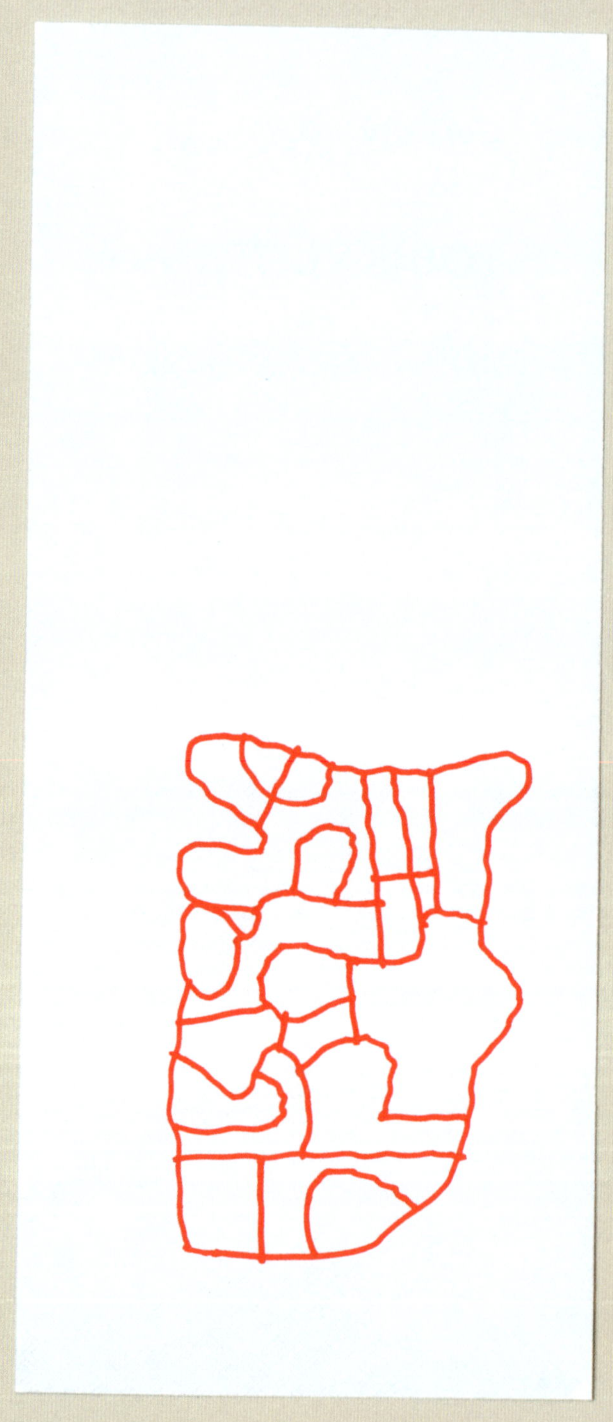

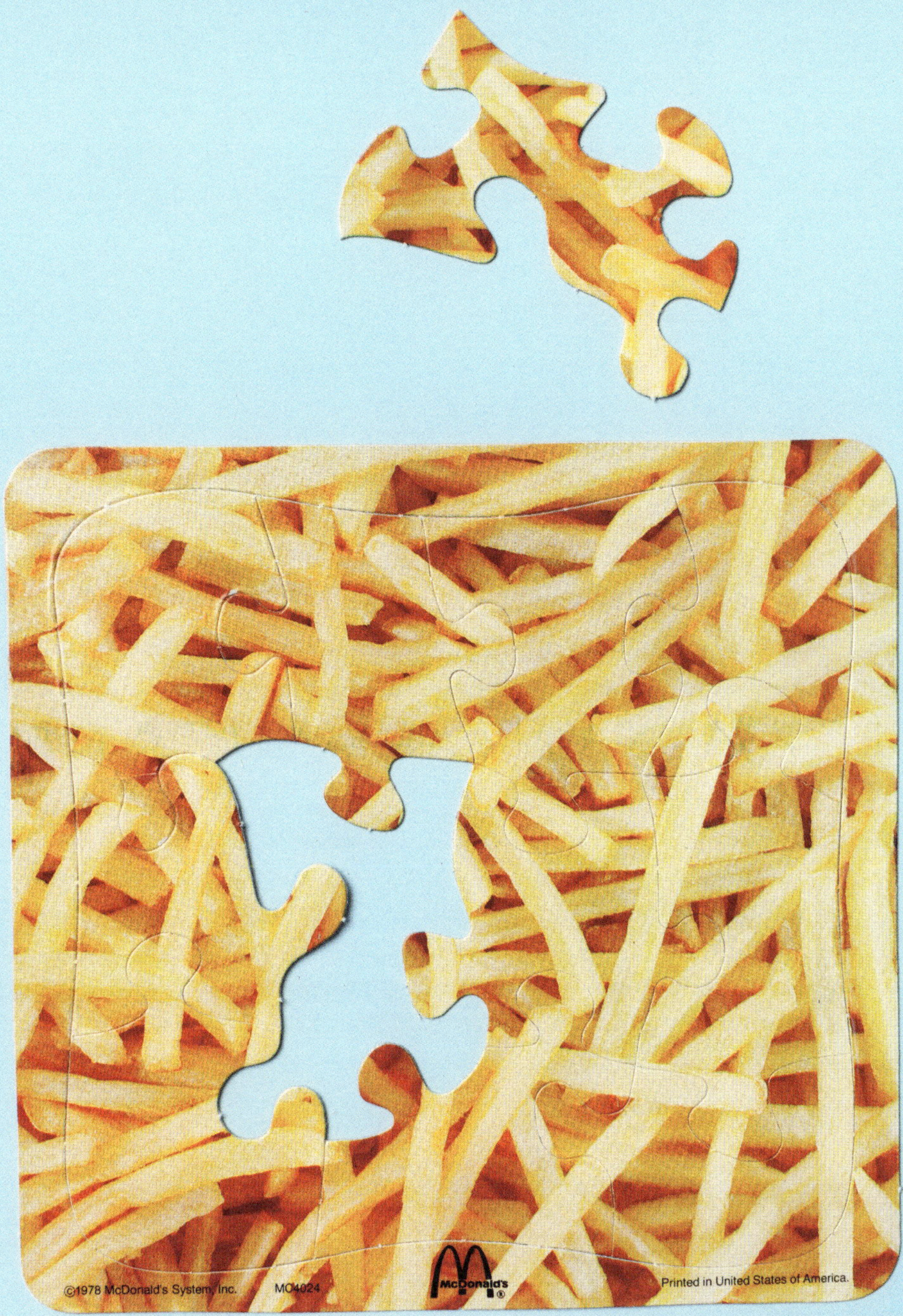

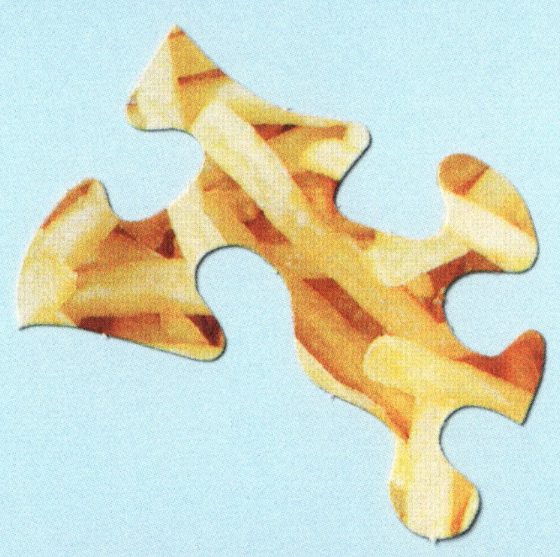

©1978 McDonald's System, Inc.
MC4024
McDonald's®
Printed in United States of America.

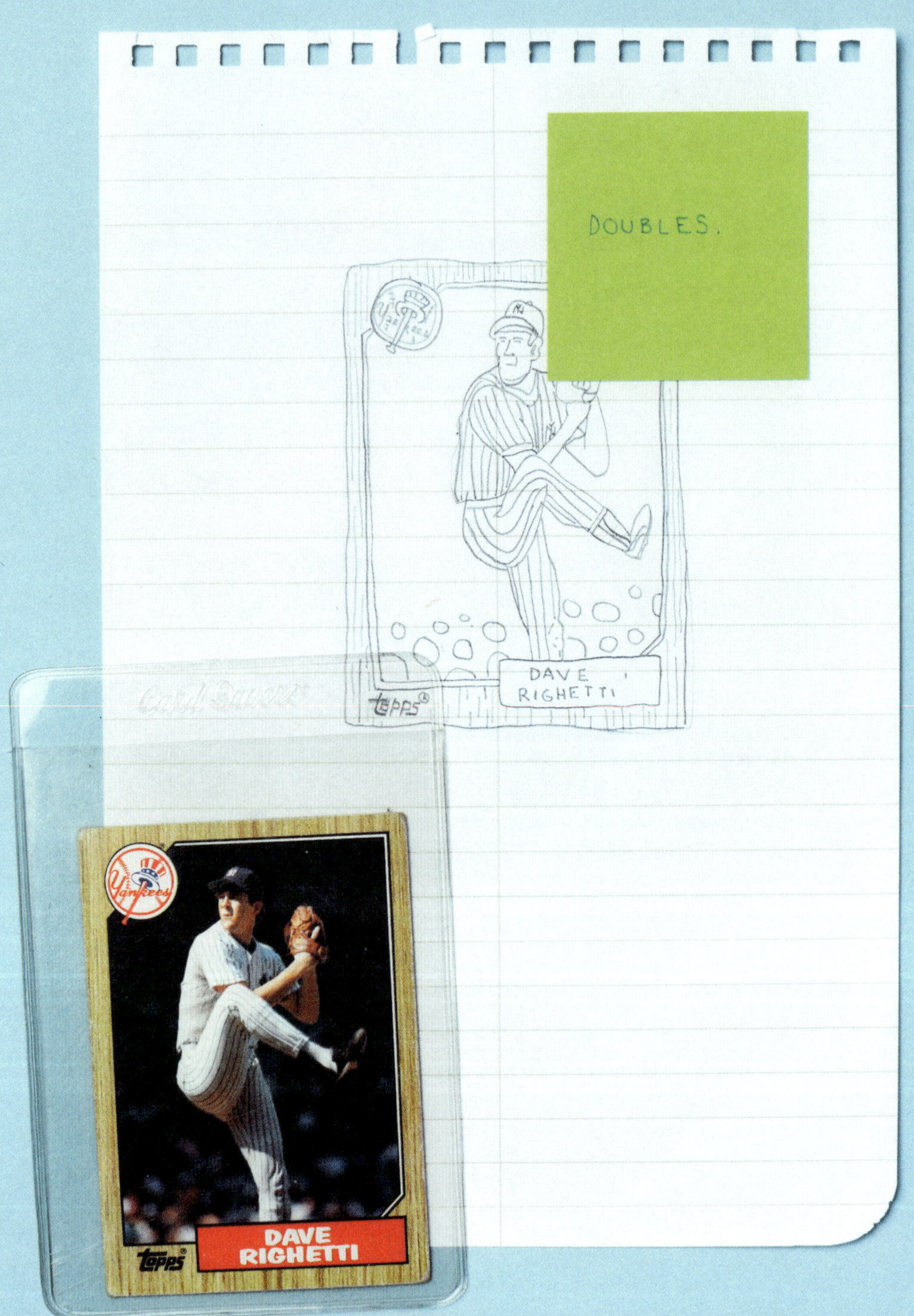
DOUBLES.
DAVE
RIGHETTI
Topps
DAVE
RIGHETTI
Topps
Yankees

I STARTED A CLUB. IT'S CALLED "WHENEVER I HAPPEN TO FIND A RARE, EDITIONED COPY OF 'THE PLIGHT OF THE CREATIVE ARTIST IN THE UNITED STATES OF AMERICA' BY HENRY MILLER, I'M GOING TO SEND IT TO ONE ~~[illegible]~~ LUCKY BASTARD CLUB."

THE PLIGHT OF THE CRE-ATIVE ARTIST IN THE UNIT-ED STATES OF AMERICA • BY HENRY MILLER

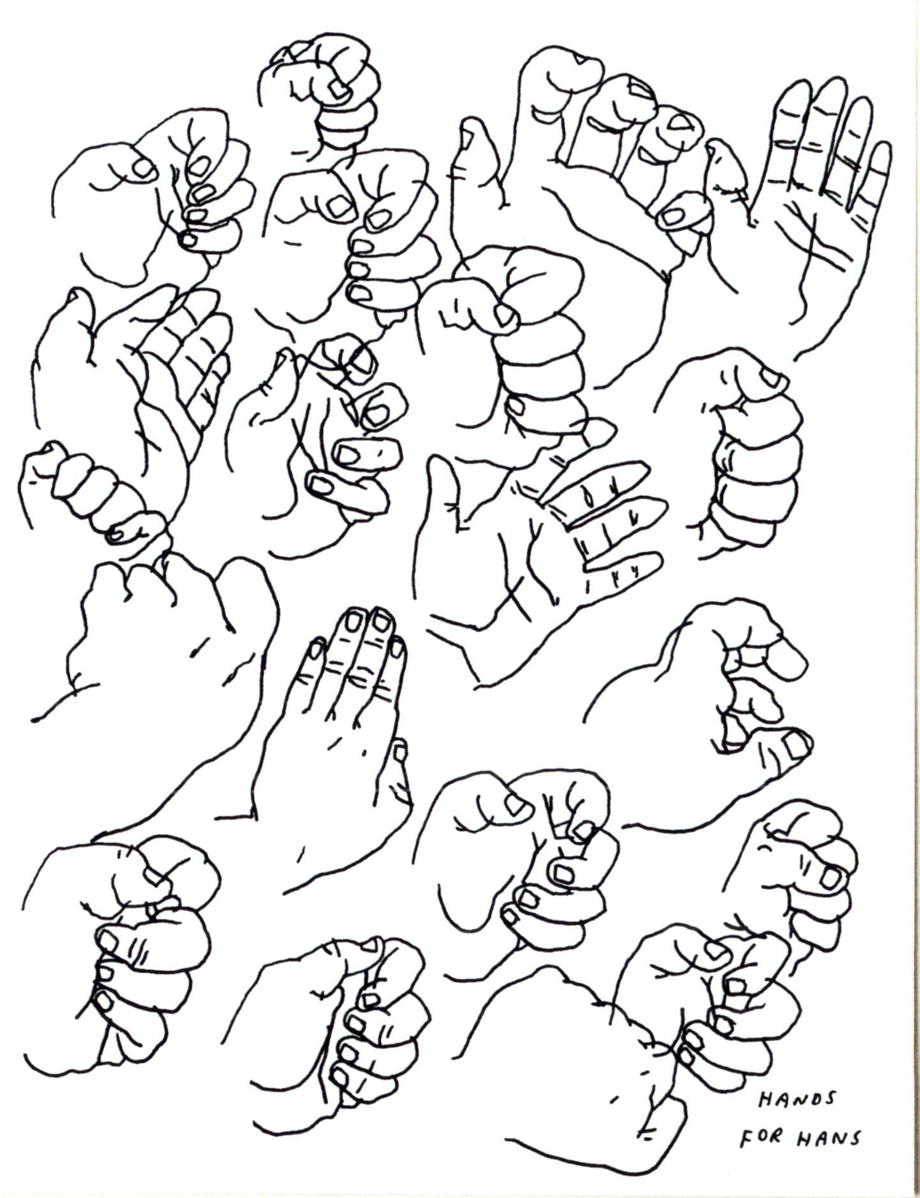
HANDS
FOR HANS

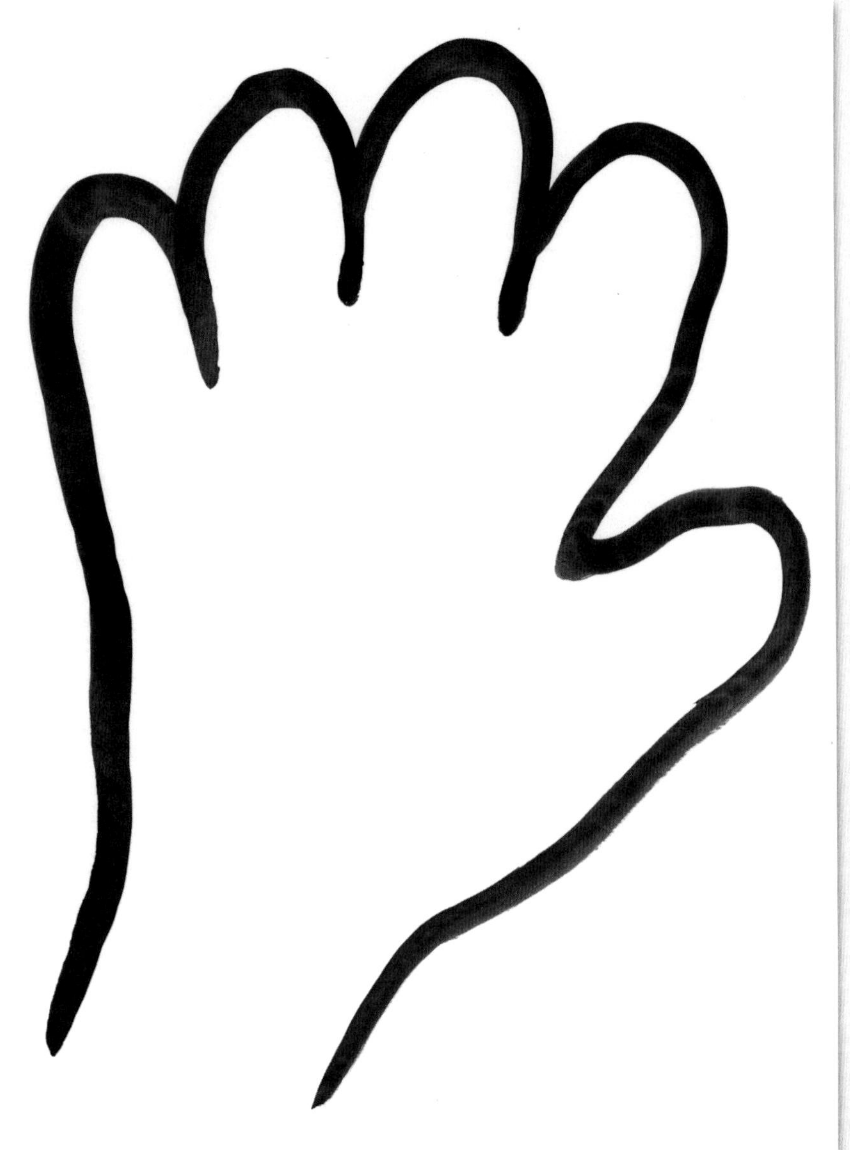

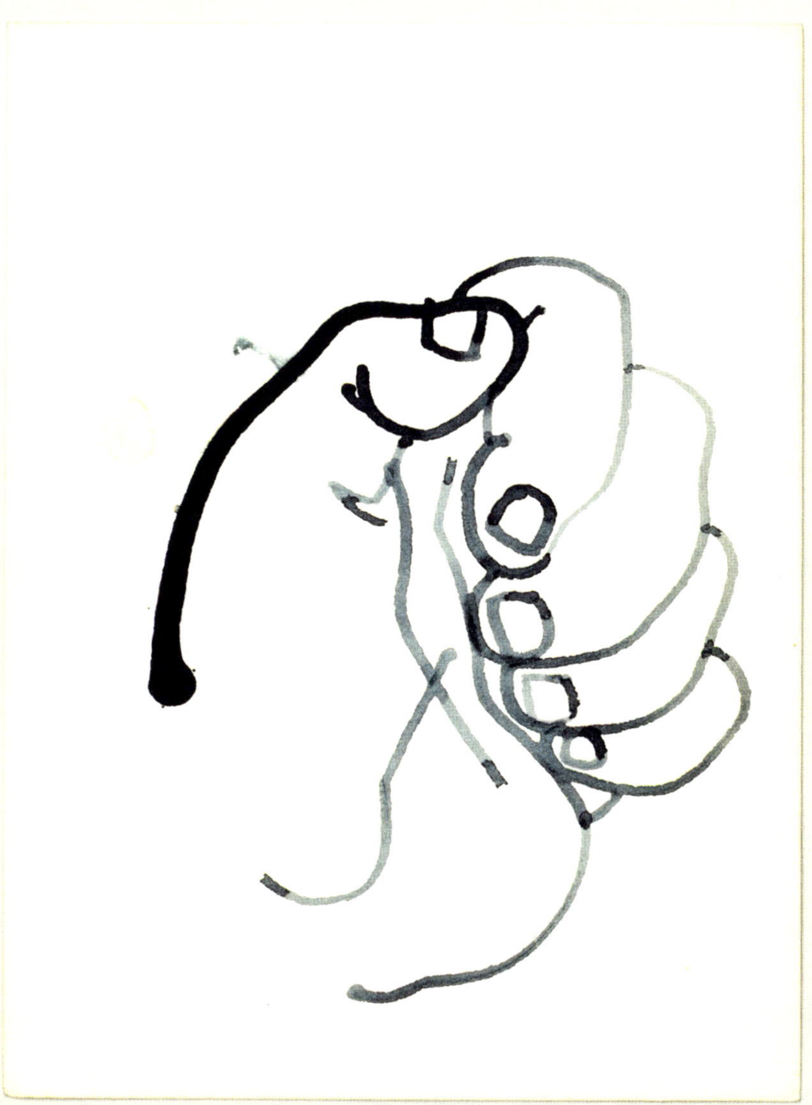

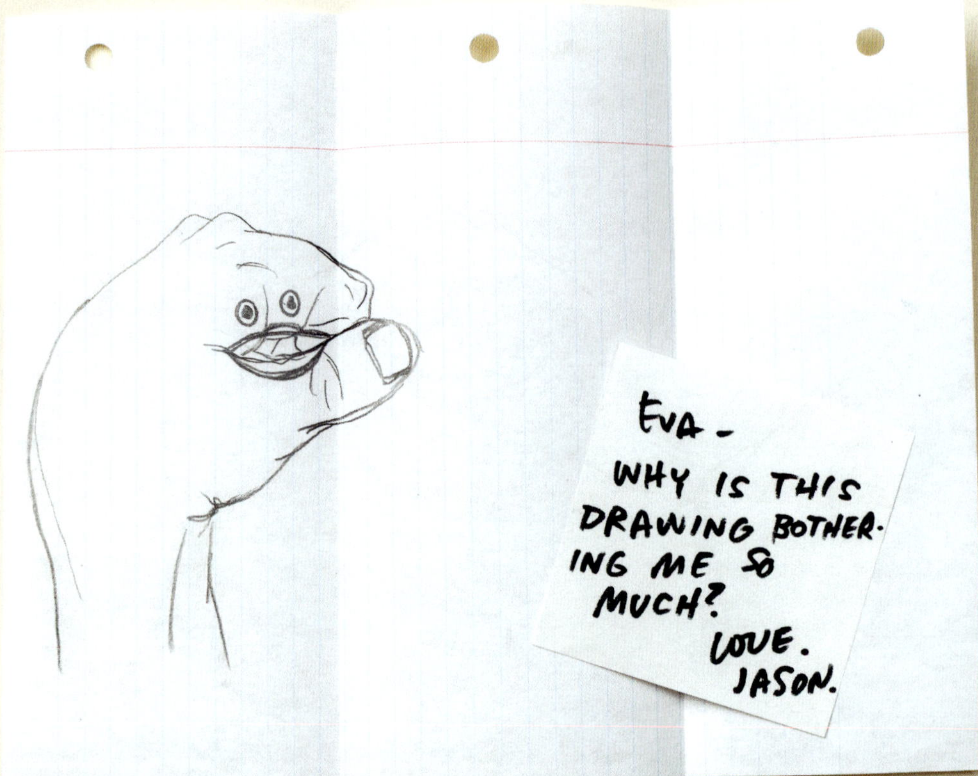
EVA -
WHY IS THIS
DRAWING BOTHER-
ING ME SO
MUCH?
LOVE.
JASON.

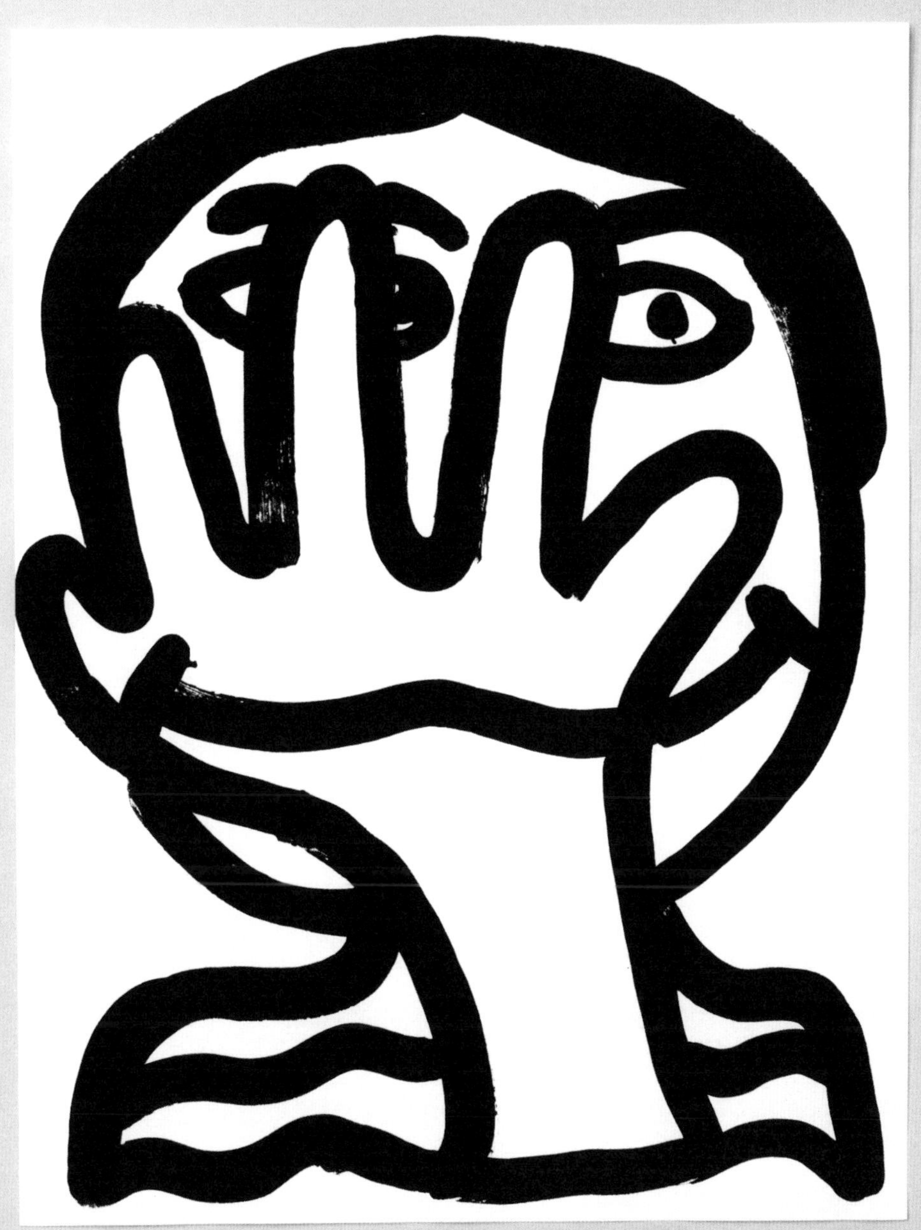

VISIT THE BEAUTIFUL STATE OF TENNESSEE
There's much to see and do in Tennessee, from Memphis, the home of Elvis, to Nashville, Country Music U.S.A., to East Tenn. and the beauty of the Smokey Mountain Range.

Photo: ©1981 Steve Caldwell

NASHVILLE TN 372
PM
29 OCT
2011

© 1991 Richard & Southern

A mocking bird?
What kind of state
is rep'd by a wise
ass bird like that!?

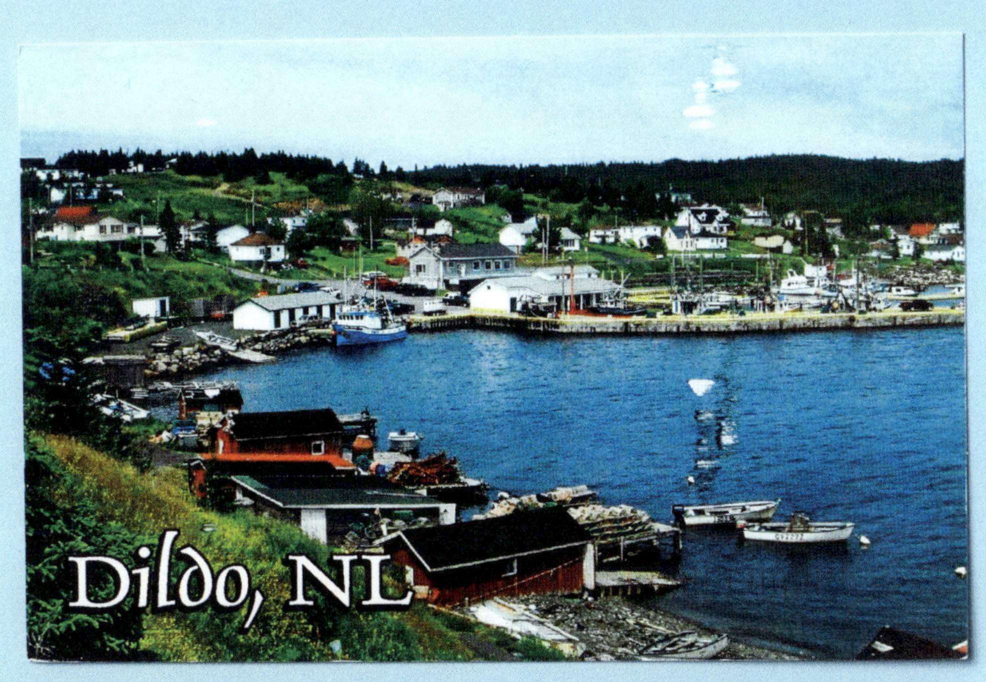

On way to, not kidding.

Spread Eagle!

Hello! Here's a letter all about falconry. Enjoy.

- In England during the 1600s, falconry was governed by a strict set of rules:
  - a King could fly a gyrfalcon
  - an earl could fly a peregrine
  - a yeoman could use a goshawk
  - the sparrowhead was reserved for priests
  - servants could have a kestral.

- Falconry plummeted with the growing popularity of firearms and the decline of the aristocracy.

- The hood is the most important of the falconer's aids. It is used during the manning process (acclimating to humans) to keep the raptor calm throughout training.

MICHAEL.

CAN I HAVE YOUR AUTOGRAPH?

THANKS SO MUCH,
JASON POLAN

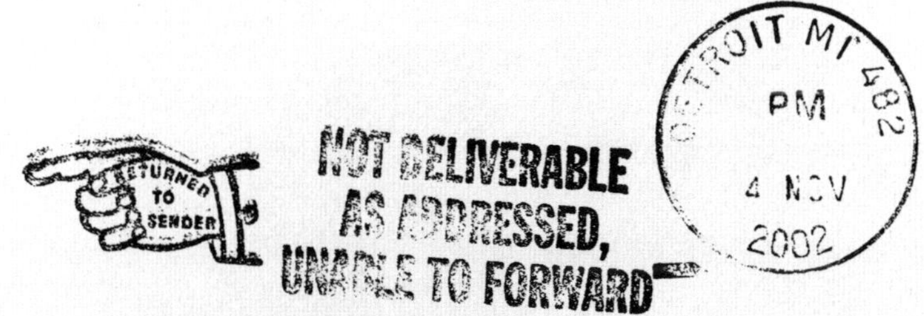

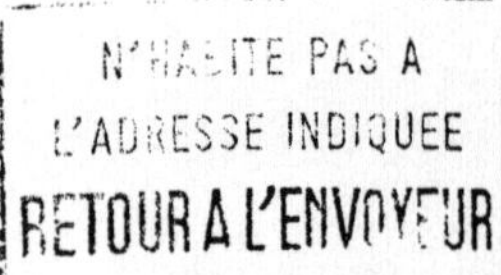

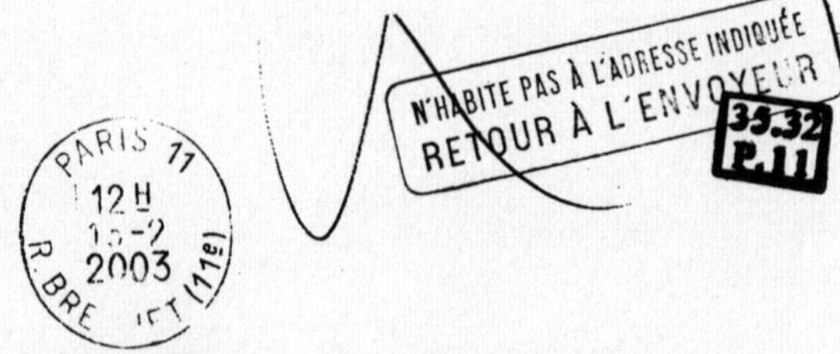

space invader.

i enjoy your work. i wanted to know if i could have your autograph?

thank you,
jason polan

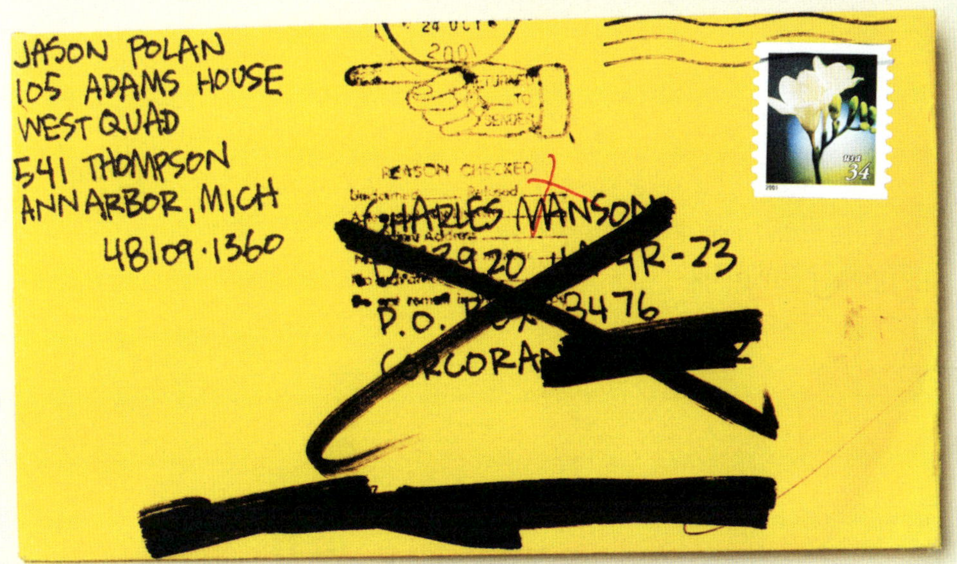

MR. MANSON

I AM INTERESTED + CONFUSED BY YOU.

CAN I HAVE YOUR AUTOGRAPH?

THANKS, JASON POLAN
105 ADAMS HOUSE
WEST QUAD
541 THOMPSON
ANN ARBOR, MICH 48109-1360

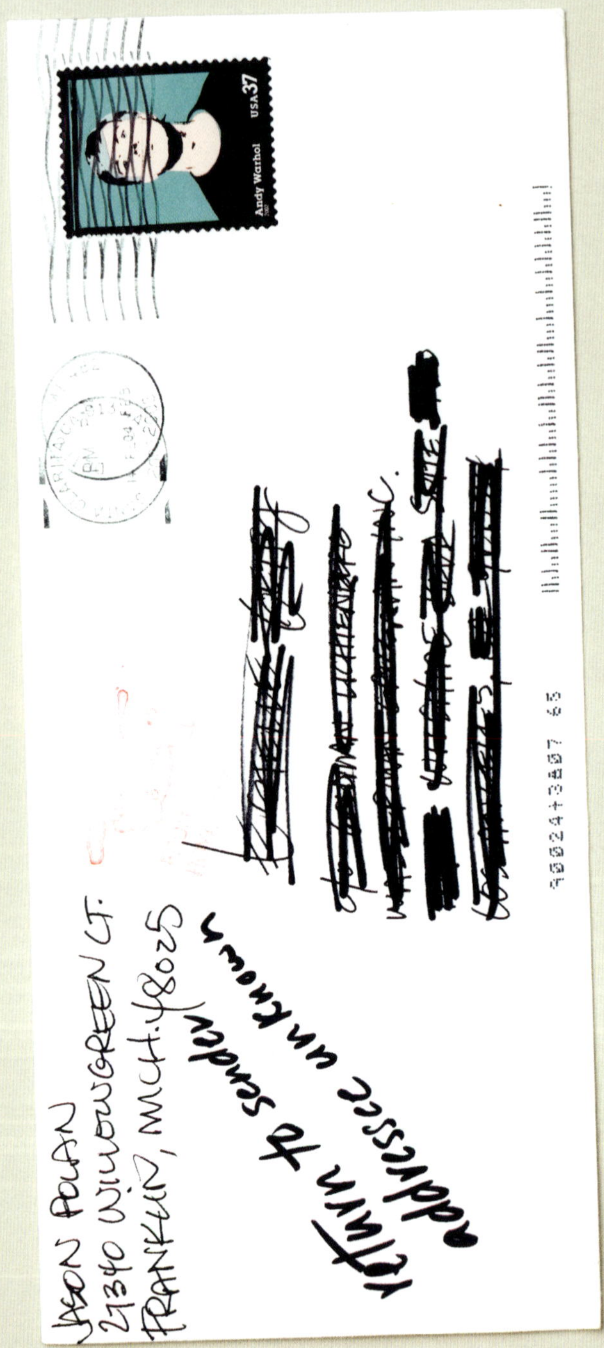
Andy Warhol
USA37
JASON POLAN
27340 WILLOWGREEN CT.
FRANKLIN, MICH. 48025
return to sender
addressee unknown

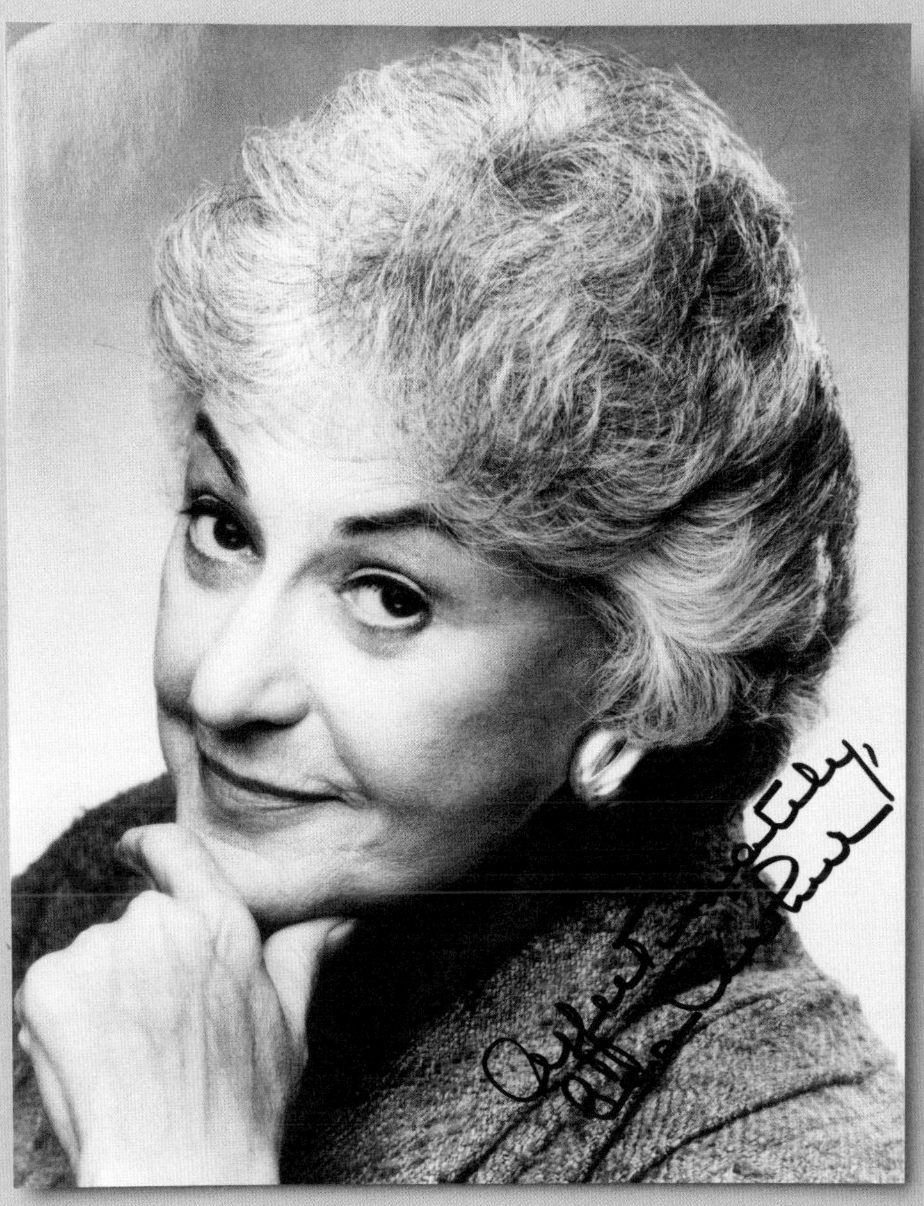

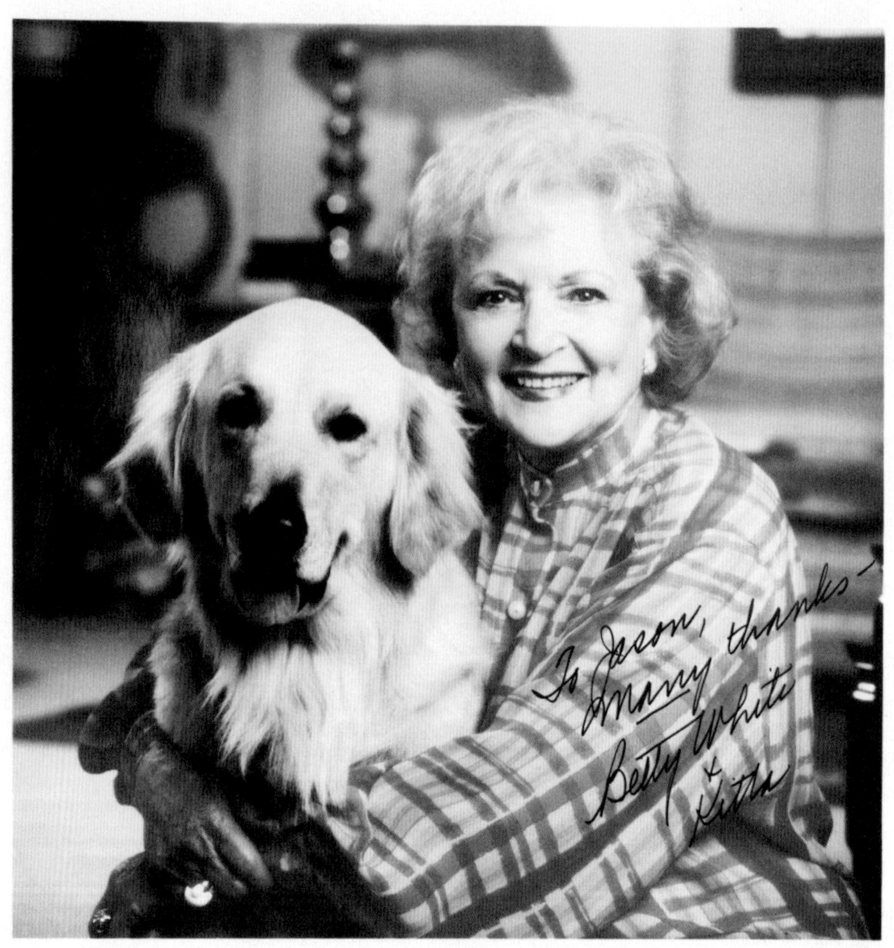
To Jason,
Many thanks—
Betty White
+ Kitta

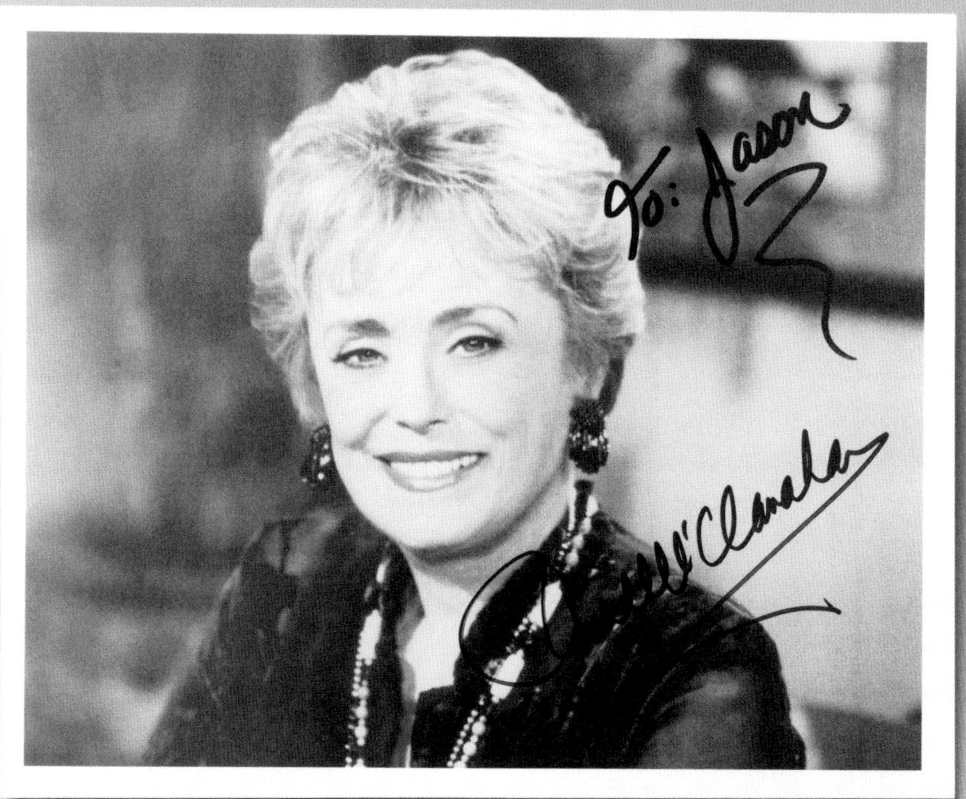
To: Jason

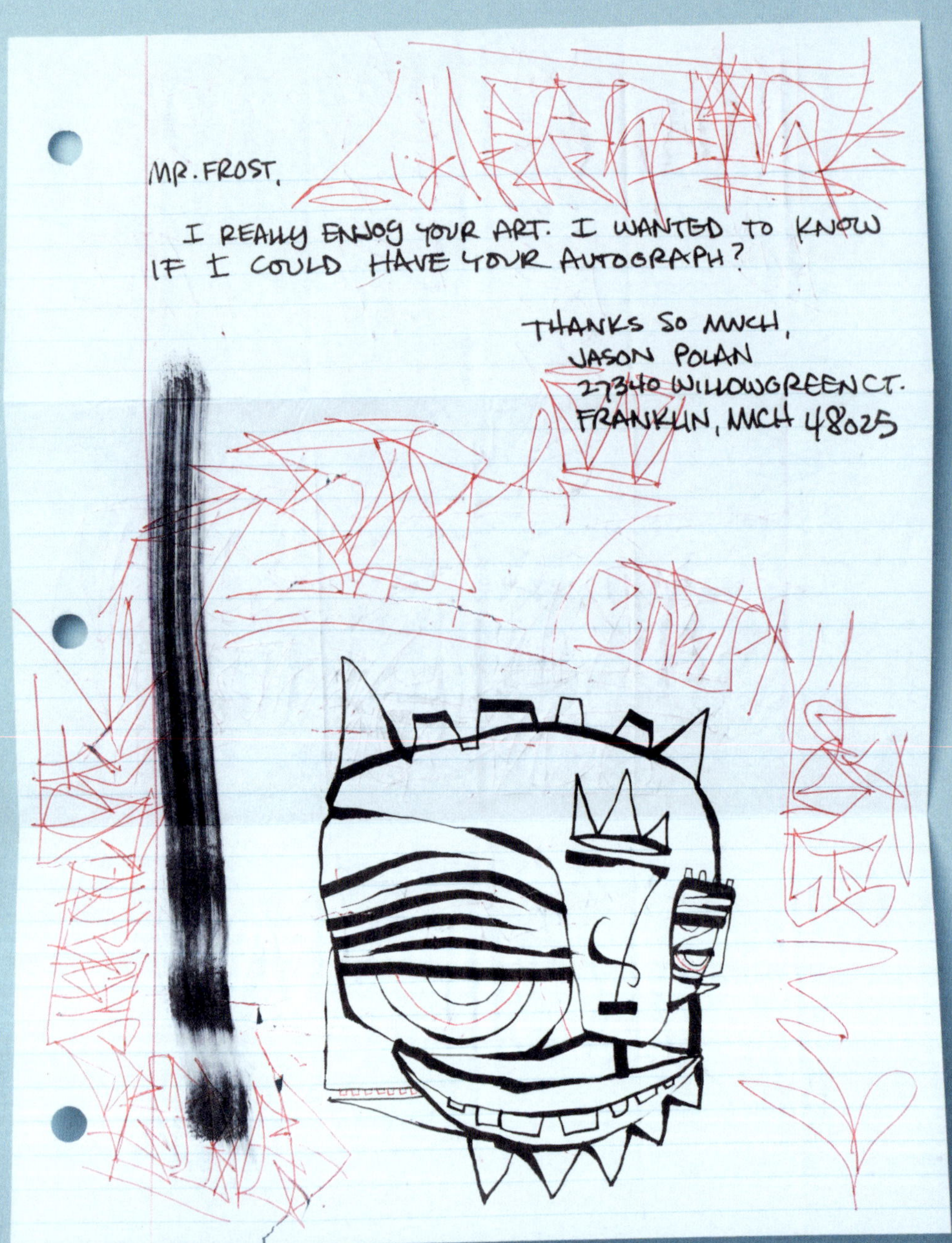

MR. FROST,

I REALLY ENJOY YOUR ART. I WANTED TO KNOW IF I COULD HAVE YOUR AUTOGRAPH?

THANKS SO MUCH,
JASON POLAN
27340 WILLOWGREEN CT.
FRANKLIN, MICH 48025

Dear Mr. Allred,

I just wanted to ask if there was any way to get a sketch or an autograph. I would love any kind of thing you can get to me. thank you!

thanks again,

Jason Polan

JASON POLAN
27340 Willowgreen Ct.
Franklin Mi.
48025

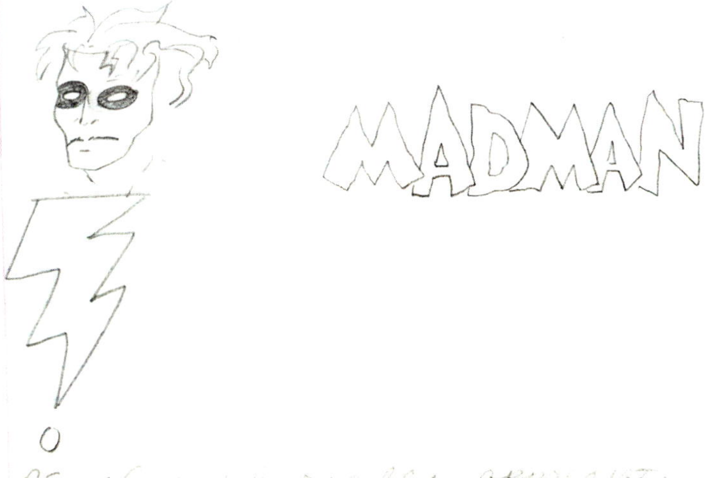

MADMAN

P.S.- I would really appreciate a list of where you will be appearing at shows & cons.

DANIEL JOHNSTON,

I LIKE YOUR MUSIC + DRAWING A LOT, I AM INCLUDING SOME THINGS FOR YOU, I HOPE THAT YOU ARE DOING WELL.

SINCERELY,

JASON POLAN.

Hey Jason,
My autograph
as you
requested!

Ted L. Nancy

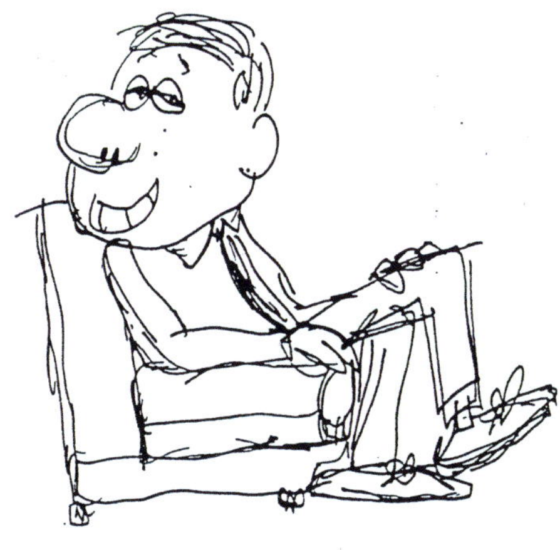

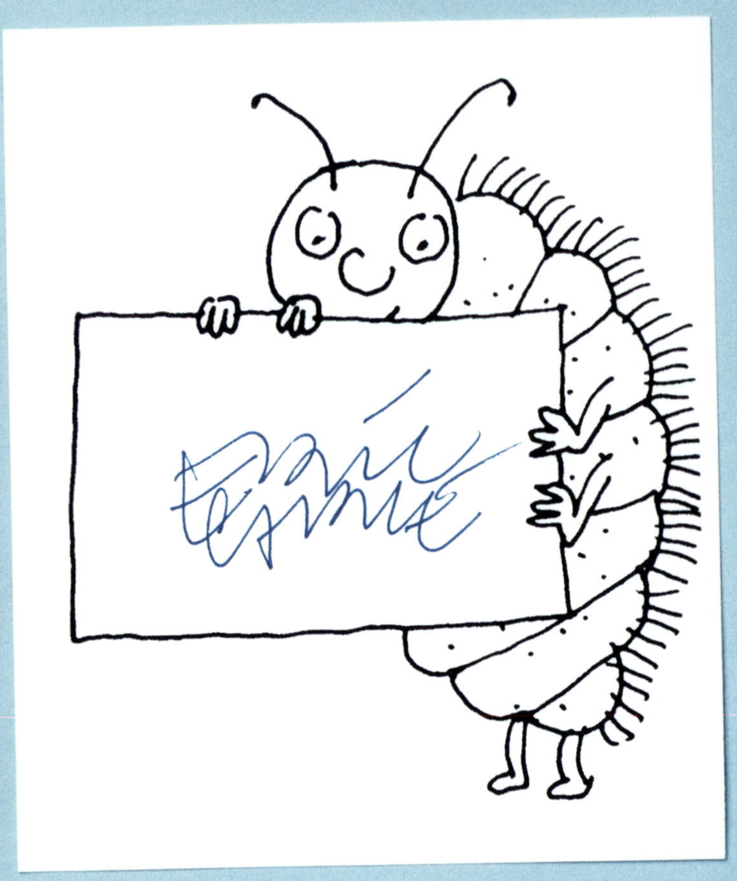

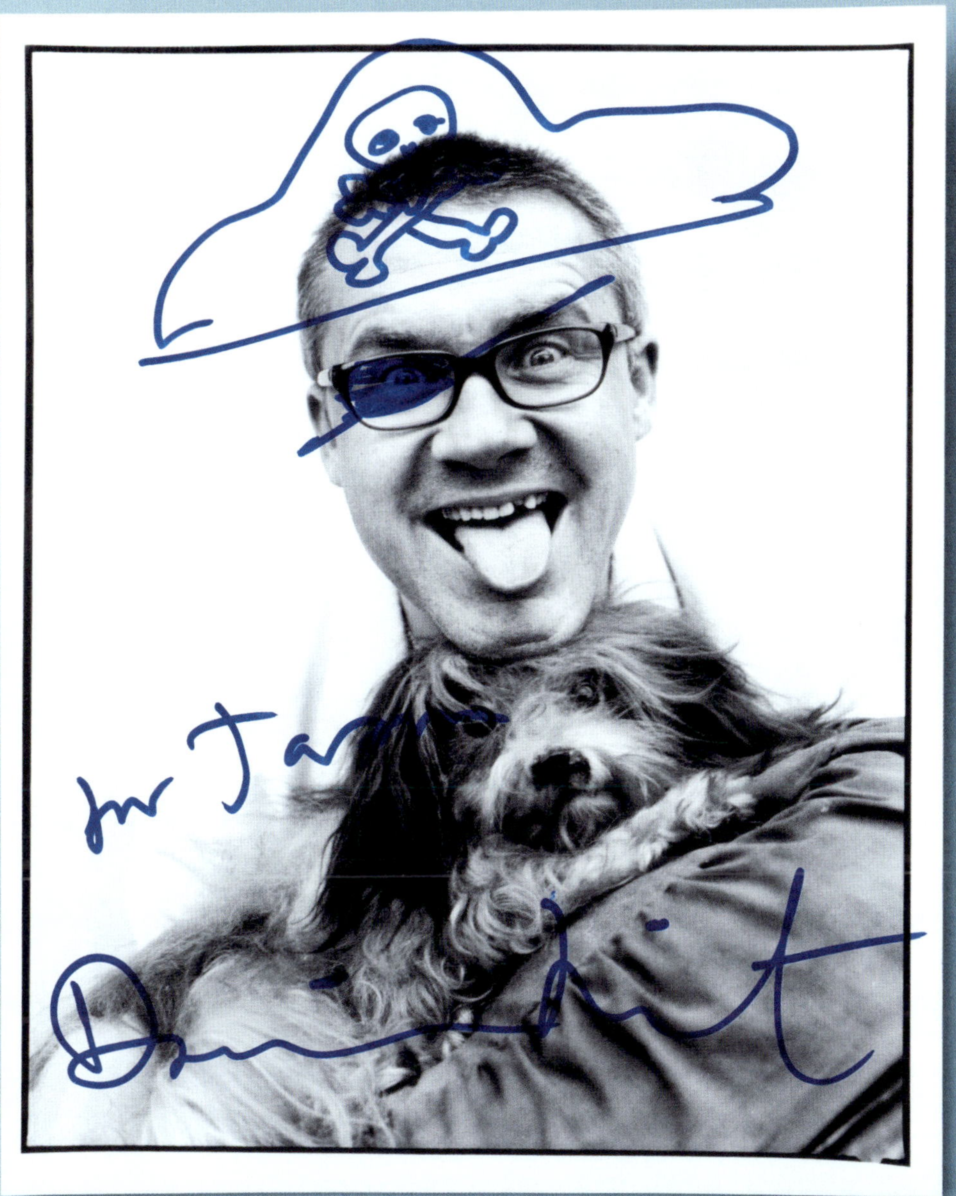

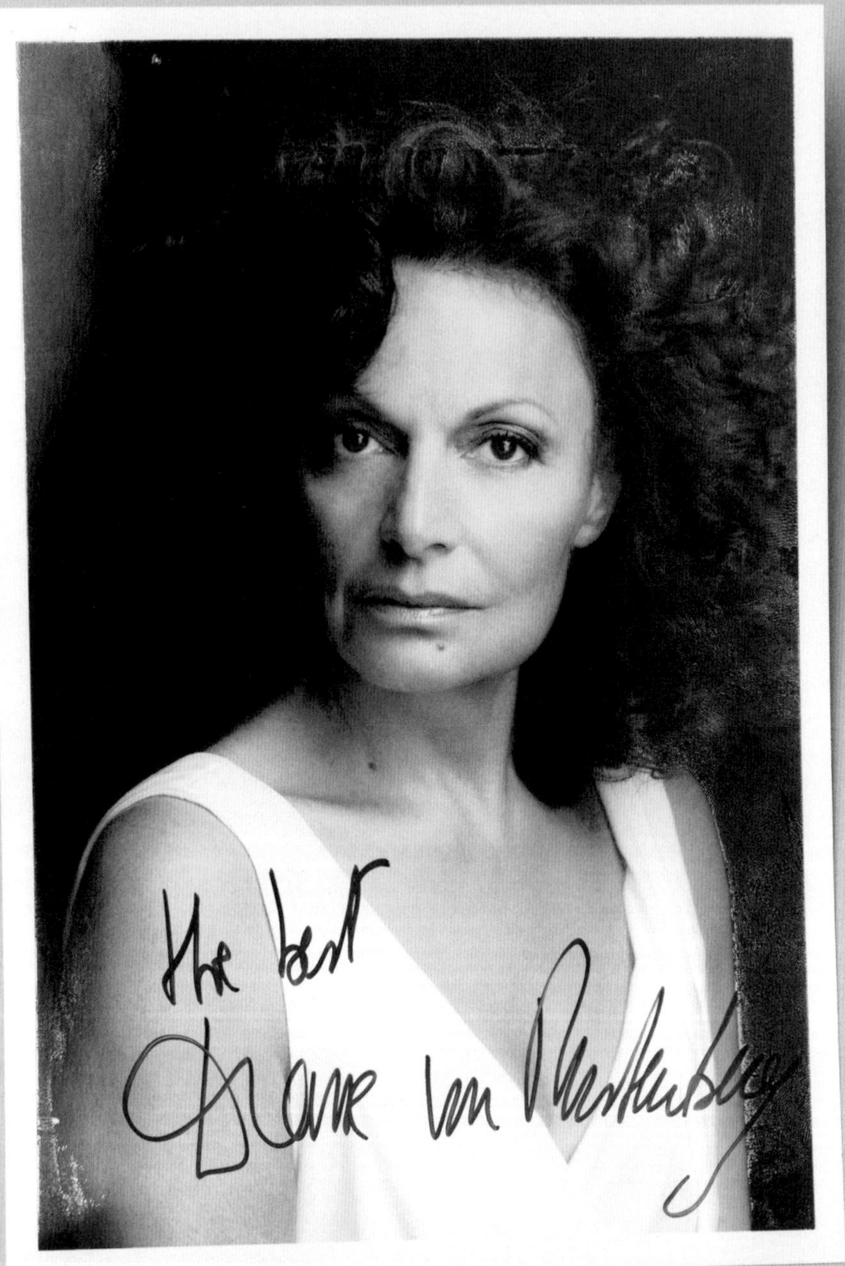

 Diane von Furstenberg to JP

SAM HSIEH PUNCHING HIS TIME CLOCK ON THE HOUR
ONE YEAR PERFORMANCE APRIL. 11, 1980 - APRIL. 11, 1981
PHOTOGRAPH BY MICHAEL SHEN

Performance Space 111 Hudson St. 2 Fl. New York, N.Y. 10013

Dear Jason Polan,

Thank you so much for your support,

Best wishes!

Tehching Hsieh

4. 2004

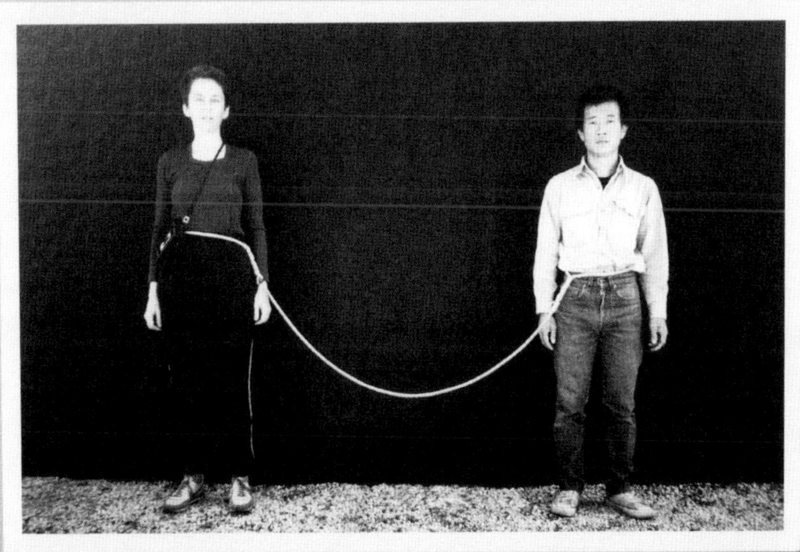

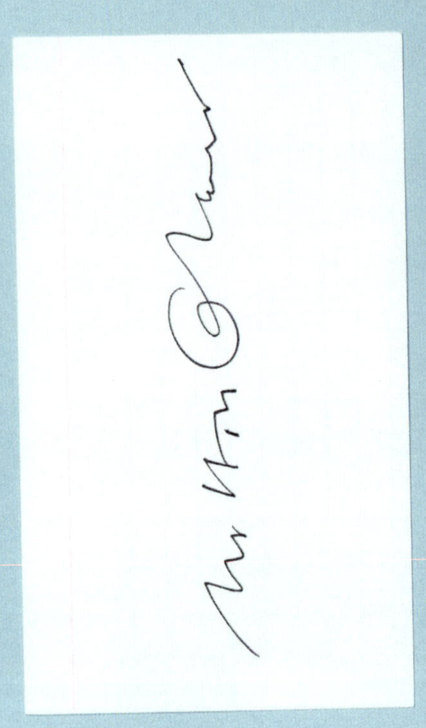

207
EAST 32ND STREET
NEW YORK, N.Y. 10016
TEL. (212) 889-3161
JASON POLAN
105 ADAMS HOUSE
WEST QUAD
541 THOMPSON
ANN ARBOR, MICH
48109-1360
$00.340
MAILED FROM NEW YORK NY 10016

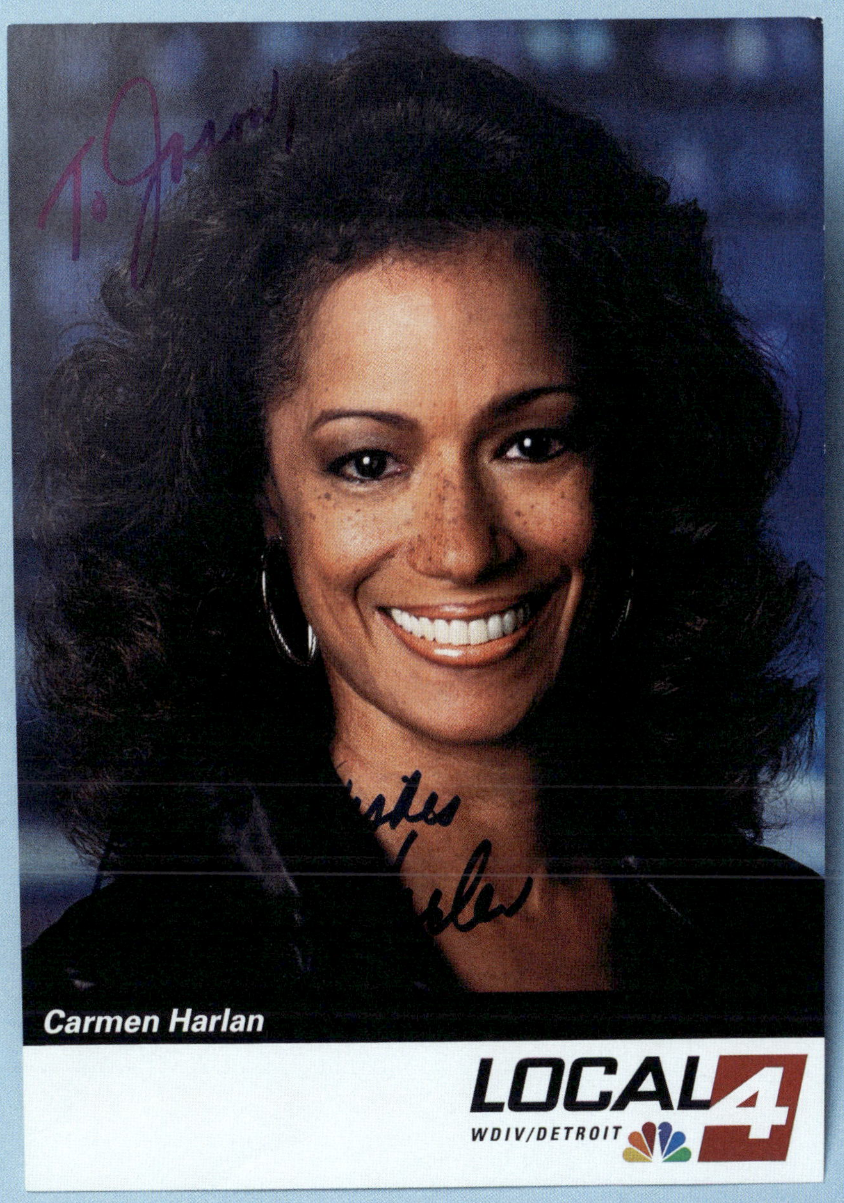
Carmen Harlan
LOCAL 4
WDIV/DETROIT

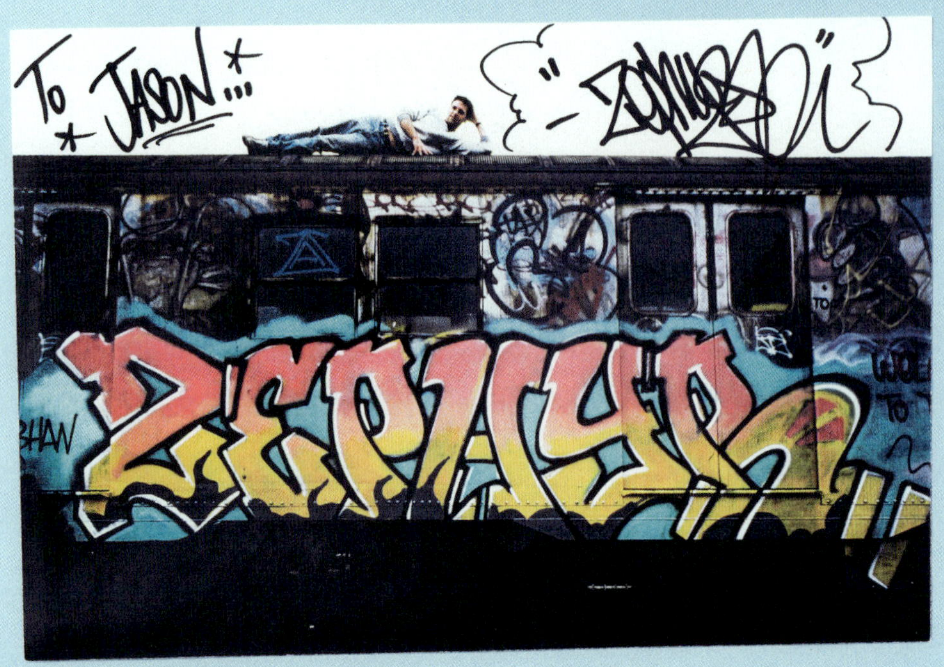

JASON—

Info on respirators:
I like the double cartridge type →
make sure it's tight. Replace cartridges. Replace respirator also, after much use. When you first put it on, blow into it. You should hear the valves "click" a little. They get sticky & lock up. Make sure they're "breathing" freely.

Unfortunately, I can't set up a meeting. I prefer to stay underground...

Thanks,

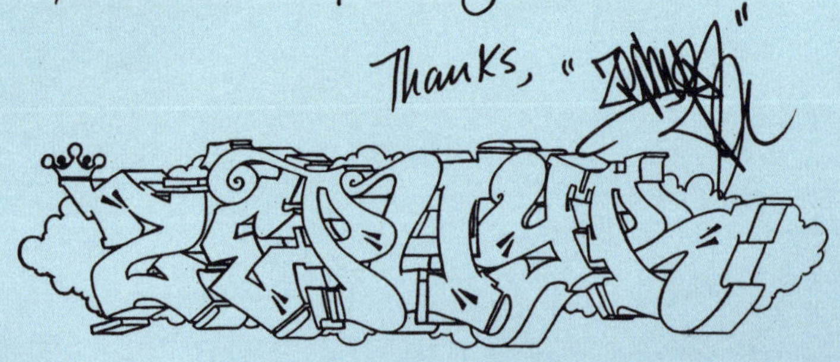

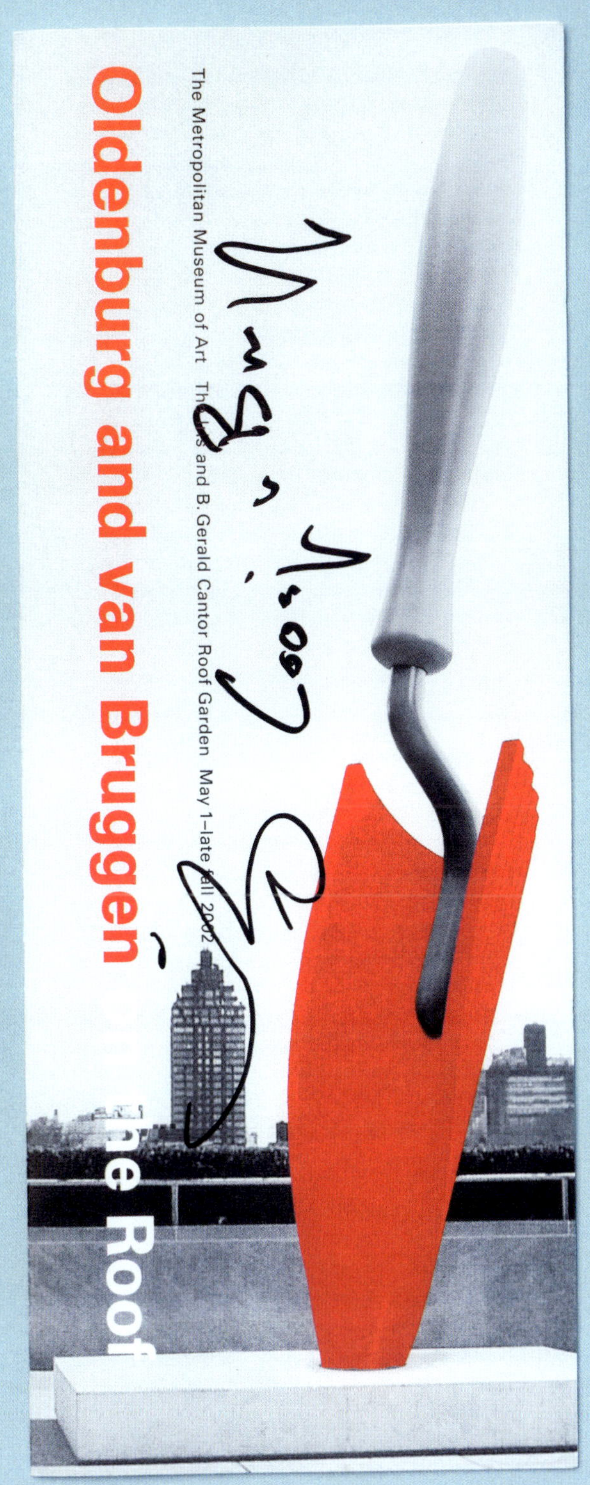
The Metropolitan Museum of Art
Oldenburg and van Bruggen

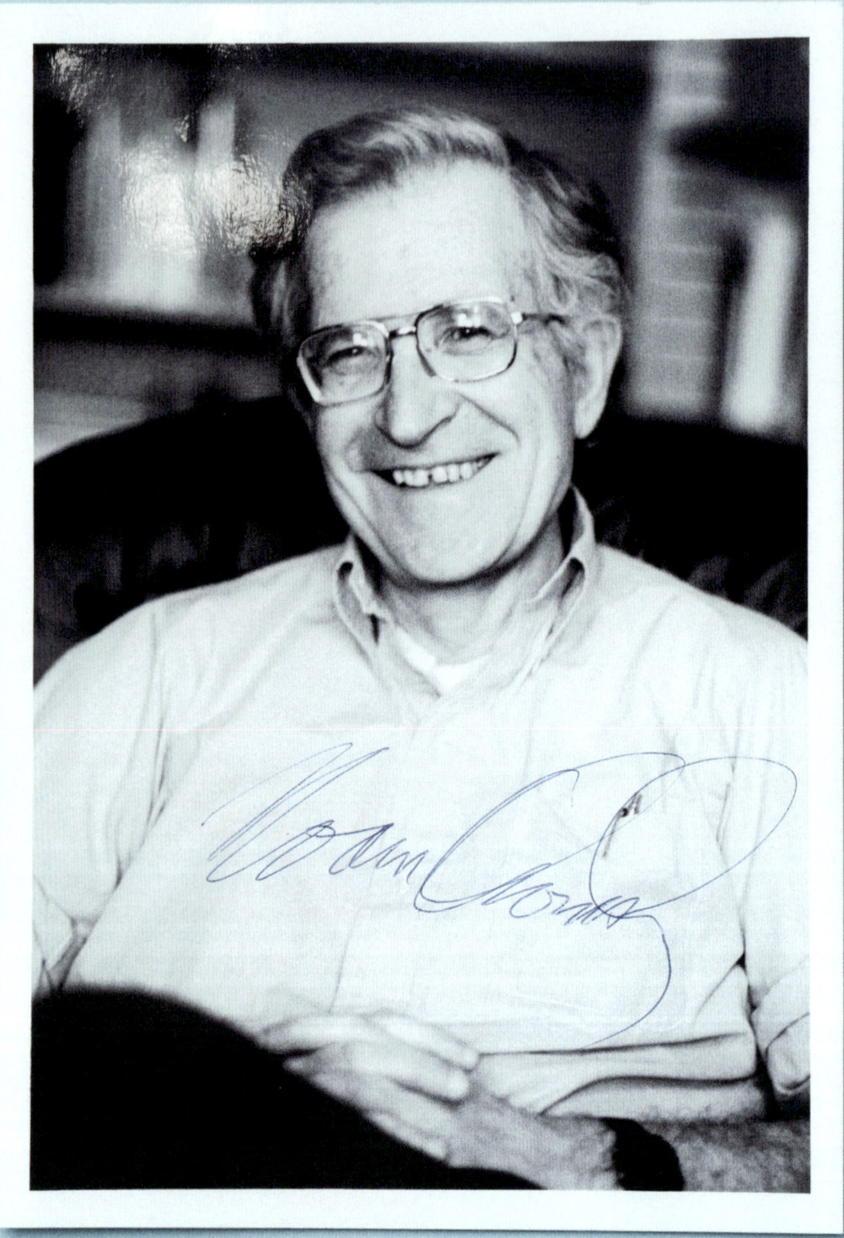

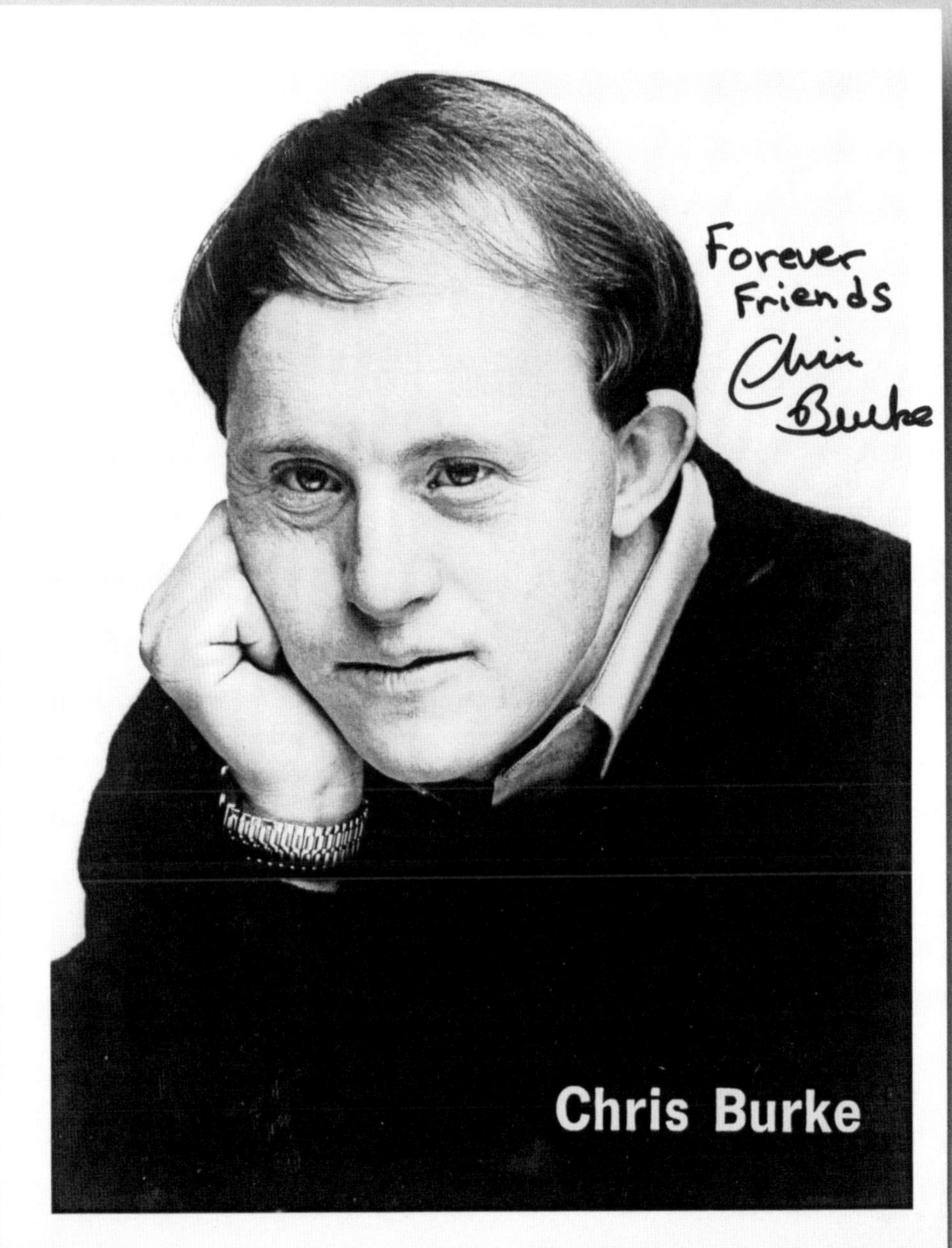
Forever
Friends
Chris
Burke
Chris Burke

MR. COPELAND,

I ENJOY YOUR ART WORK.
YOUR SKETCHBOOKS ARE AMAZING.
I WANTED TO KNOW IF I
COULD HAVE YOUR AUTOGRAPH?

THANKS SO MUCH,
JASON POLAN
27340 WILLOWGREEN CT.
FRANKLIN, MICH
48025

HERE YA GO,

JOHN COPELAND

DJ SHADOW,

I ENJOY YOUR WORK. I WANTED TO KNOW IF I COULD HAVE AN AUTOGRAPH.

THANKS SO MUCH,

JASON POLAN
27340 WILLOWGREEN CT.
FRANKLIN, MICH 48025

All the Best,

12/16/02

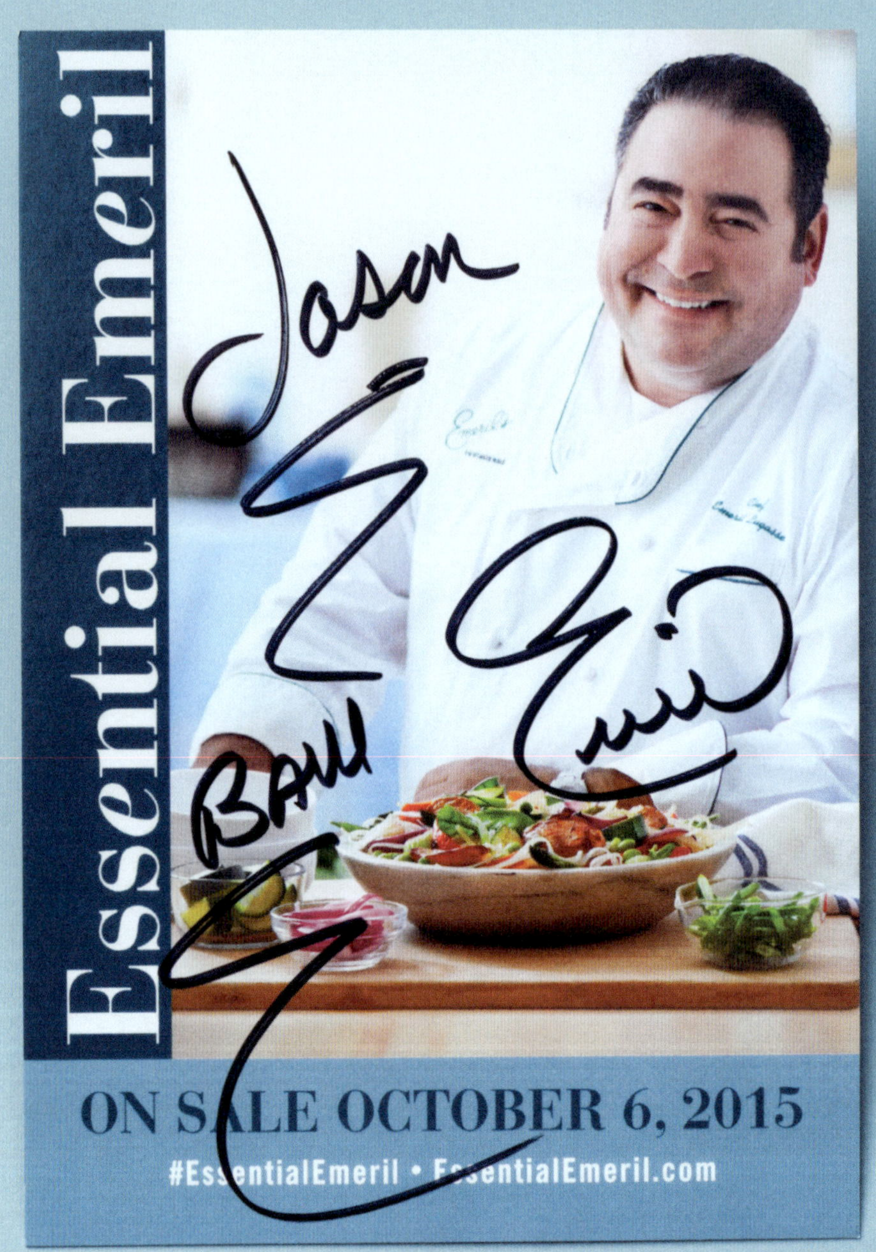
Essential Emeril
Jason
BAM
ON SALE OCTOBER 6, 2015
#EssentialEmeril • EssentialEmeril.com

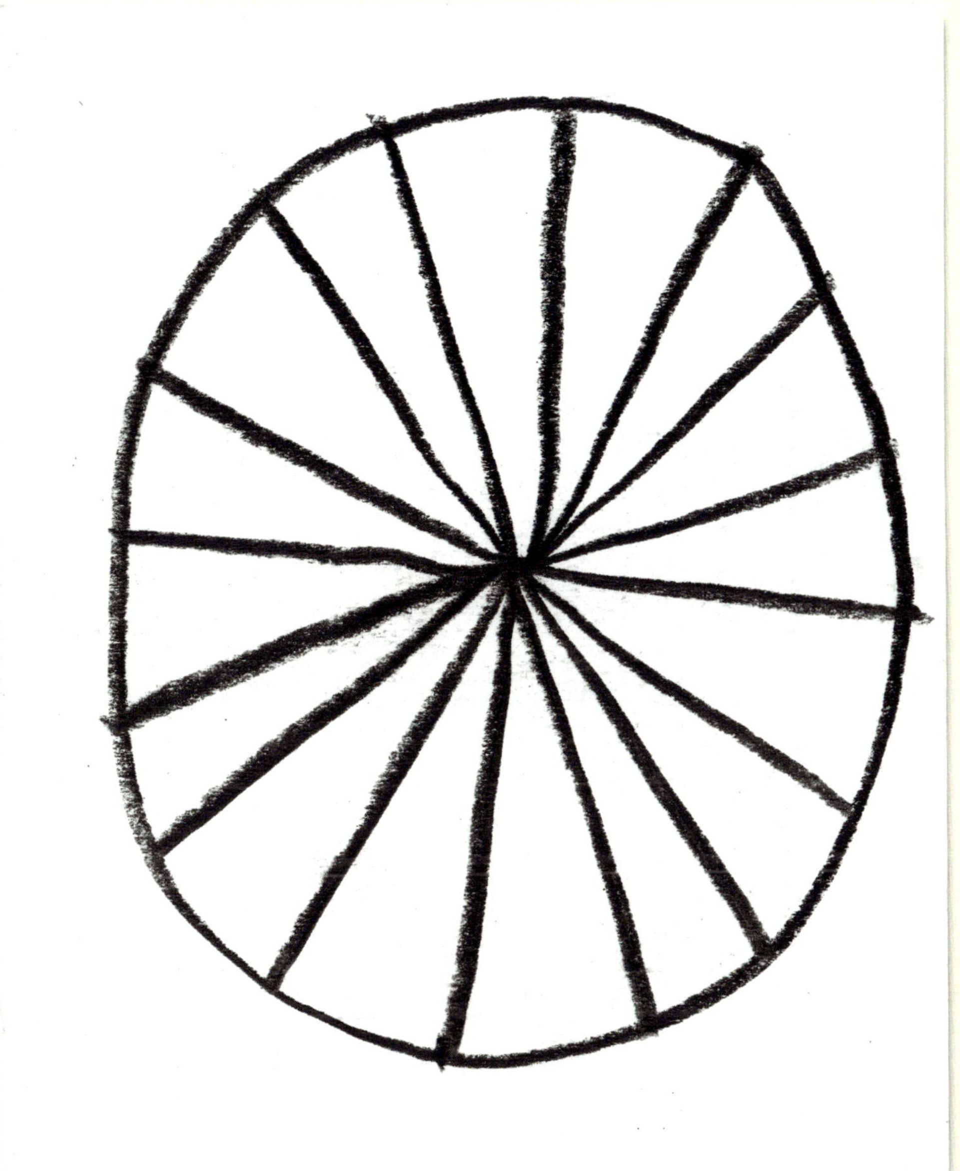

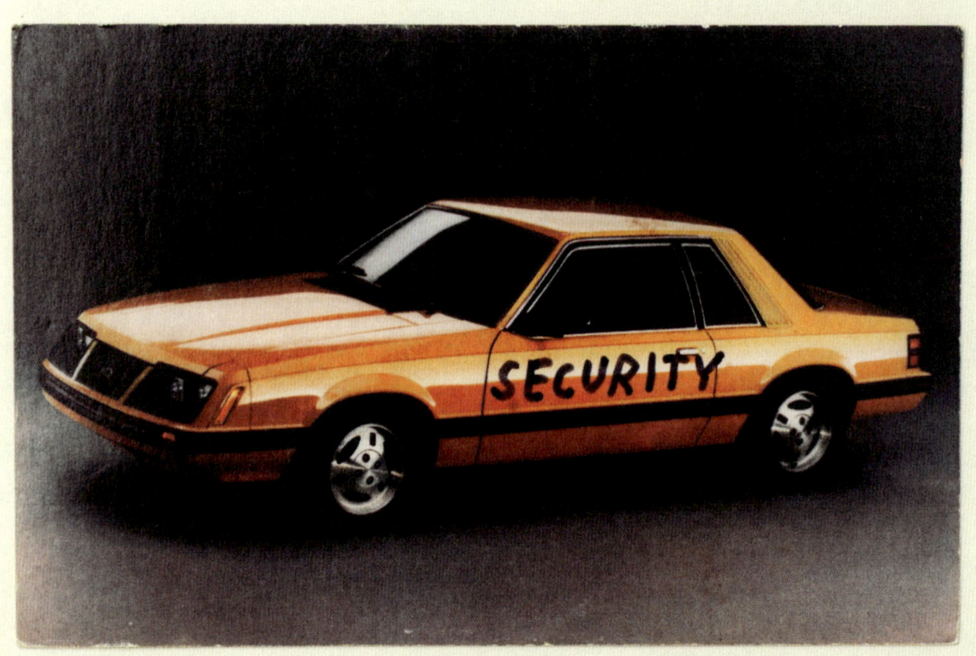
SECURITY

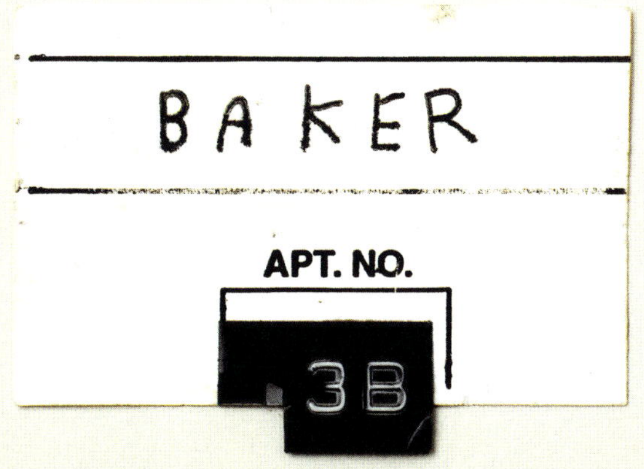
BAKER
APT. NO.
3B

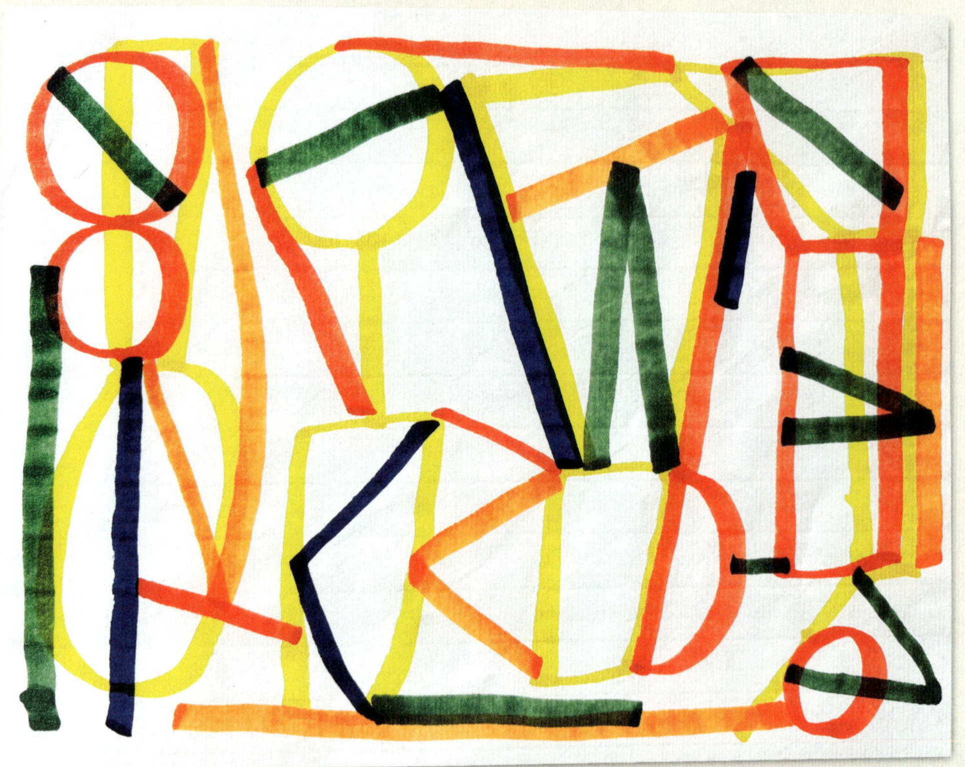

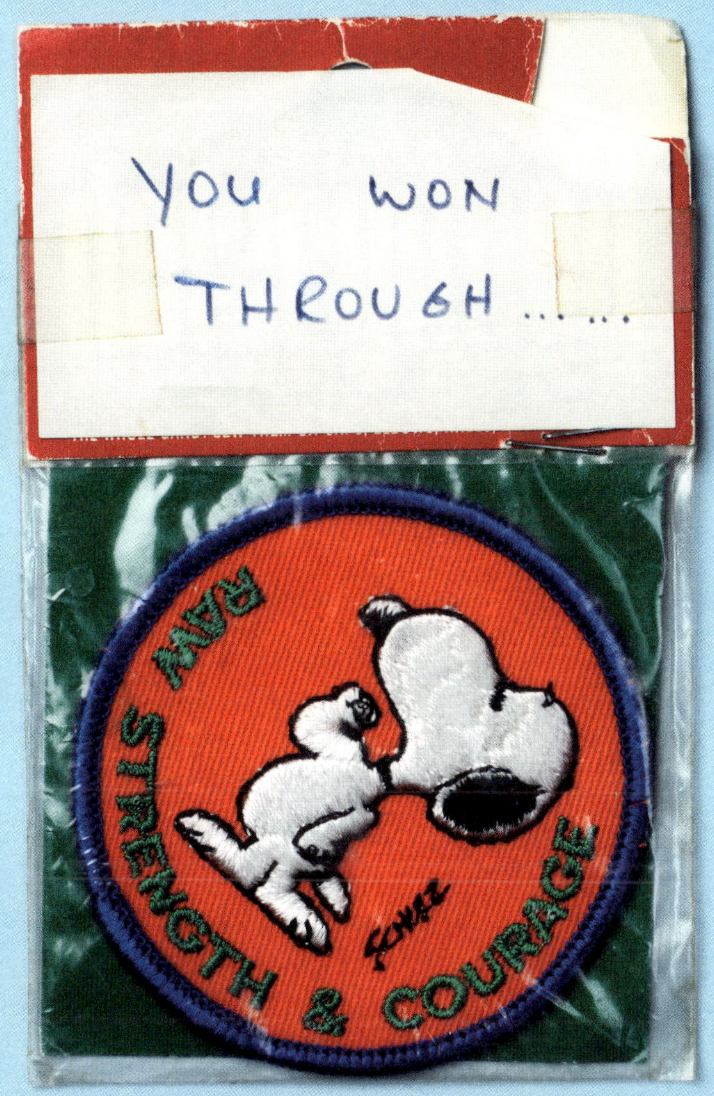
YOU WON
THROUGH ......
RAW
STRENGTH & COURAGE
SCHULZ

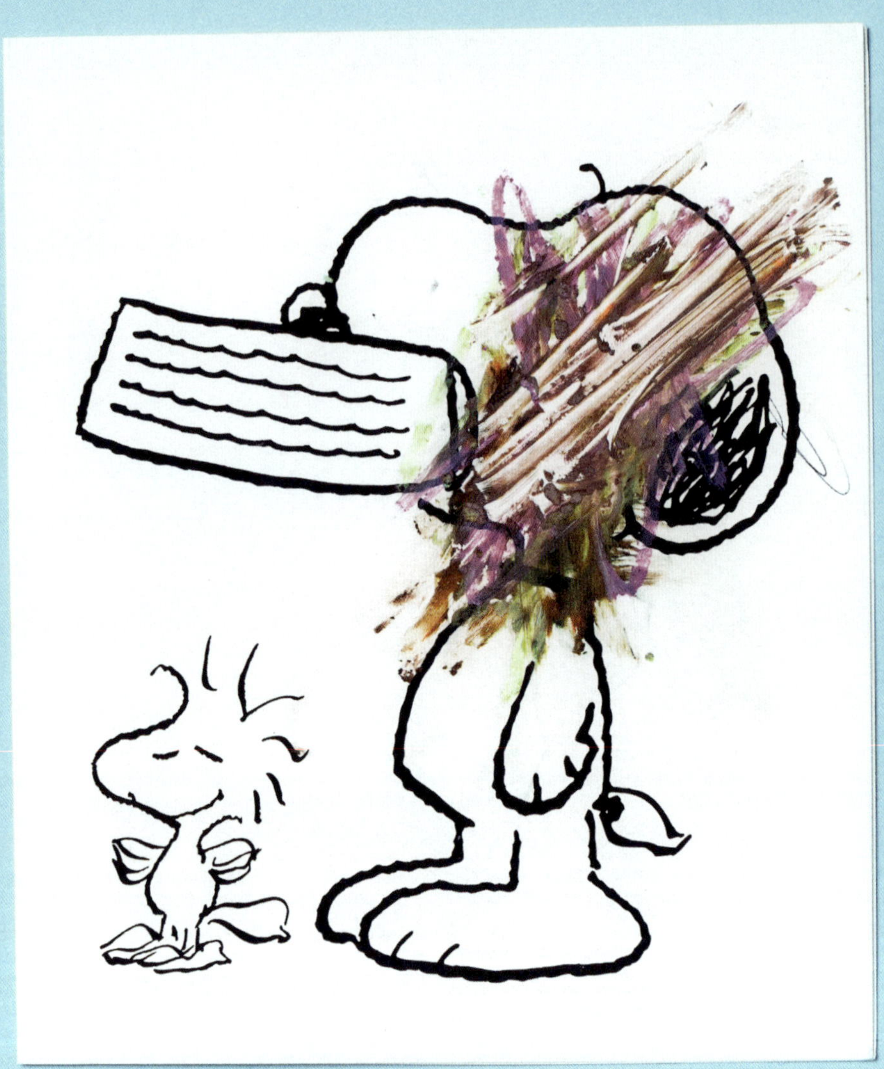

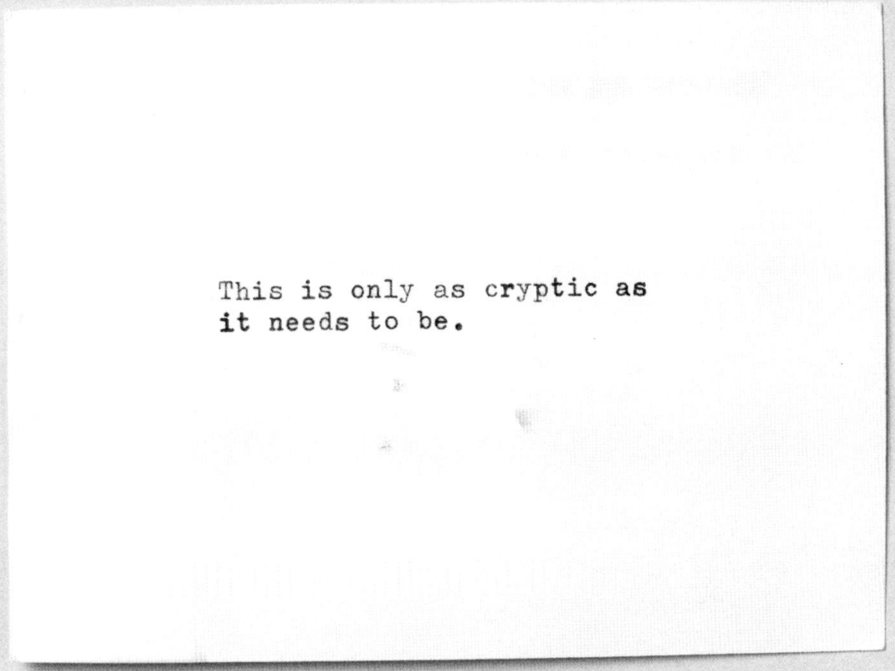

This is only as cryptic as
it needs to be.

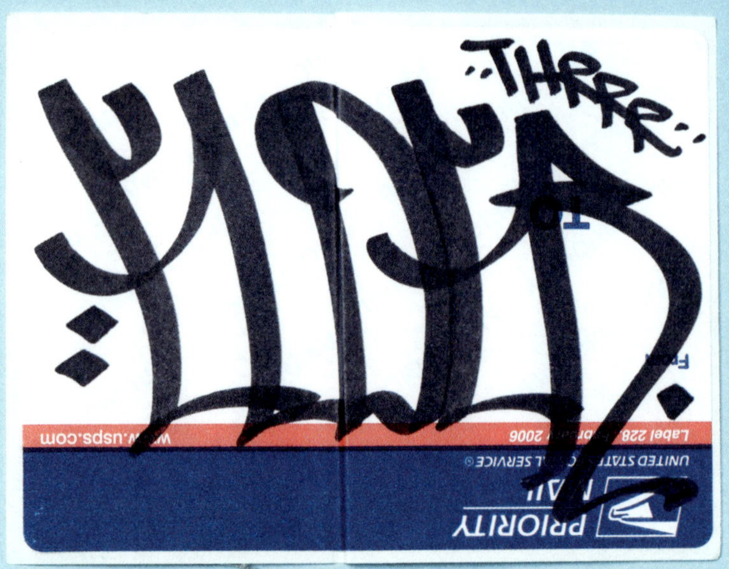
THRRR
PRIORITY
MAIL
www.usps.com

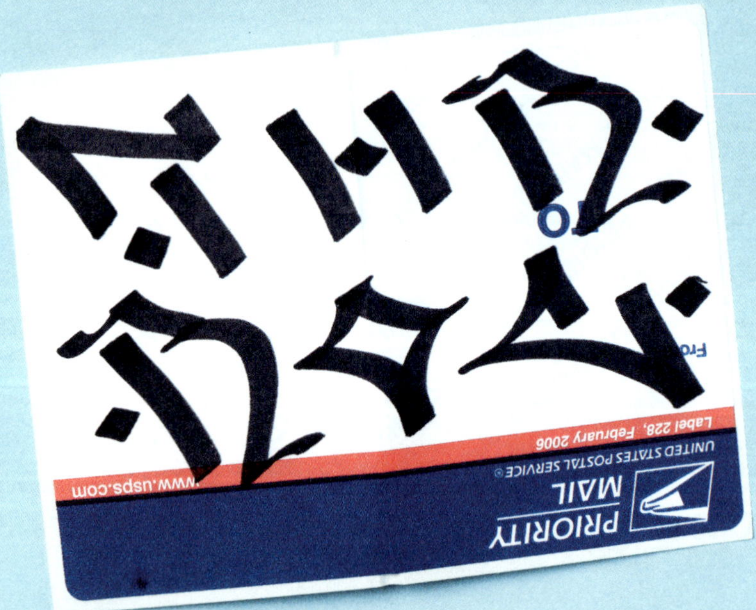
TO
PRIORITY
MAIL
UNITED STATES POSTAL SERVICE®
Label 228, February 2006
www.usps.com

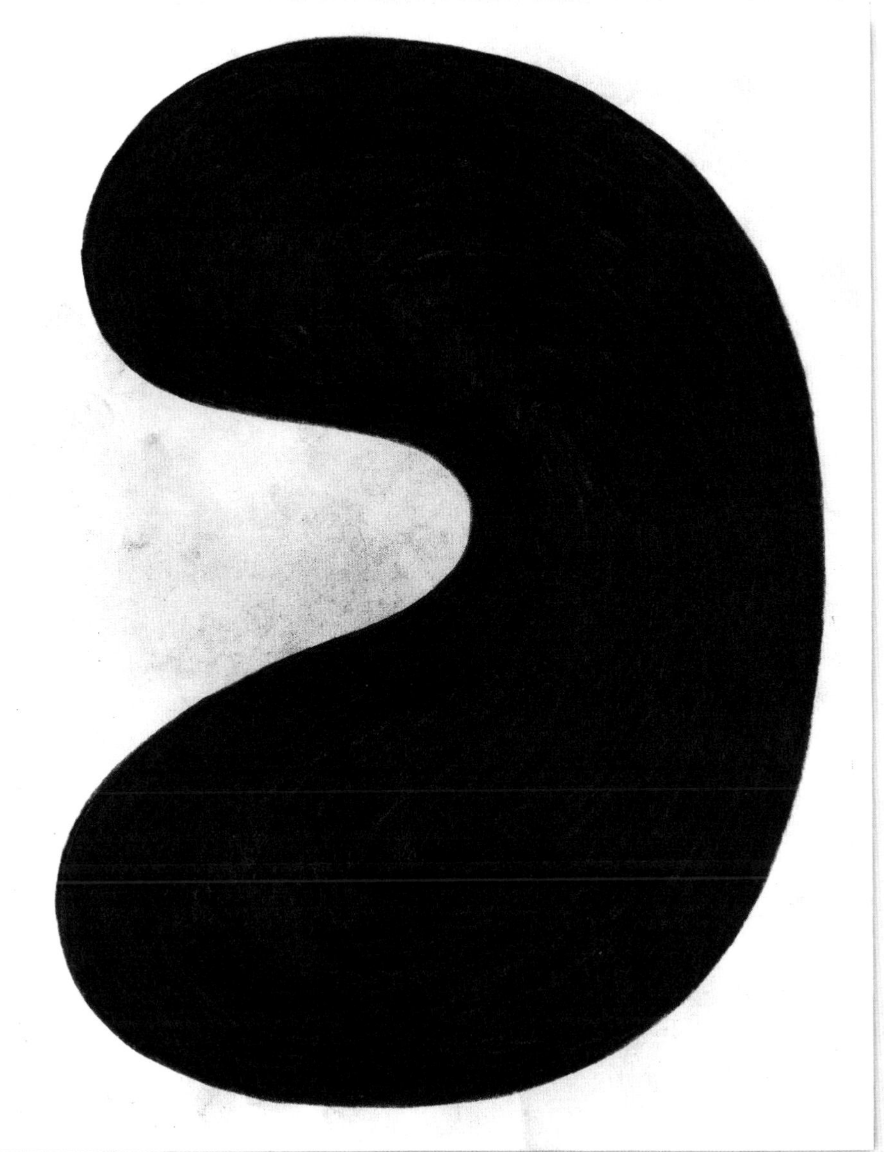

MOUNT!

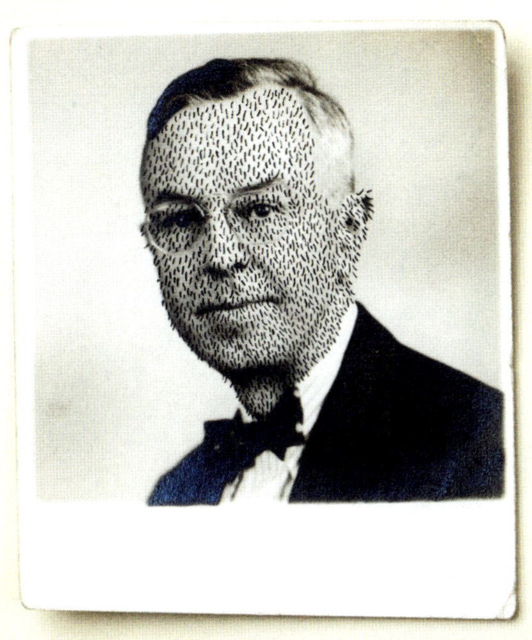

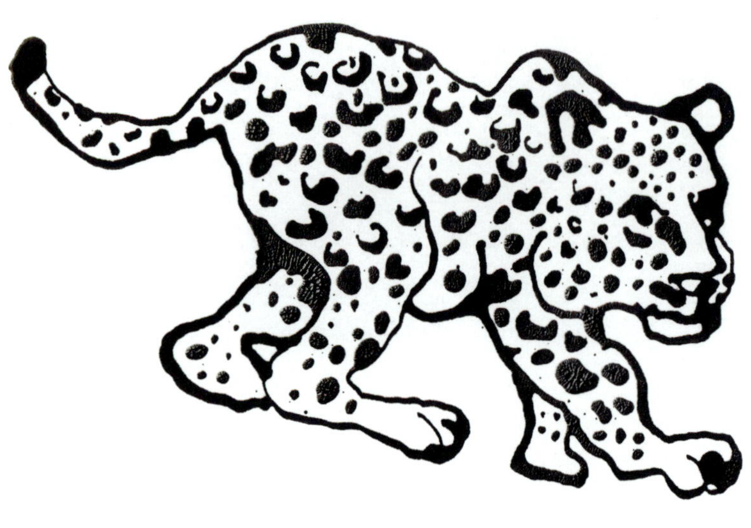

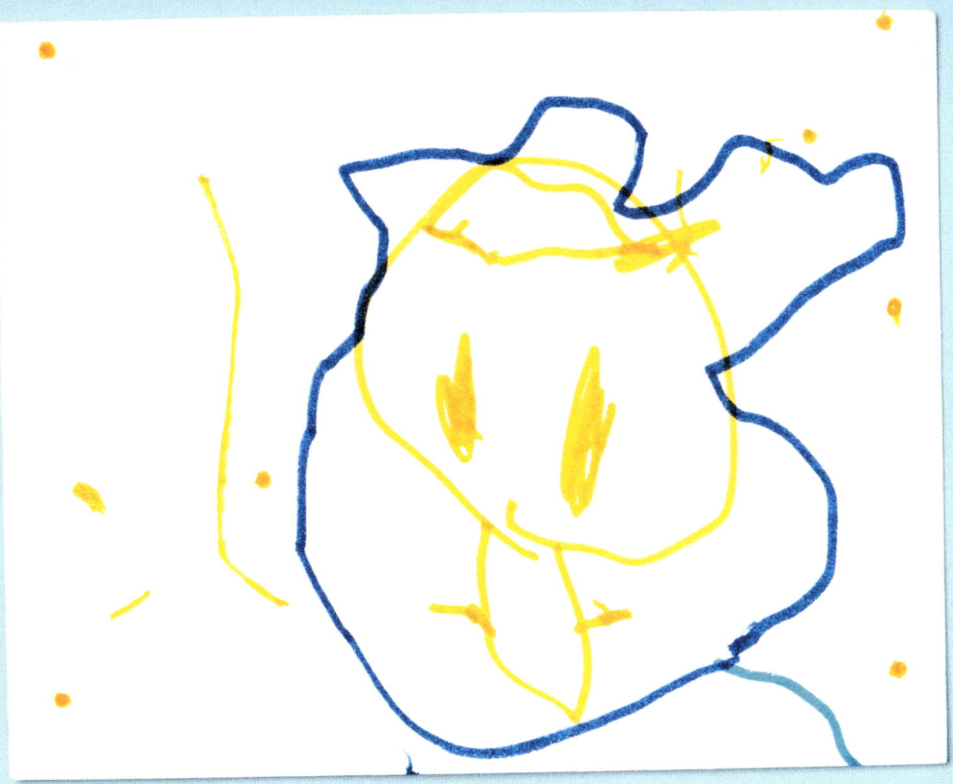

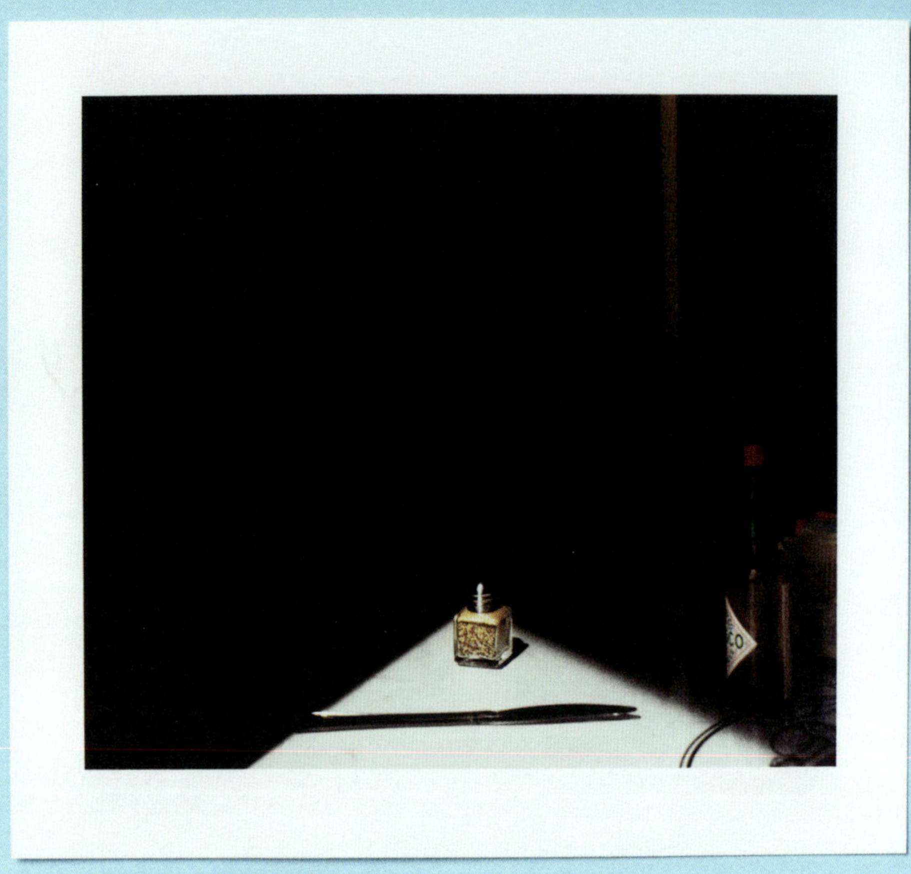

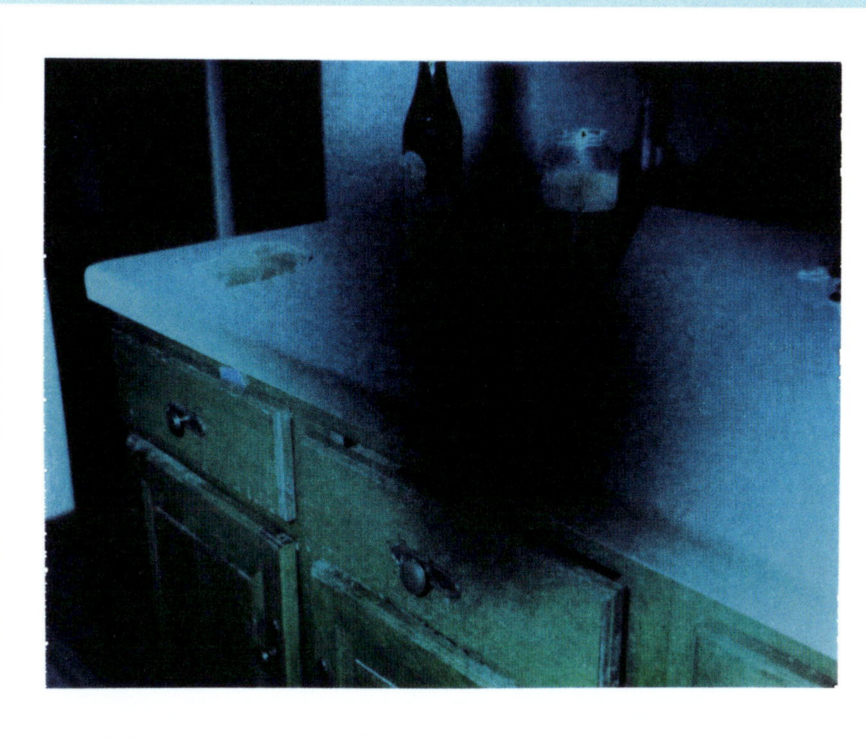

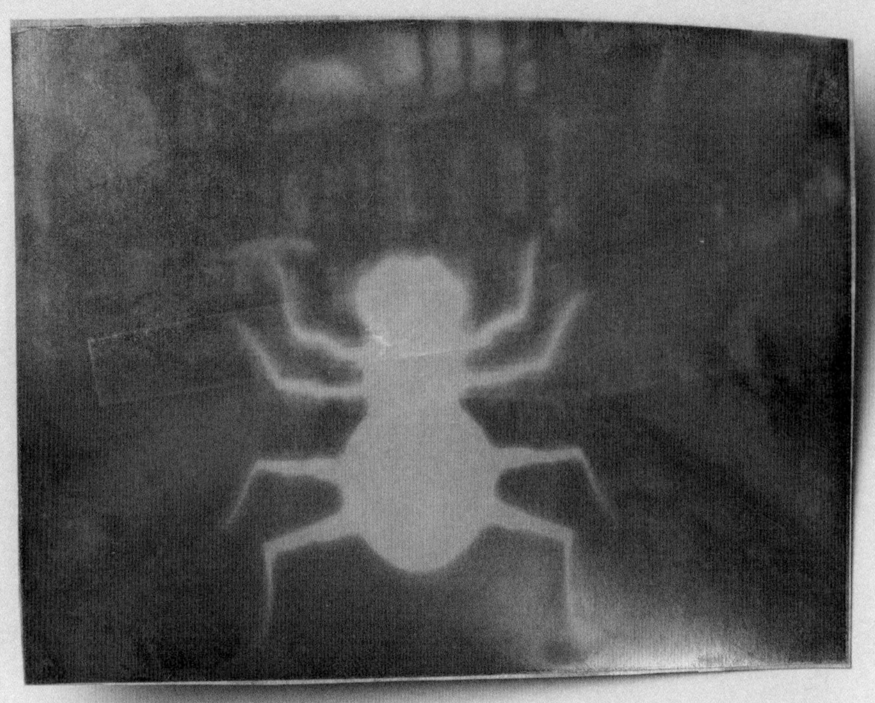

Walker art

Minneapolis Tribune

● Best Buys . . . . . 12 ● Ann Landers . . 13 FRIDAY, MARCH 18, 1966 ★ 11

POP-GUN PAINTING ARRIVES

Artist Finds New Idea Difficult

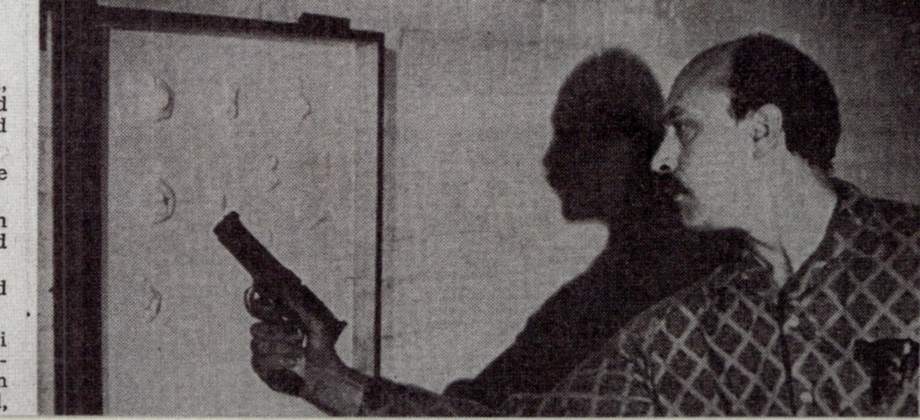

By MIKE STEELE
Minneapolis Tribune
Staff Writer

He aimed the pellet gun, released the safety and shot, again and again. Red oozed out.

"It's great," shouted one woman.

"Needs another shot in the upper left corner," said a well-dressed gentleman.

Thus pop-gun art arrived in Minneapolis.

THE IDEA is that of Niki de St.-Phalle, a Paris painter, with local help from artist Hollis MacDonald,

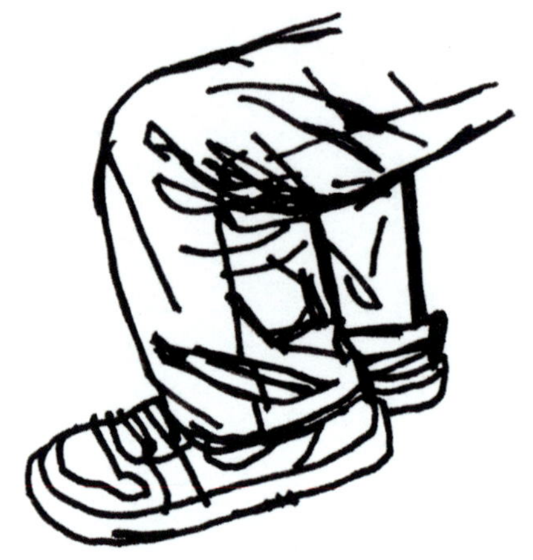

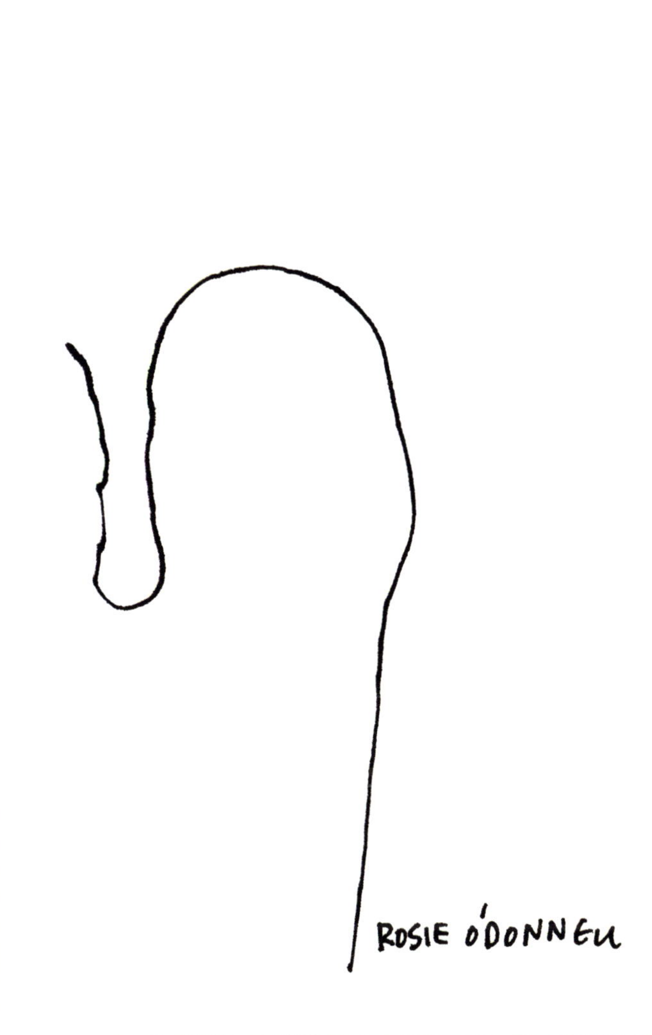
ROSIE O'DONNELL

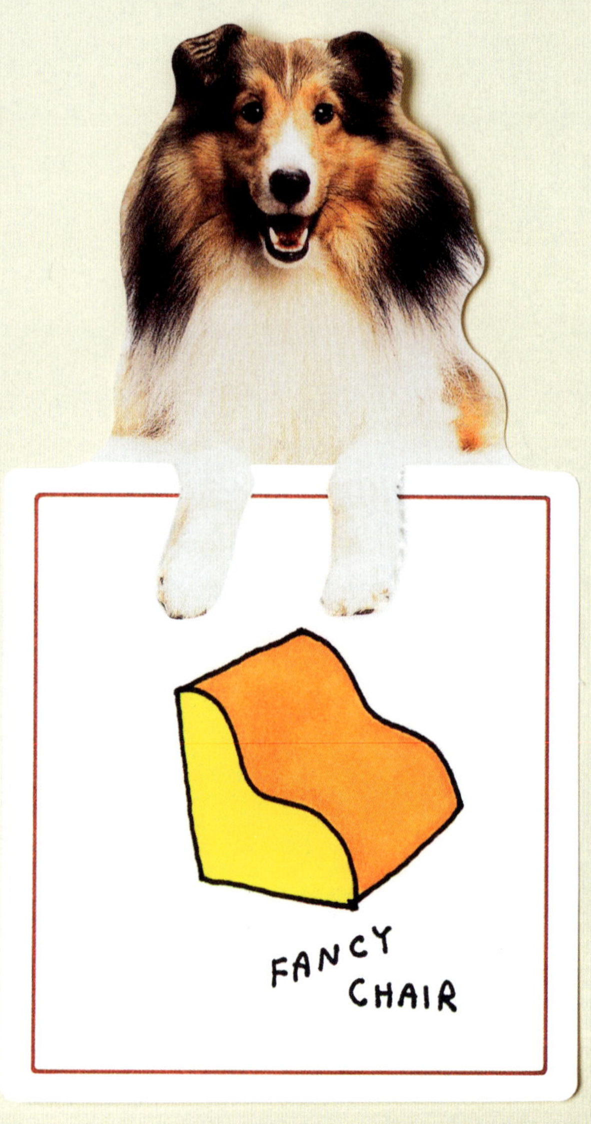
FANCY
CHAIR

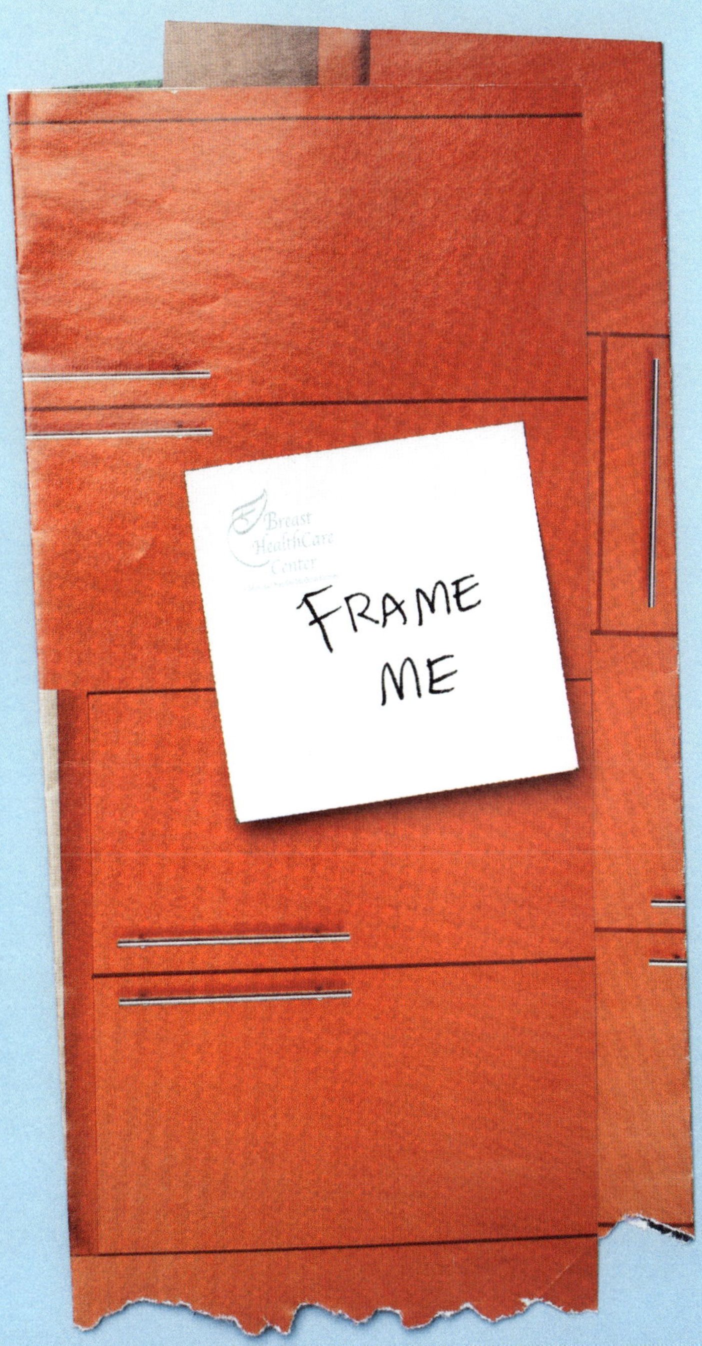
Breast
HealthCare
Center
FRAME
ME

JASON!!!

I'm SUCH a bad friend. sorry. I feel like a JERK! I've been meaning to send this for TWO months now, It's terrible. I'm not sure why but I thought you need to have a yo-yo.

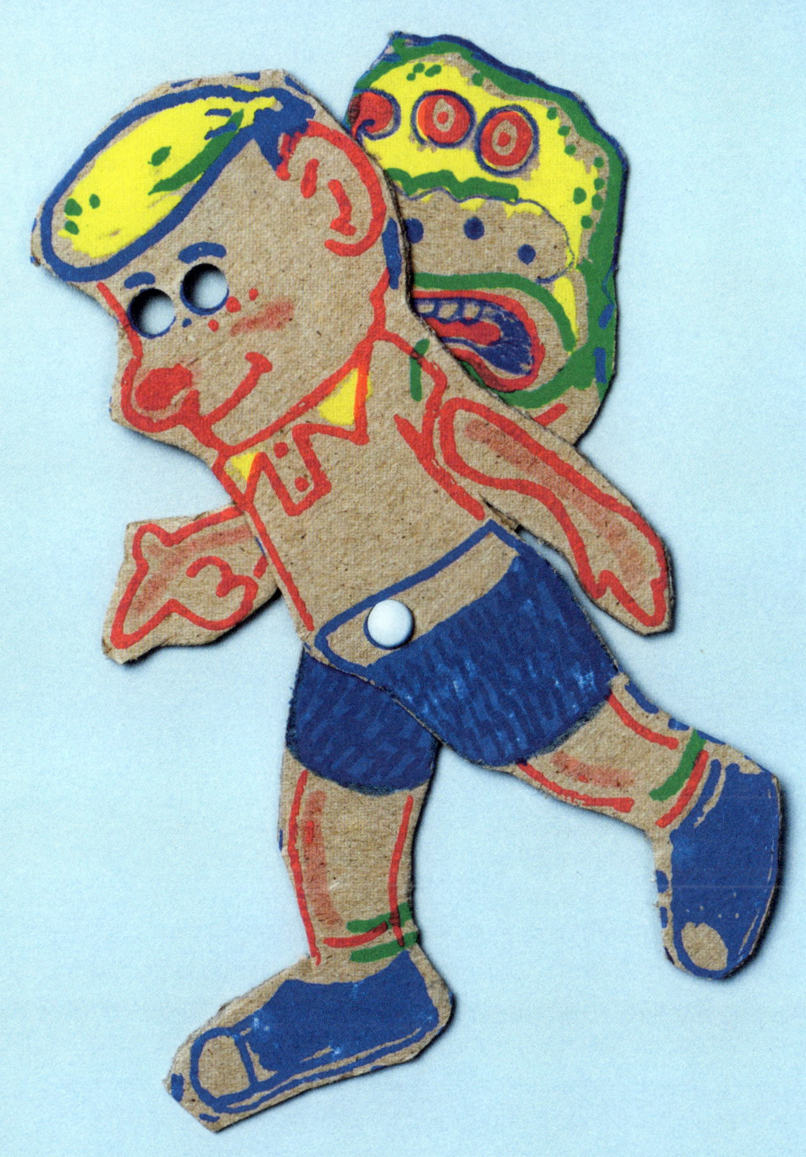

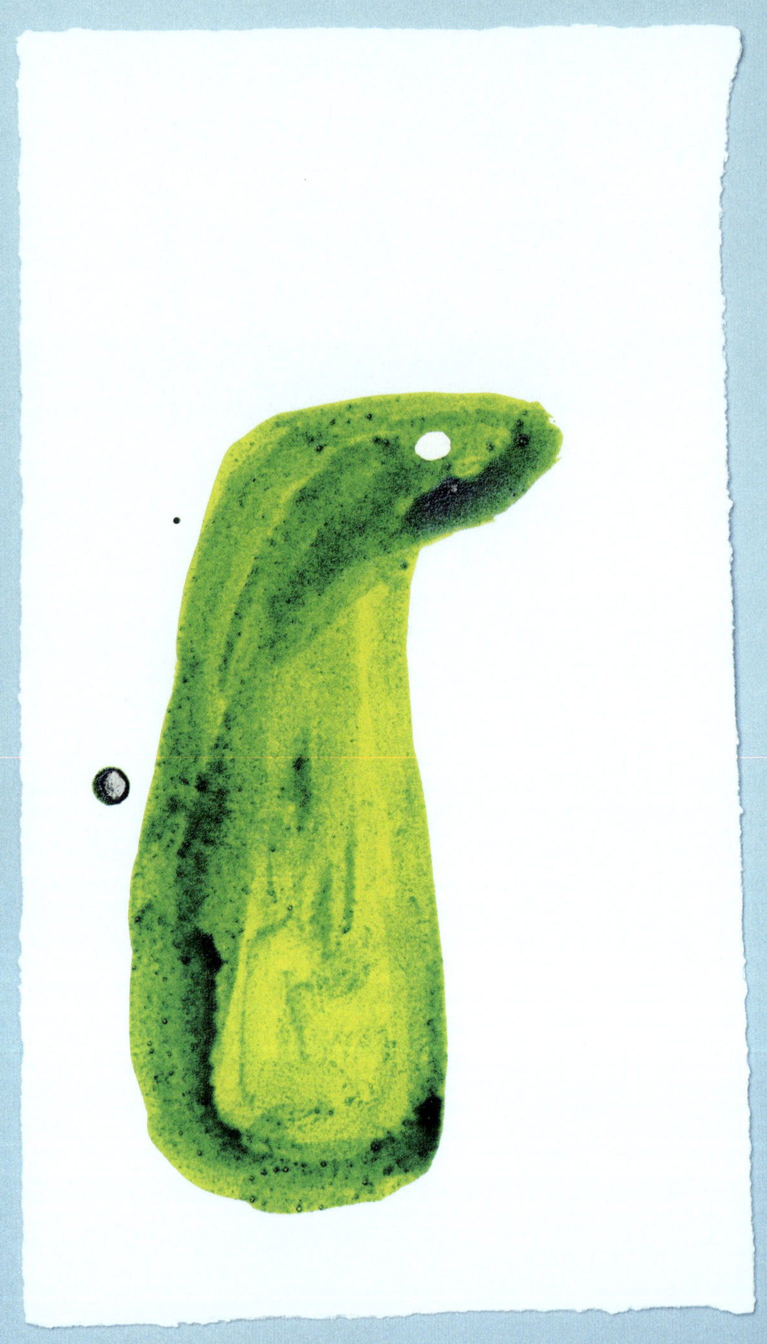

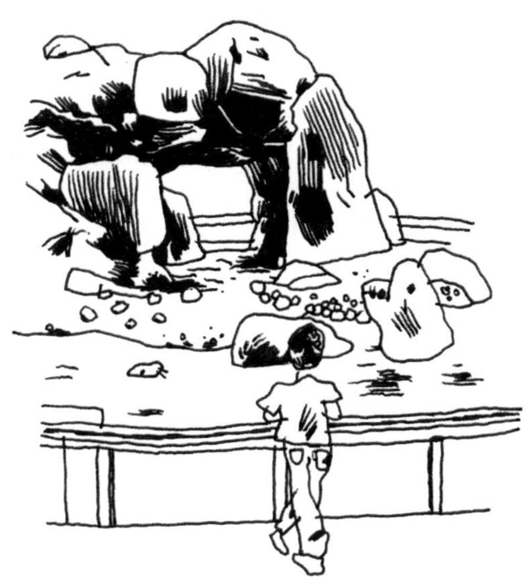

BOY WATCHING
THE SEA LIONS
IN THE CENTRAL
PARK ZOO
JUNE 15. 2012

conceptual artists can't draw.

JASON D. POLAN
SOLO SHOW

THIS WEDNESDAY NIGHT
AUGUST 4. 2004 6:32 P.

LIVE.

"IN HIS BACK LEFT POCKET"

THE EVENT WILL BE CATERED.
TEN PIECES WILL BE EXHIBITED.

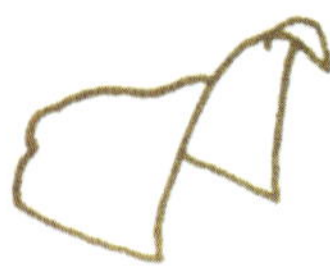

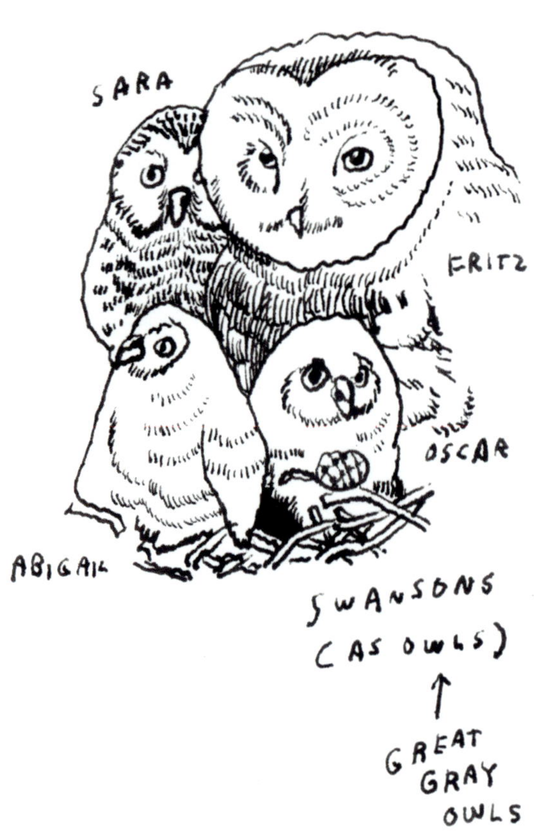
SARA
FRITZ
OSCAR
ABIGAIL
SWANSONS
(AS OWLS)
↑
GREAT
GRAY
OWLS

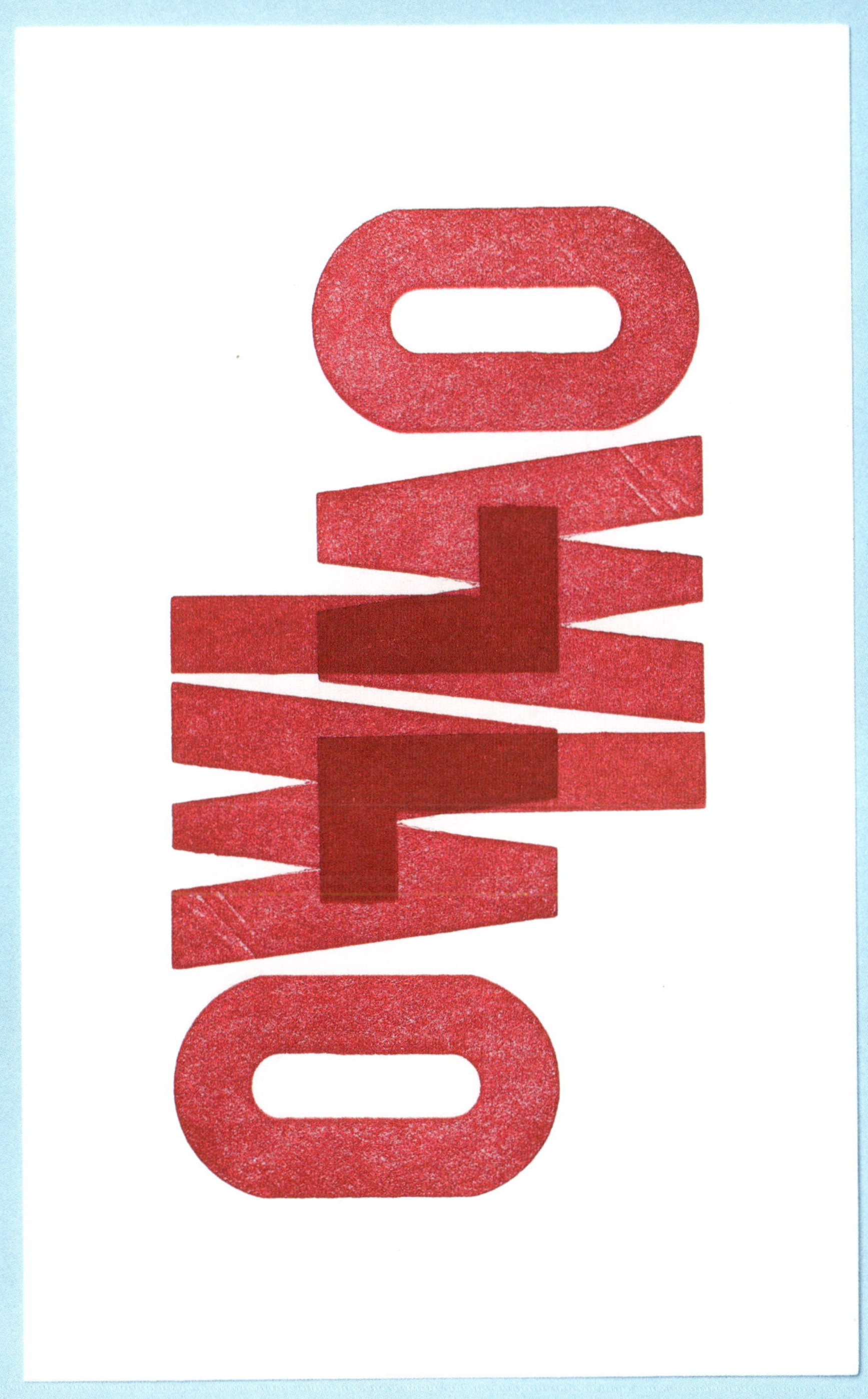

TUCSON AZ 85726
PM
20 JUL
2005

Pal-O,

Forget what I said about werewolves. Just wing it.

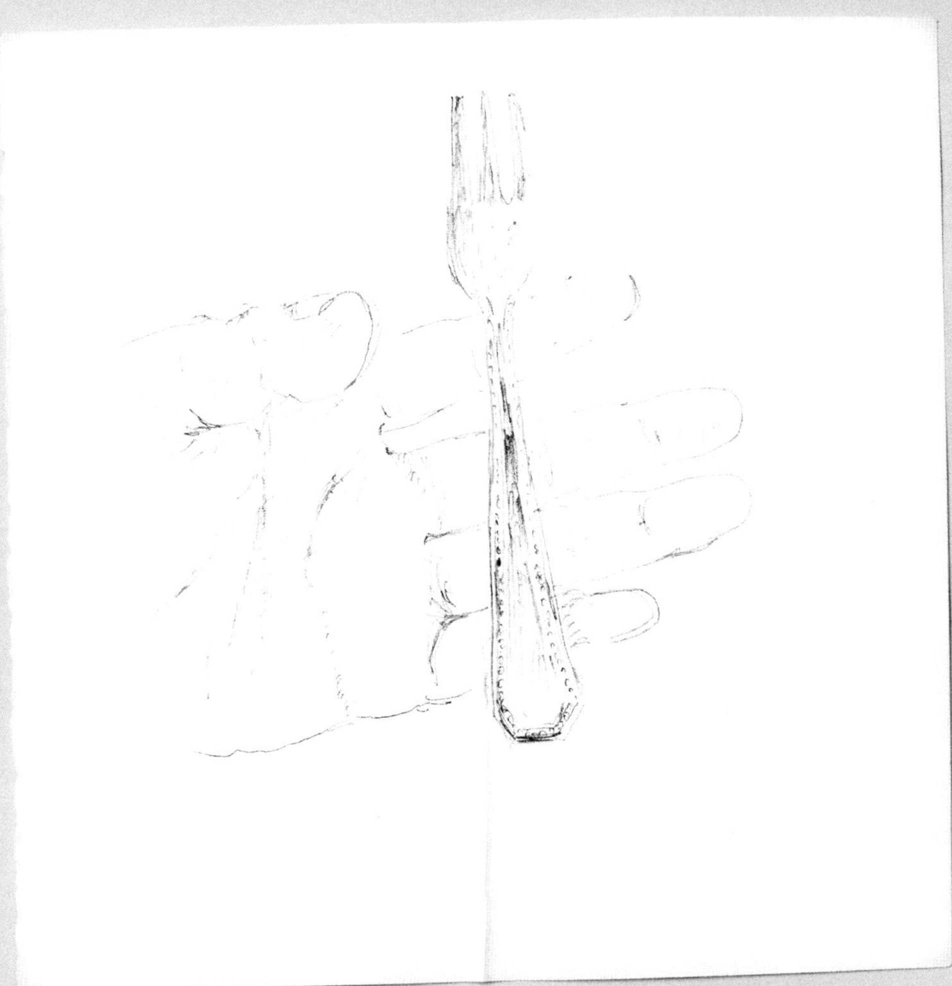

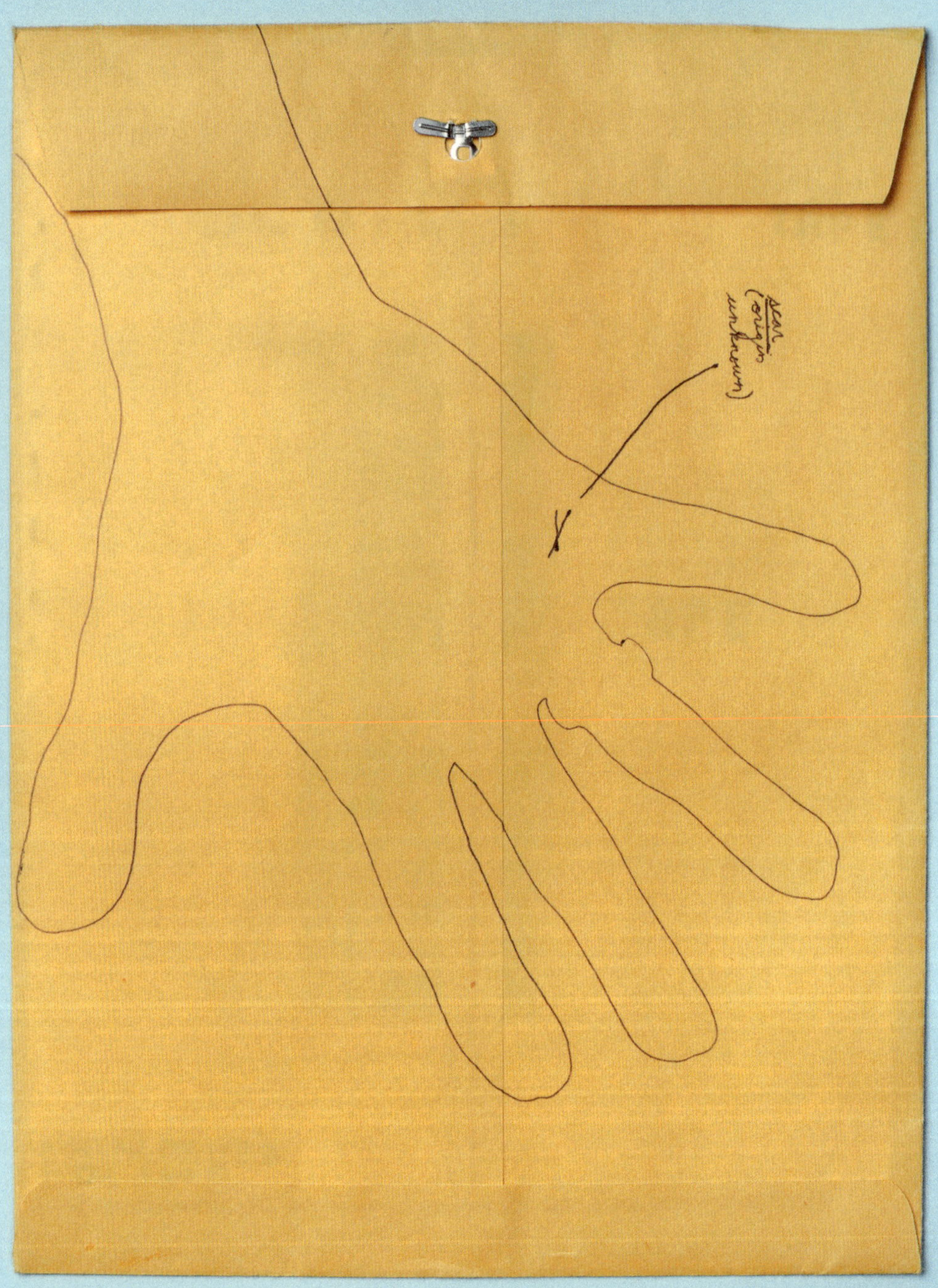

144 • Jess Smiley to JP

21. FEB 15

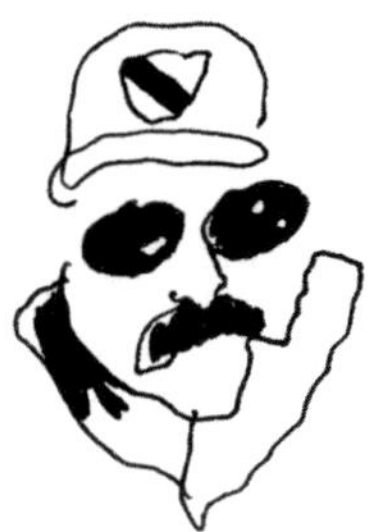

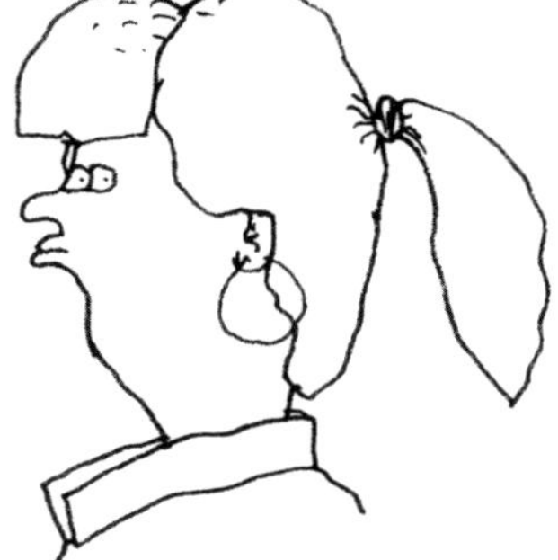

PEOPLE AT TACO BELL
14TH STREET
FOR NANCY
HI NANCY!
FROM:
JASON & STEFAN

Dear Taco Bell,

More than three years ago, I started a club called the Taco Bell Drawing Club here in Manhattan. I realized I was spending a lot of my time eating and drawing at Taco Bell and thought it might be a fun idea to invite friends to eat and draw with me. We now have more than 80 members across America, and several members from other countries who eat and draw with us while visiting the States. I have had club meetings at Taco Bells all over. (The farthest north we have ever gotten together was at one of your locations in North Pole, Alaska!) Now there are regular weekly meetings in Michigan, Illinois, Oklahoma, Ohio, and New York.

Our members include artists, writers, moms, and Emmy-award winners. We invite anybody who would like to draw with us. To become a member, all you need to do is go to Taco Bell and draw! Official members have laminated membership cards with their names on them. We even have a blog.

We have assembled three volumes of Taco Bell Drawing Club drawings. I will include the most recent one, number three (a fourth is already being planned), for you to see some of the great work that is being made while at a Taco Bell.

Over the past three years, the club has brought many people to Taco Bell that do not usually eat there and now regularly enjoy your food.

While putting together the most recent volume, I was trying to figure out a way to raise some money for printing costs and mailing the volumes to members around the country. We do not have dues, and the costs add up when I am printing and sending the books to all of the members. I tried to think of a company that would want to contribute to the club, some company that would appreciate and benefit from the Taco Bell Drawing Club. I then thought that Taco Bell may be that company.

We are always expanding, and this seems like the right time to approach your corporation about helping the club with some of the things we are already doing but may have trouble with if we continue to grow at the current rate. Also, we would love to make T-shirts ("Official Member Taco Bell Drawing Club" T-shirts) to give to members. We have ideas about art exhibitions to further showcase the work being made. We would like to put together a Taco Bell Drawing Club Tour to travel across America, having more meetings all over on a more regular basis.

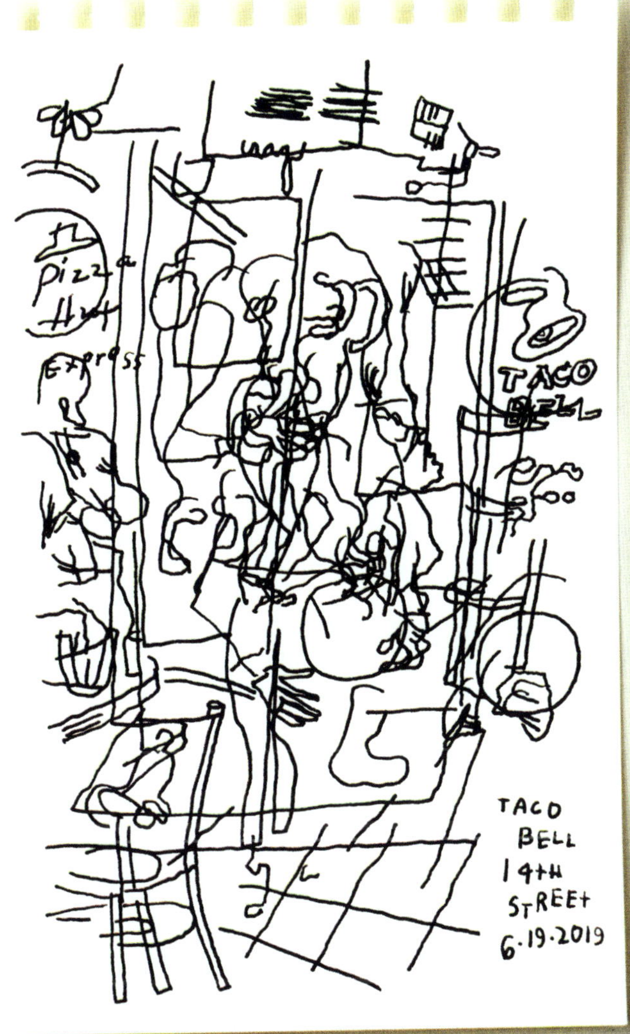
TACO
BELL
14th
STREET
6·19·2019

OFFICIAL MEMBER
TACO BELL DRAWING CLUB

CHRISTINA

POST OFFICE
GOT CONFUSED
AND DELIVERED
THIS POSTCARD
TO <u>MY</u> HOUSE.
OOPS.

— BRIAN

I got married and turned green. What can I do about it?? This is not what I look like. My hat is blue, not green. You're my only hope.

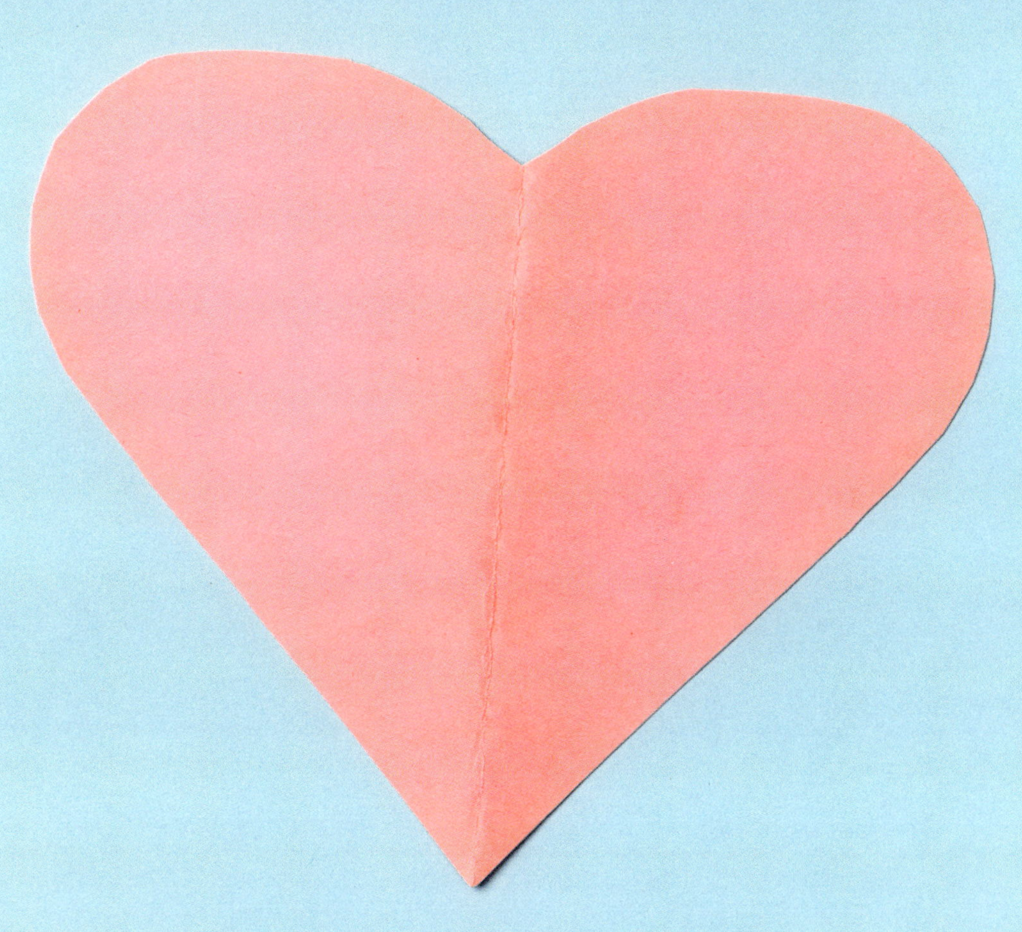

YOU ARE AN ART ASSIGNMENT. AND YOU WILL LIKE IT.

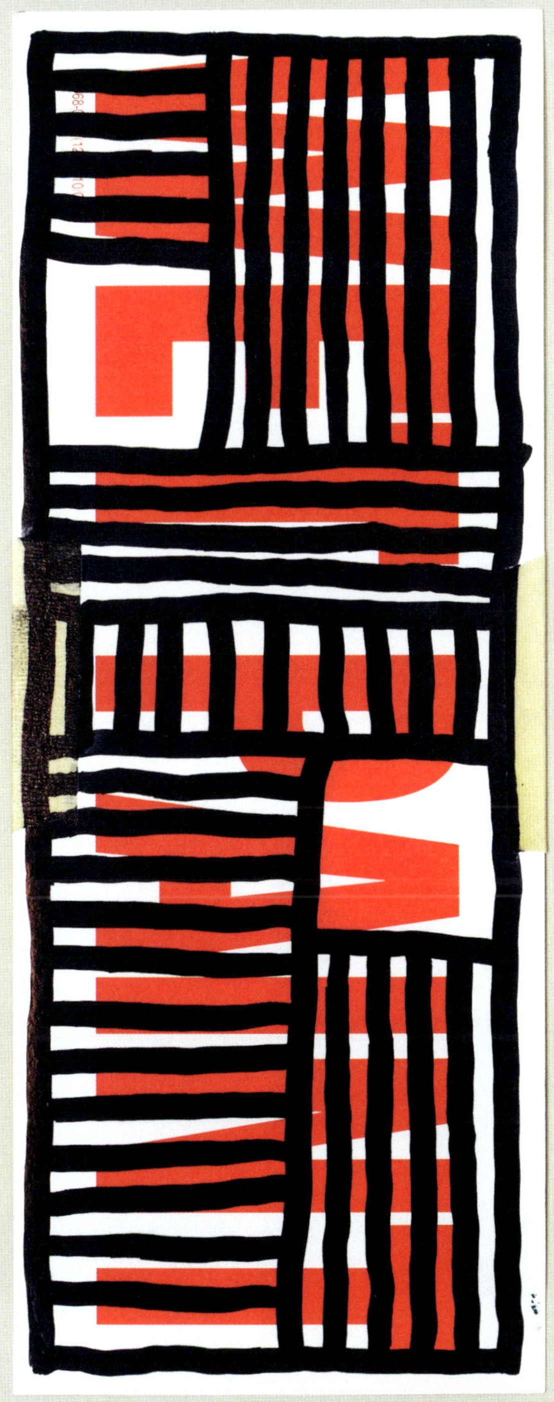

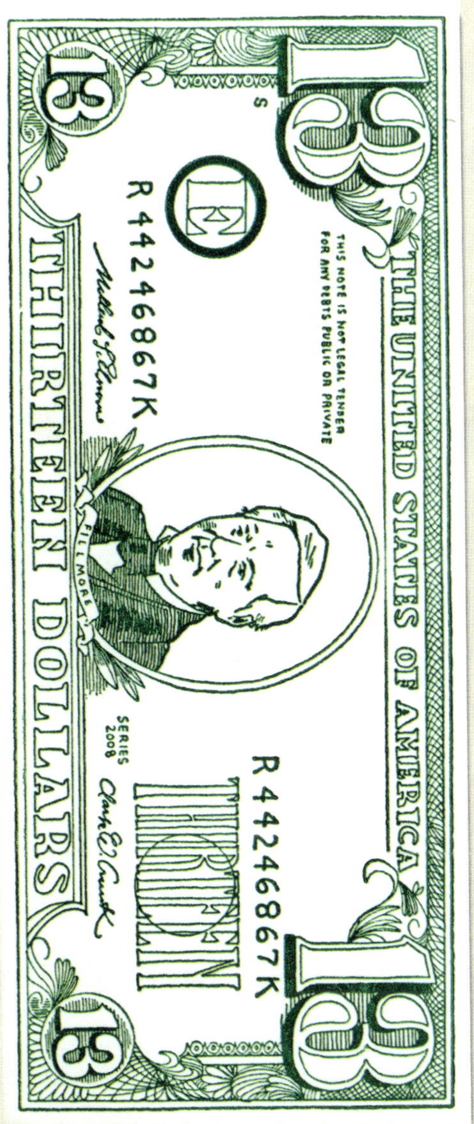

13
THE UNITED STATES OF AMERICA
THIS NOTE IS NOT LEGAL TENDER FOR ANY DEBTS PUBLIC OR PRIVATE
R 44246867K
R 44246867K
FILLMORE
SERIES 2008
THIRTEEN
THIRTEEN DOLLARS

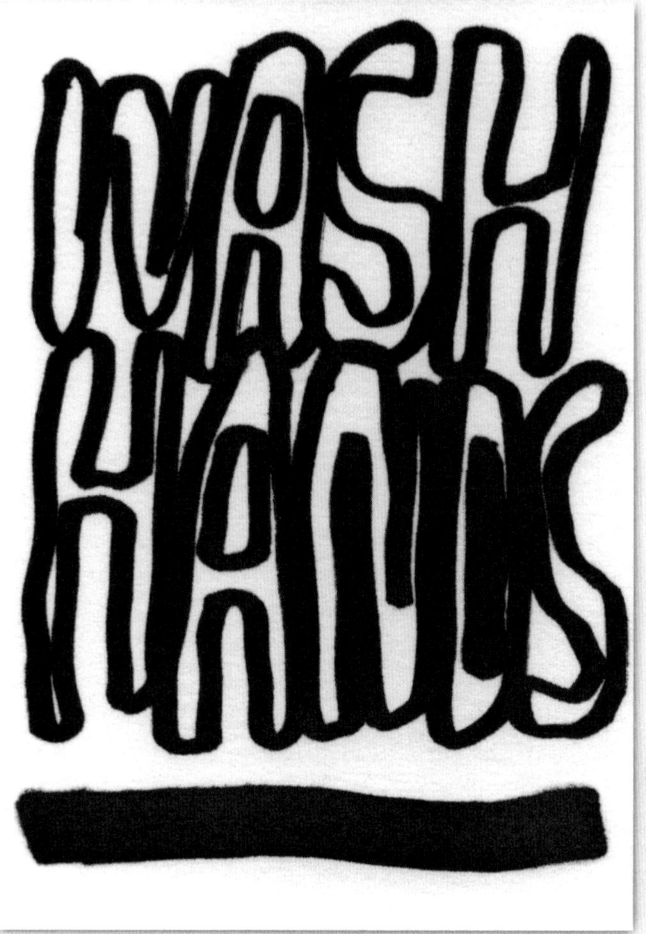
WASH
HANDS

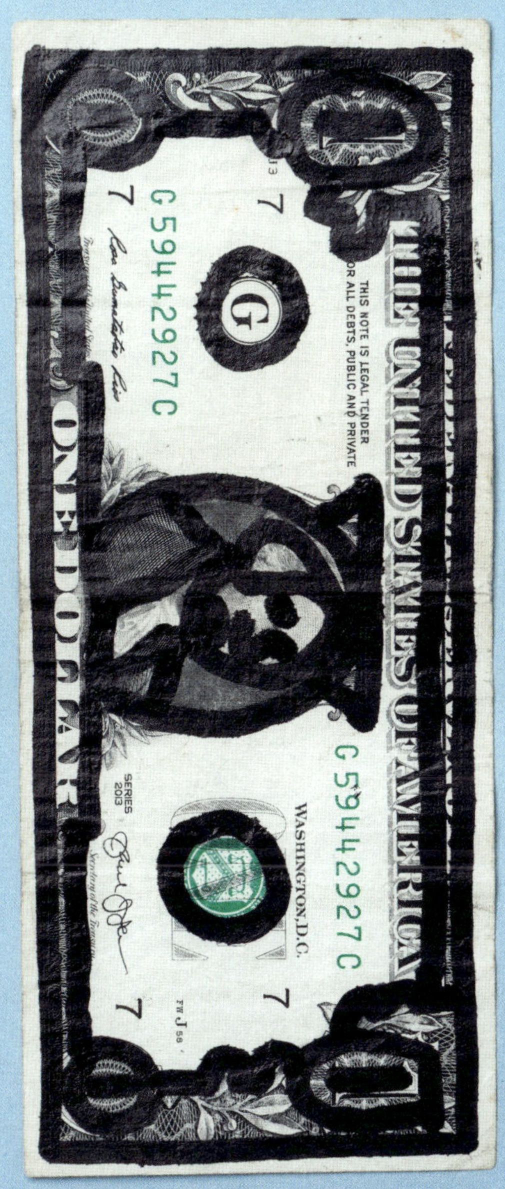
THIS NOTE IS LEGAL TENDER
FOR ALL DEBTS, PUBLIC AND PRIVATE
G 59442927 C
G 59442927 C
G
WASHINGTON, D.C.
SERIES 2013

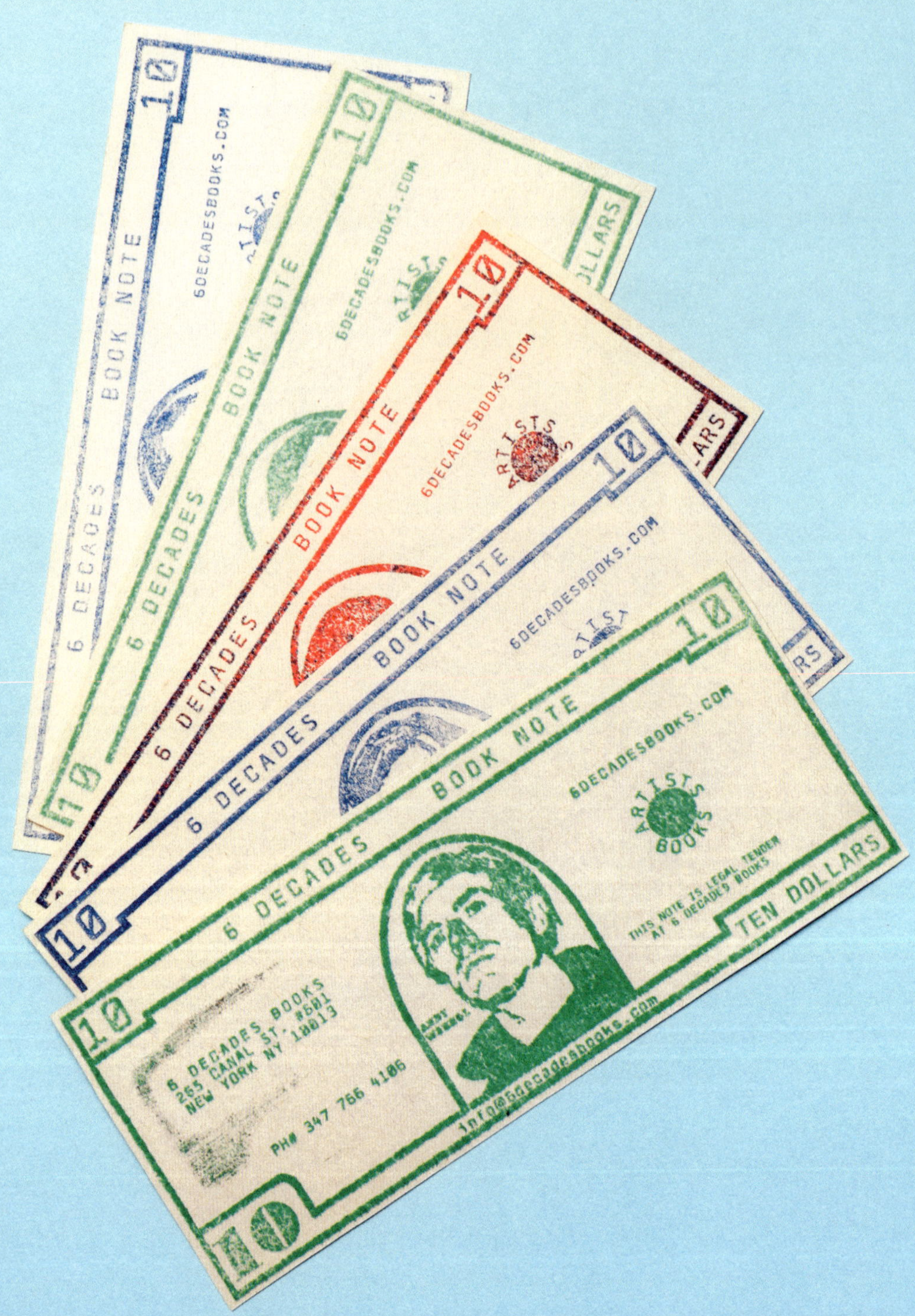
10
6 DECADES BOOK NOTE
6DECADESBOOKS.COM
ARTISTS BOOKS
THIS NOTE IS LEGAL TENDER AT 6 DECADES BOOKS
TEN DOLLARS
6 DECADES BOOKS
265 CANAL ST. #601
NEW YORK NY 10013
PH# 347 766 4106
info@6decadesbooks.com

I've enclosed a check for $60.00, for 1 Hour of Art. This is a gift for my son Alex's 21st birthday. I've been instructed _not_ to give you any information about him whatsoever so that you will draw whatever you want to.

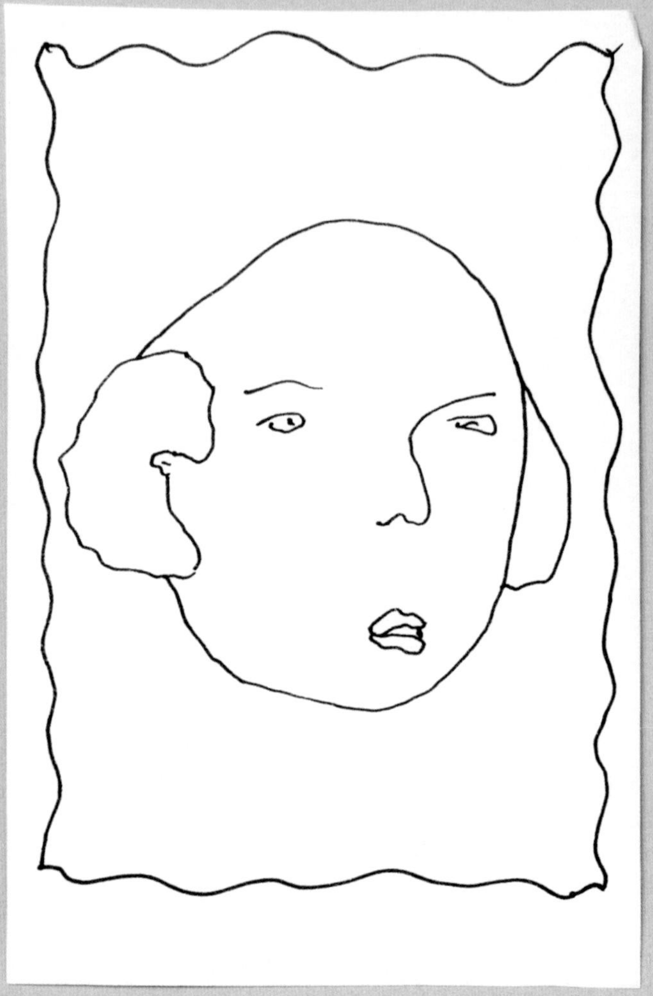

Oprah Winfrey
Harpo Productions
Harpo Studios
110 North Carpenter Street
Chicago, IL 60607-2146

January 27, 2010

Dear Ms. Winfrey,

I have been a member of your book club since 2005. I have enjoyed learning about your recommendations. I was thinking the other day that some of your faithful fans might enjoy getting to learn about some art books. I looked on your list of selected books and did not find a one! These are some of my favorites:

From Here to There by Alec Soth
The Mushroom Collector by Jason Fulford
Alpine Star by Ron Jude
Welcome to Winnipeg by Marcel Dzama
Teratoid Heights by Mat Brinkman
Invasion of the Elvis Zombies by Gary Panter
From the Mixed-up Files of Mrs. Basil E. Frankweiler by E.L. Konigsburg

That last one isn't an art book but I like it a lot so I put it on there anyway. Have you read it?

I have some others I could let you know about if you are interested.

I assume you must receive hundreds of these types of letters everyday, but how many of them include a Hershey's kiss!?

I look forward to hearing from you soon.

Best,

JASON.

Jason Polan
P.O. Box 15
Prince Street Station
New York, NY 10012
art@jasonpolan.com

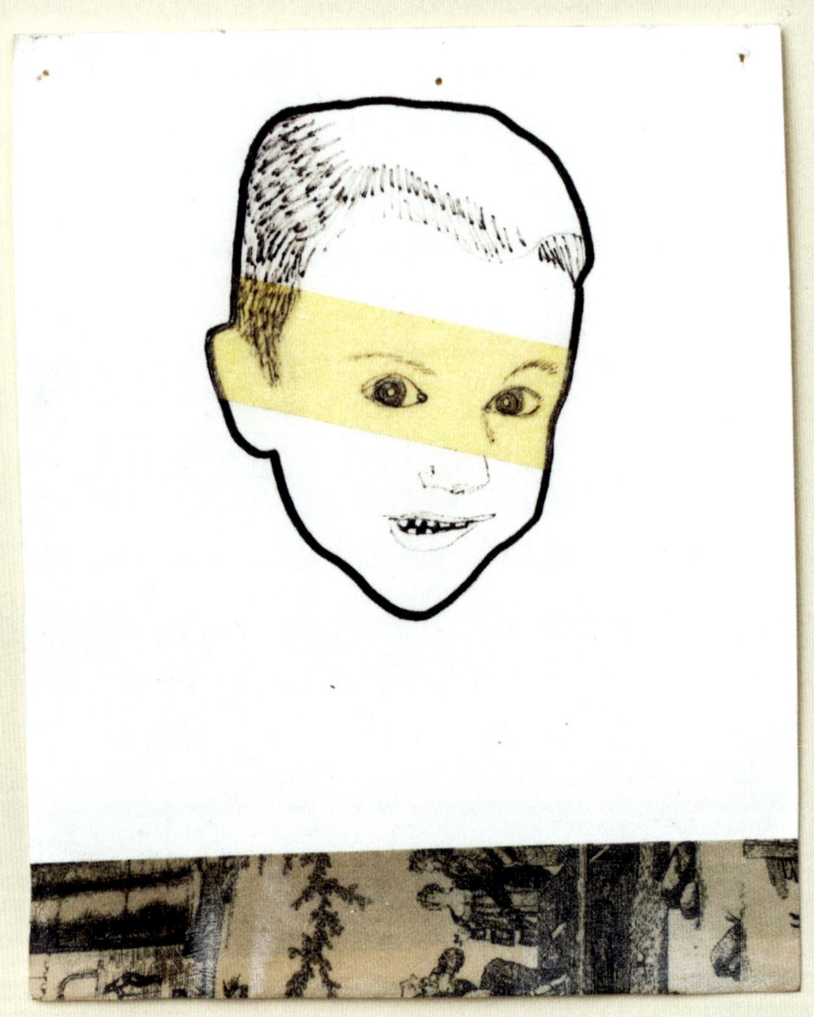

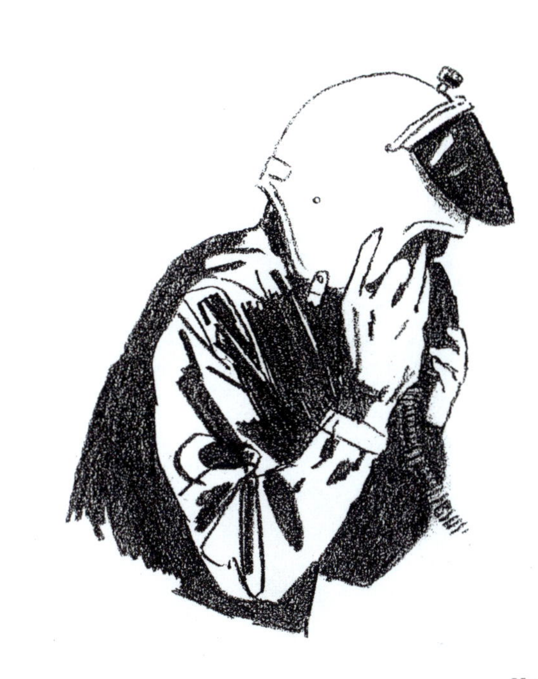

Marcel,

It was
at your e
terrific.
bat in my
like to b

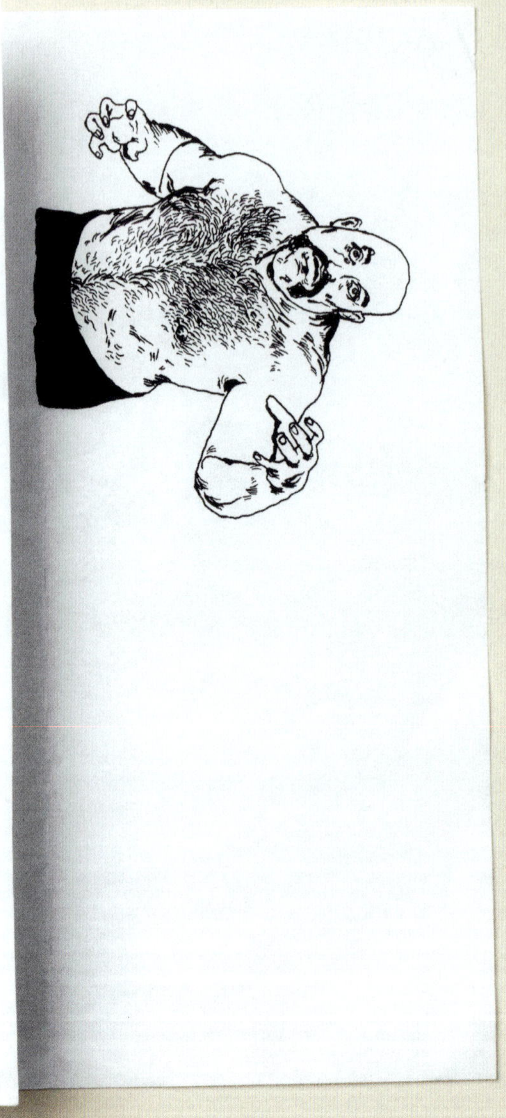

Arnold Schwarzenegger once said: "The greatest feeling you can get from a workout is the pump. All the blood flows into your muscles and it feels like your skin is going to explode. It feels fantastic."

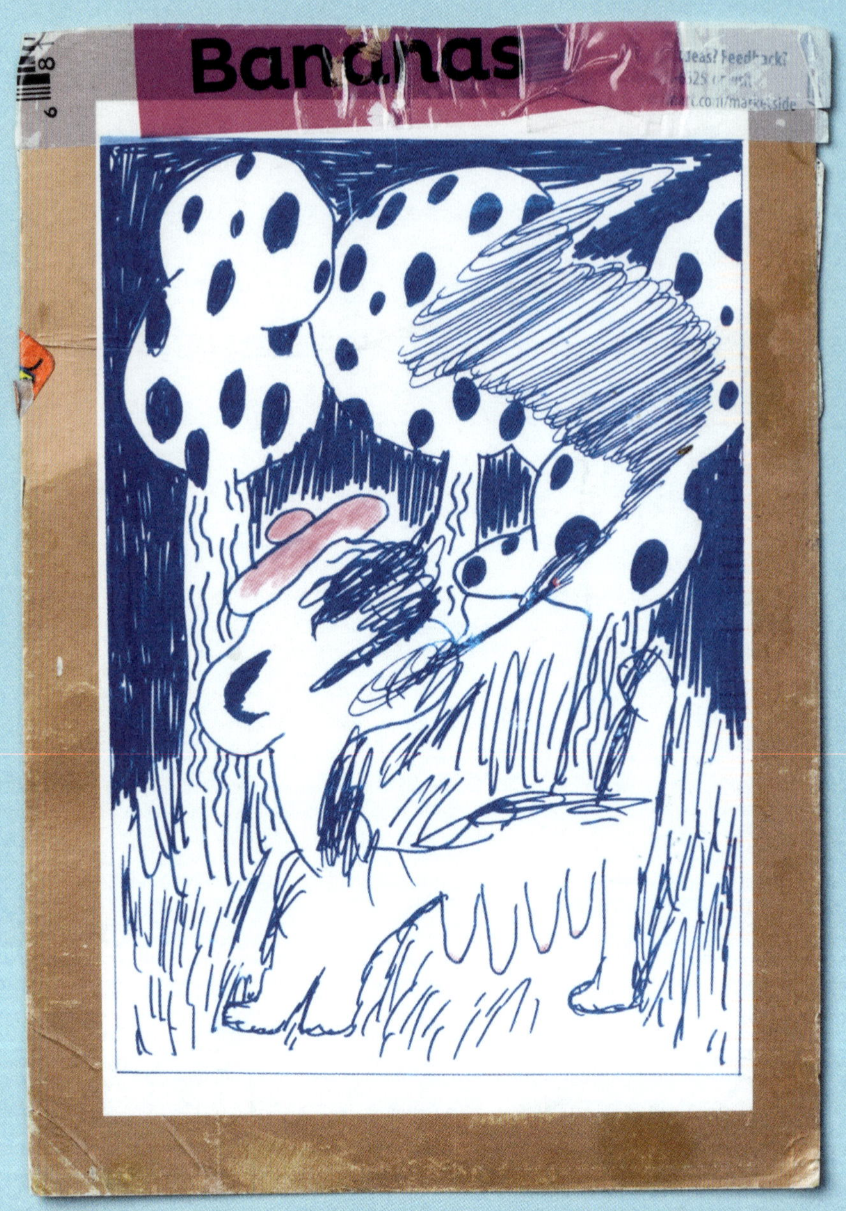
Bananas
Ideas? Feedback?

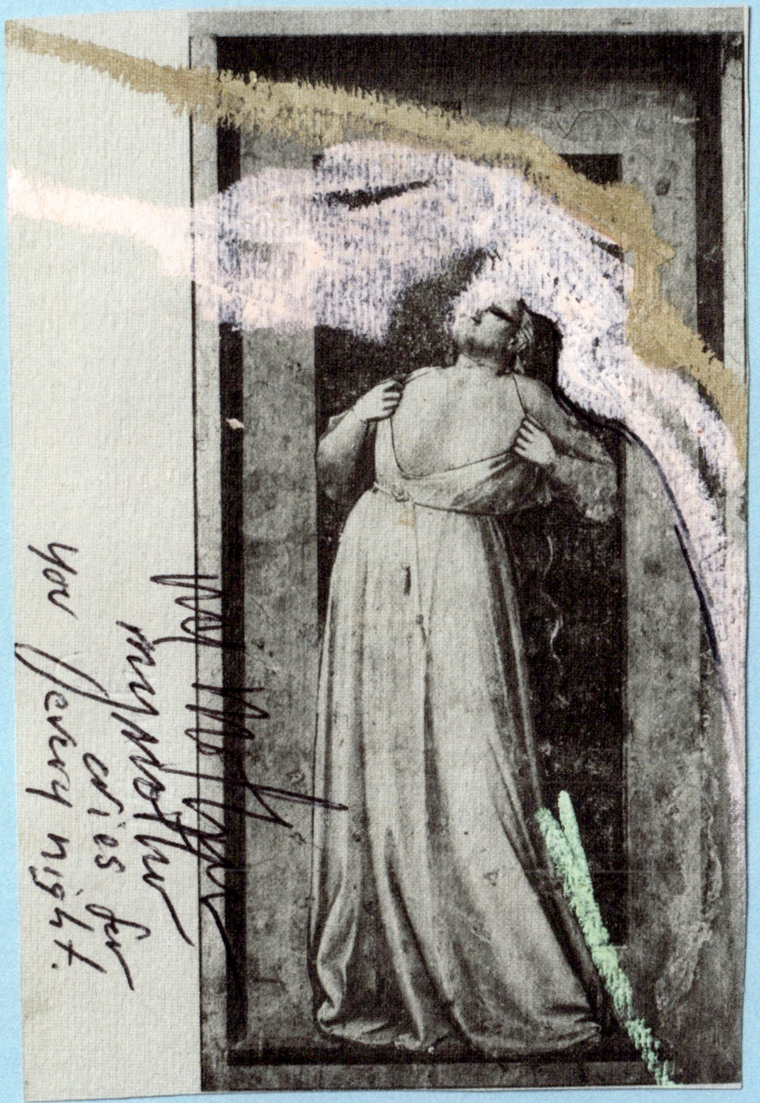
my mother
cries for
you every night.

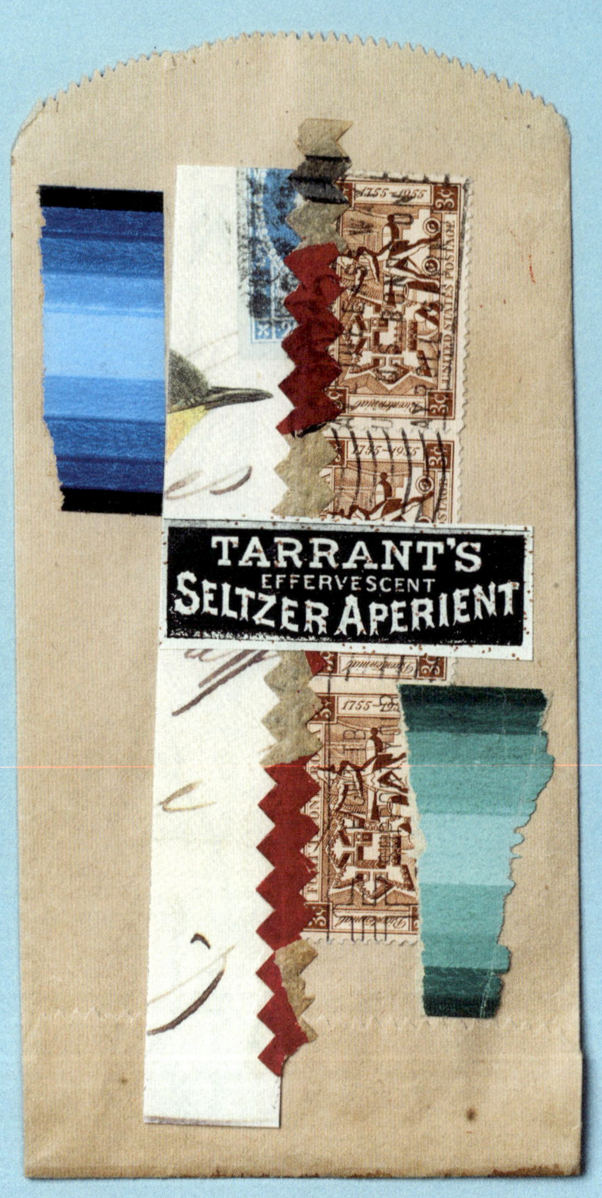
TARRANT'S
EFFERVESCENT
SELTZER APERIENT

YOU ARE SO BIG HERE.
WWW.EVASVITAMIN.COM
"Eva's has the fuel to help you do it."

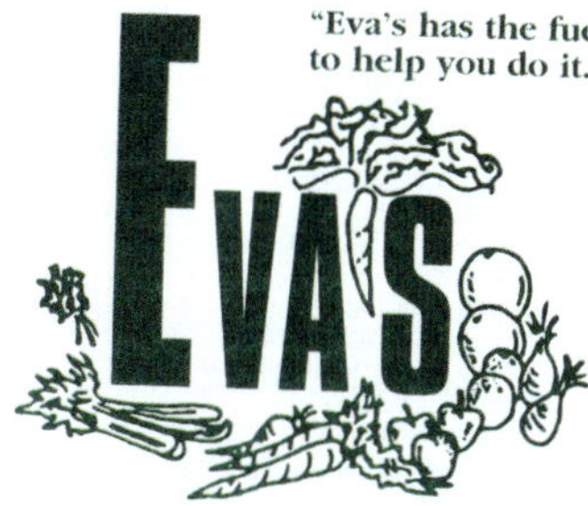

EVA'S

SINCE 1978
ALWAYS GOOD, ALWAYS FRESH,
ALWAYS DELICIOUS

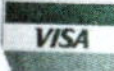

VISA

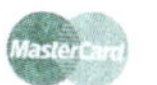

MasterCard

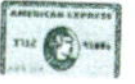
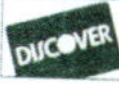

DISCOVER

NYU CAMPUS CASH
EAT IN, TAKE OUT,
sports nutrition shop
contact us @ (212) 982-2500
11 West 8th Street
New York, NY 10011
(BET. 5th & 6th Ave.)

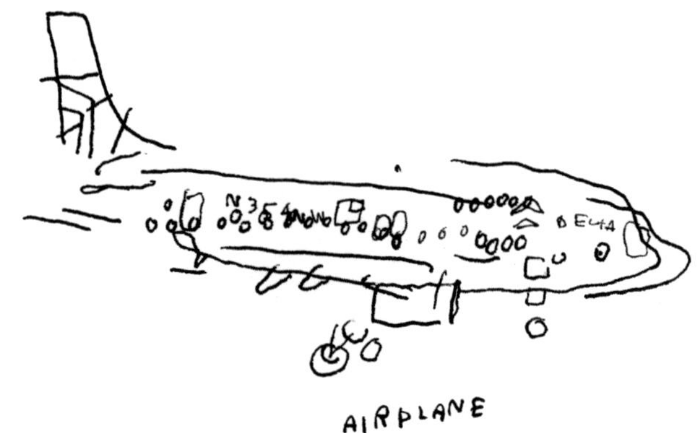
AIRPLANE
AT LAGUARDIA
AUGUST 10. 2018

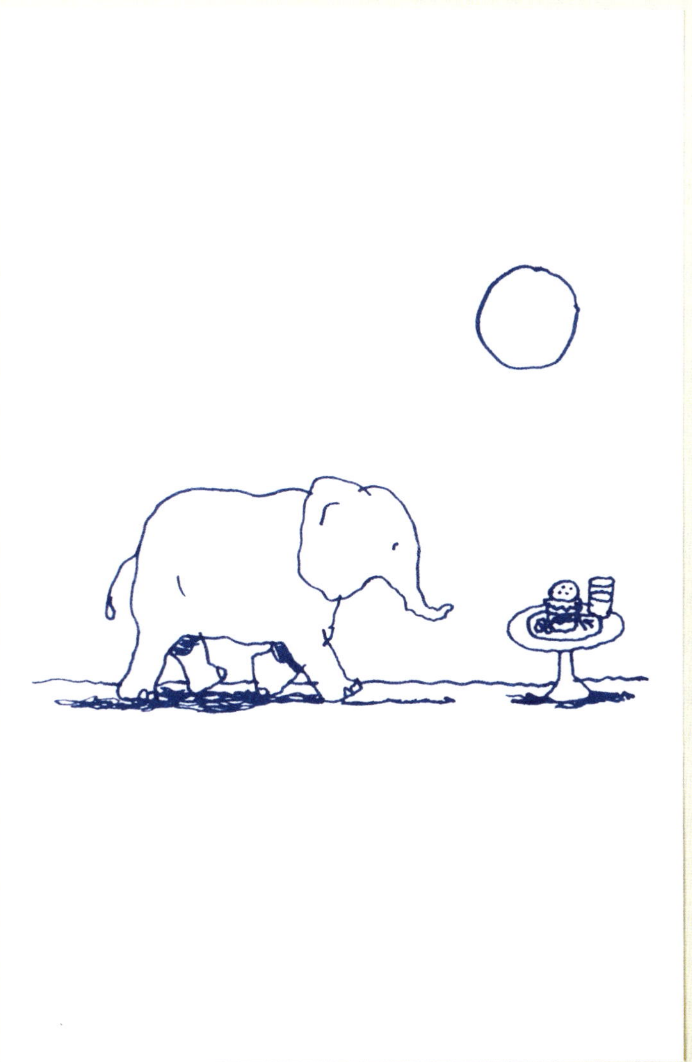

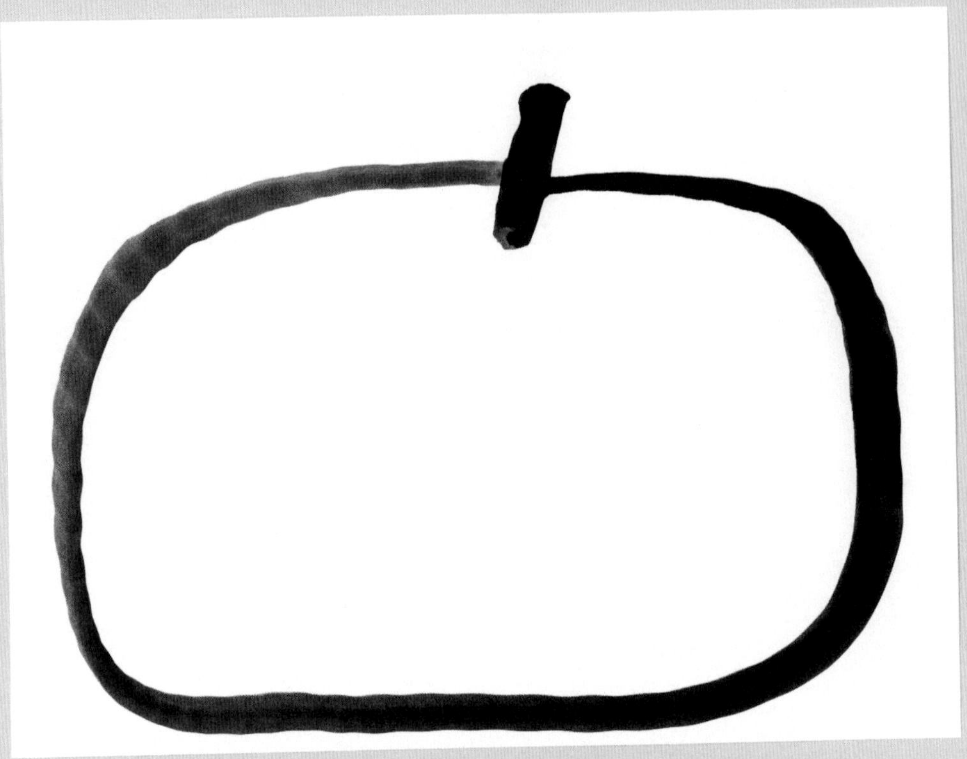

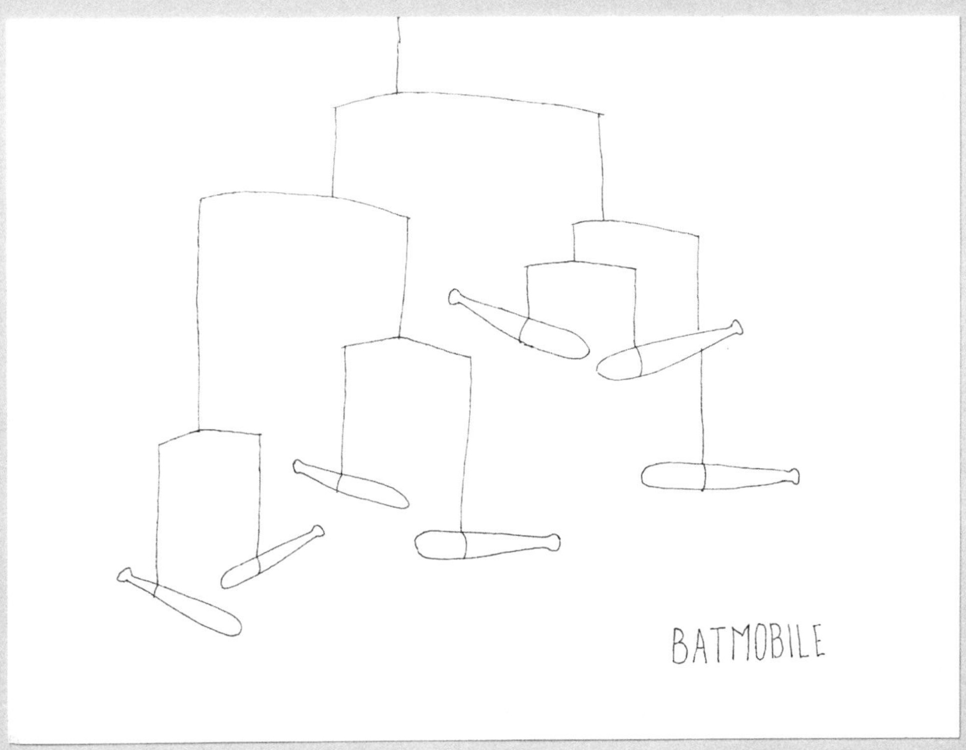
BATMOBILE

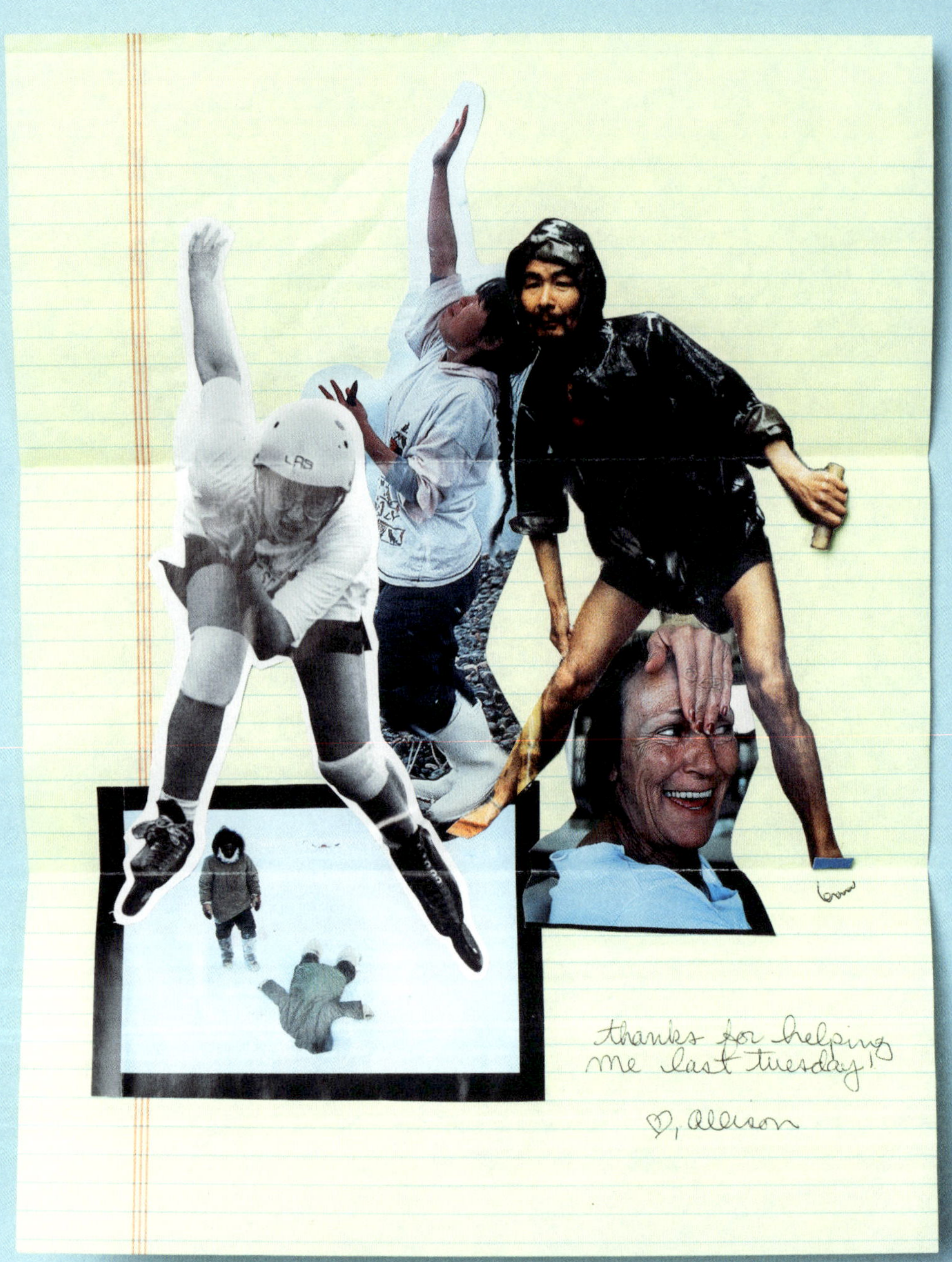
LAB
thanks for helping
me last tuesday!
♡, Allison

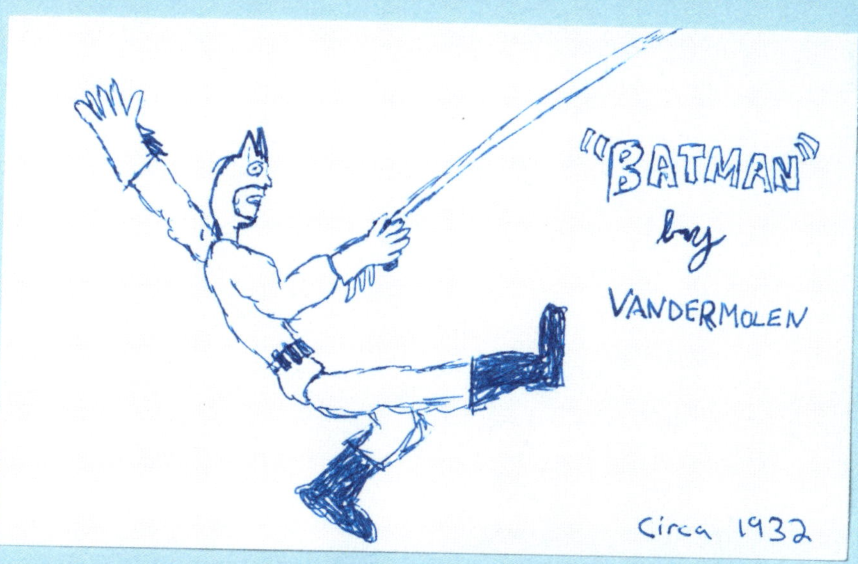

FREE NOTE CARD!

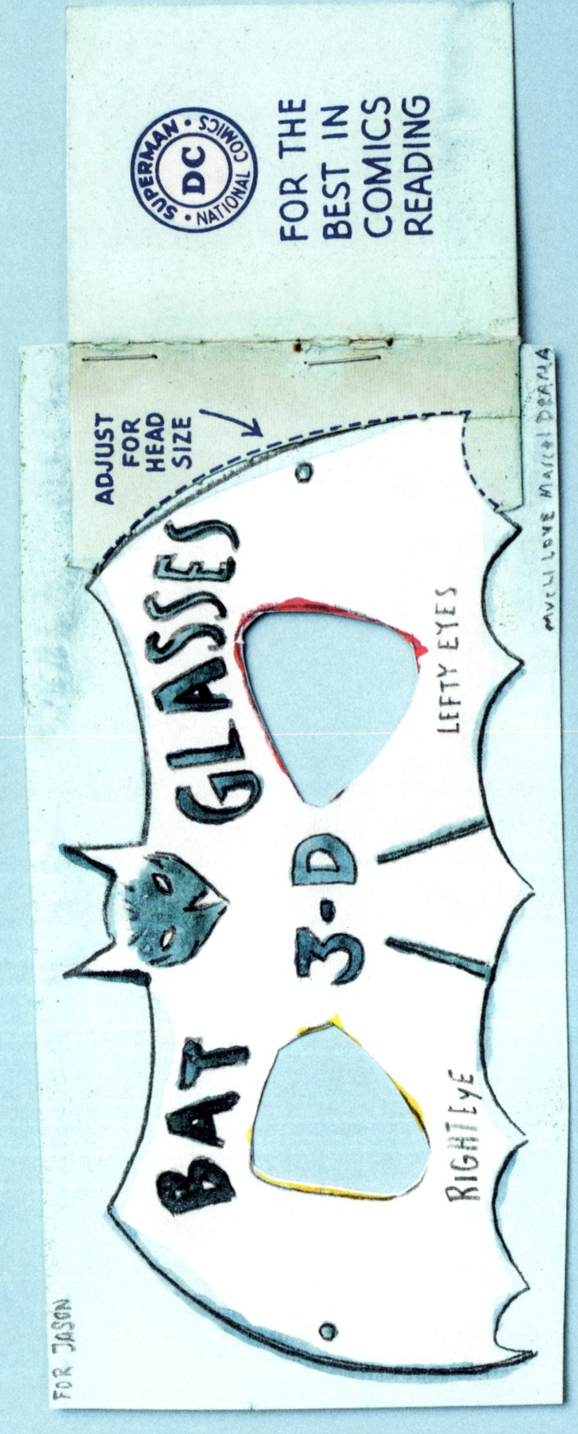
SUPERMAN • NATIONAL COMICS
DC
FOR THE
BEST IN
COMICS
READING
ADJUST
FOR
HEAD
SIZE
BAT 3-D GLASSES
LEFTY EYES
RIGHT EYE
FOR JASON
MUCH LOVE MARCEL DZAMA

Hello.

I am interested in showing my artwork at your Little Caesars Restaurant. I have included a few samples of my work. I would like to take advantage of this opportunity by creating site specific work for your restaurant. I will draw 49 portraits of people enjoying pizza. The work will be subtle as not to disturb the dining experience, but will offer a visual alternative to the white walls. The work will be installed with low tack white tape (no holes). Actual installation will not take more than one hour with take down taking even less time. Thank you very much. I look forward to working with you.

Jason Polan

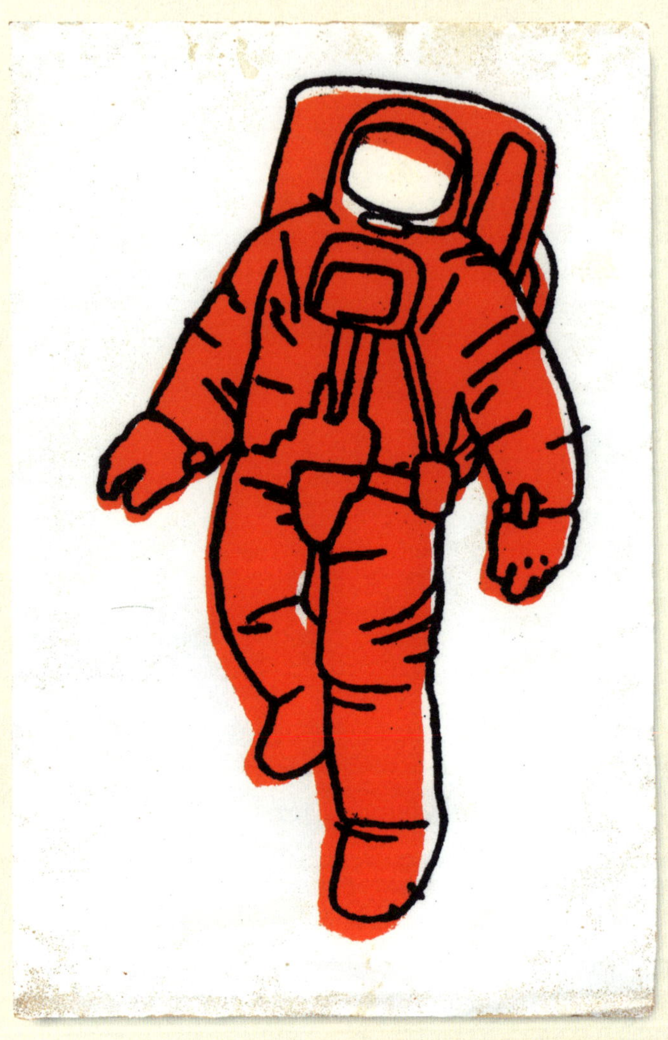

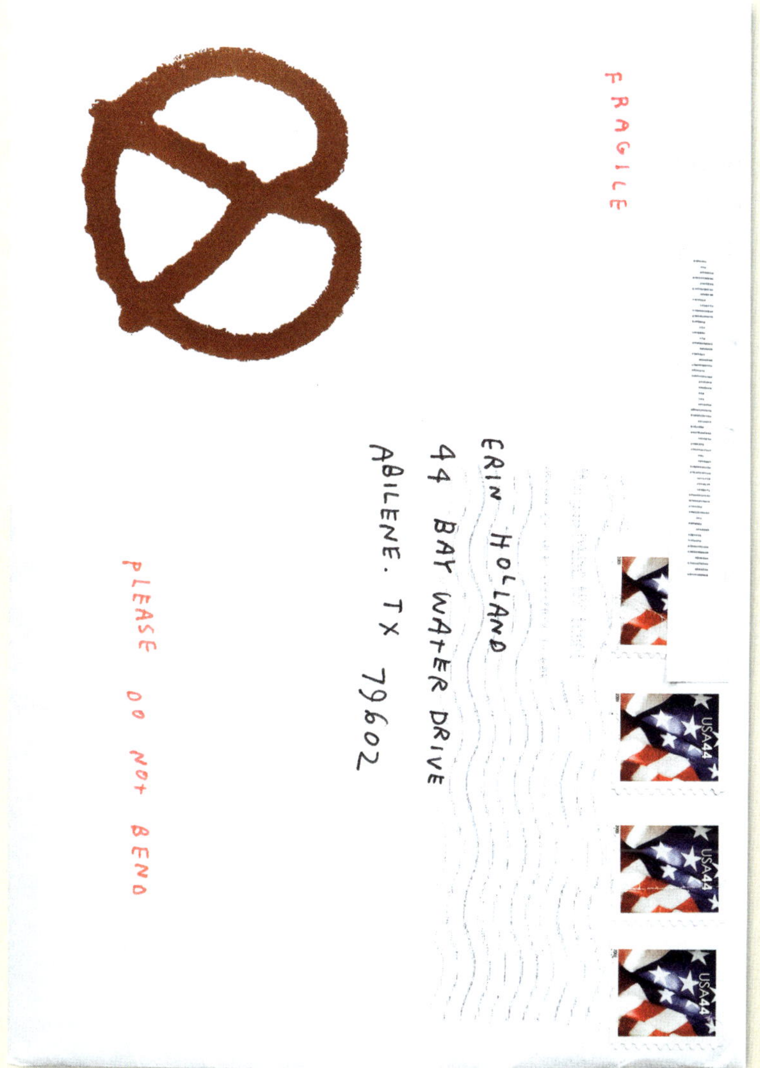
FRAGILE
ERIN HOLLAND
44 BAY WATER DRIVE
ABILENE. TX 79602
PLEASE DO NOT BEND
USA44
USA44
USA44

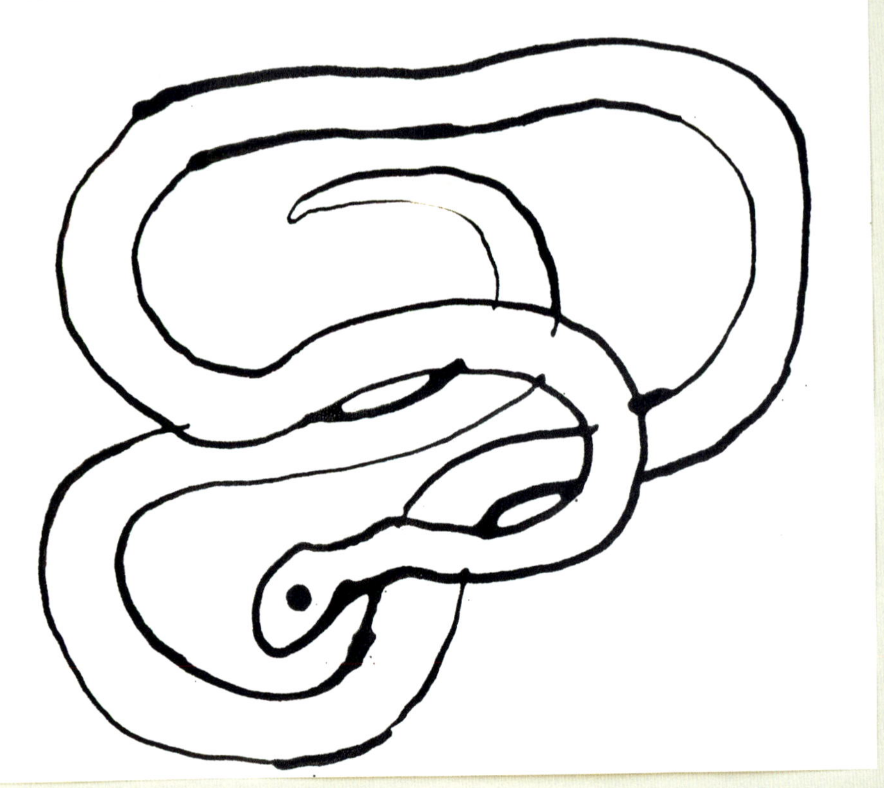

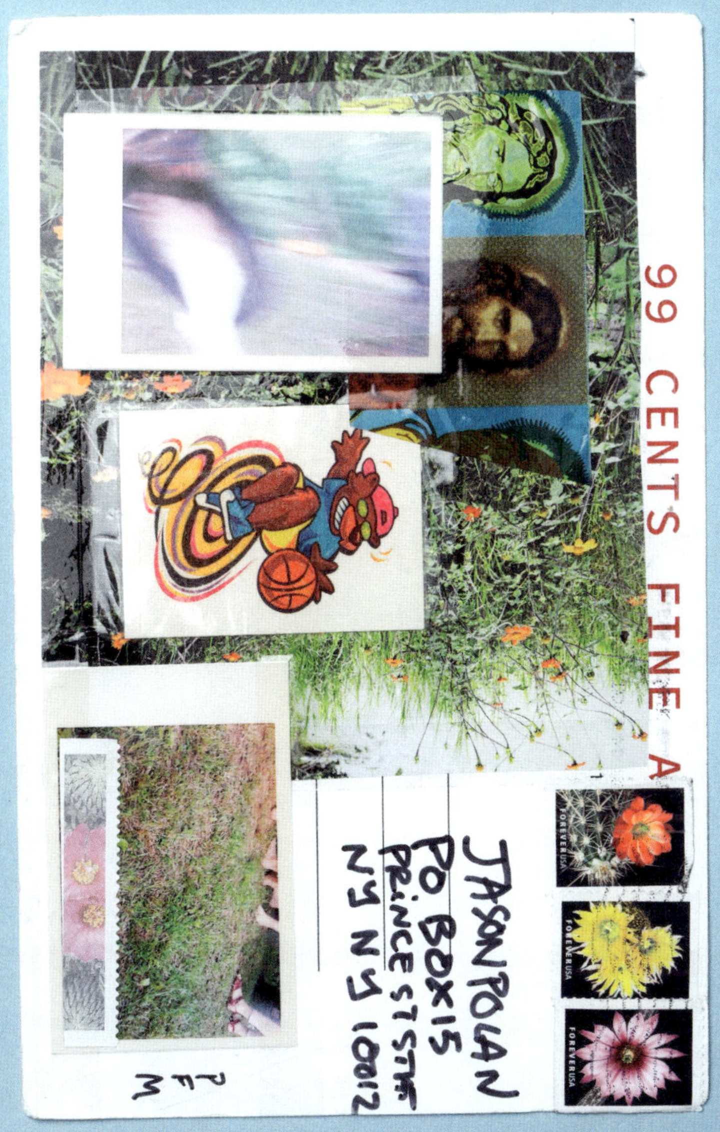
99 CENTS FINE A
JASON POLAN
PO BOX 15
PRINCE ST STA
NY NY 10012
P F M

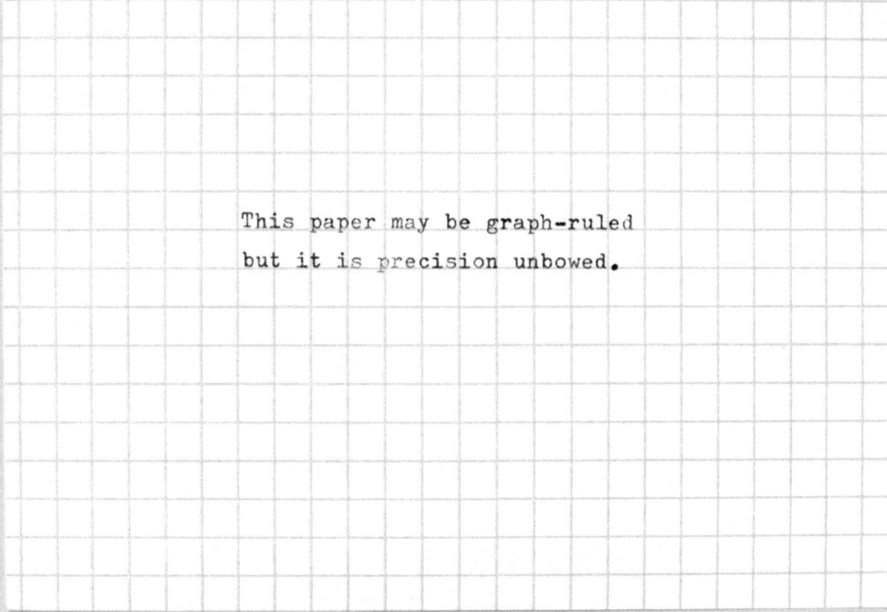
This paper may be graph-ruled
but it is precision unbowed.

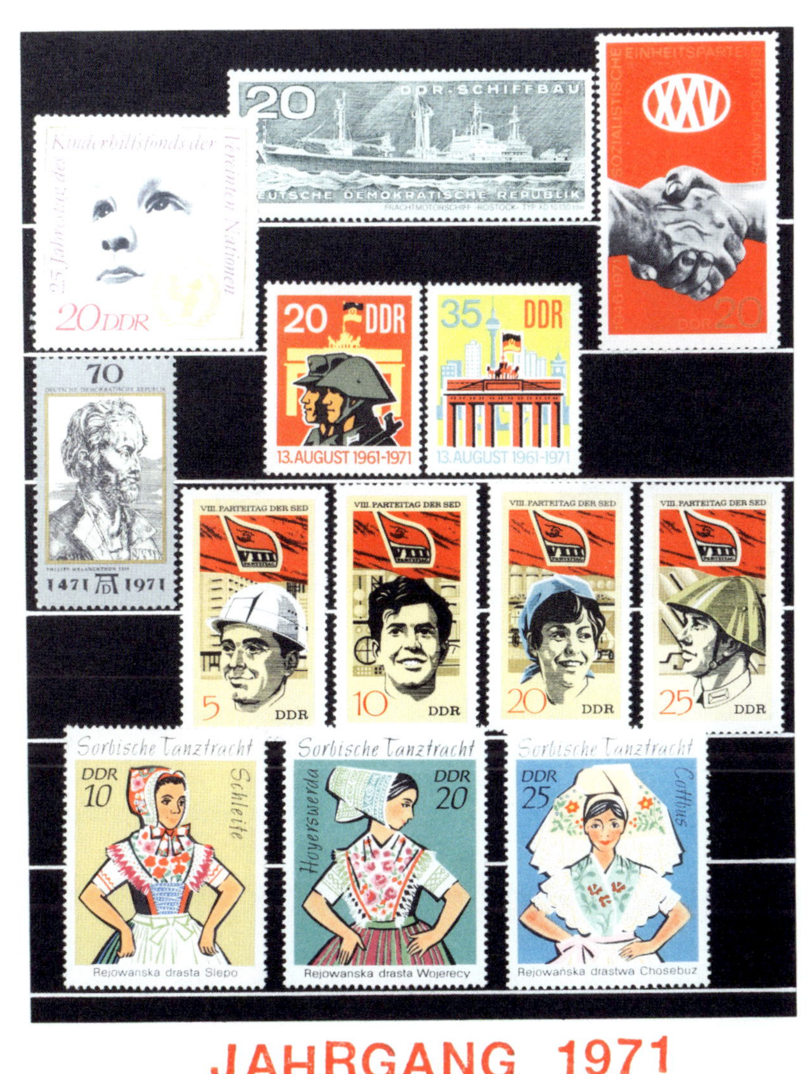
DDR
20 DDR-SCHIFFBAU
DEUTSCHE DEMOKRATISCHE REPUBLIK
SOZIALISTISCHE EINHEITSPARTEI DEUTSCHLANDS
XXV
DDR 20
Kinderhilfsfonds der Vereinten Nationen
25 Jahrestag des
20 DDR
20 DDR
13. AUGUST 1961-1971
35 DDR
13. AUGUST 1961-1971
70
DEUTSCHE DEMOKRATISCHE REPUBLIK
1471 1971
VIII. PARTEITAG DER SED
5 DDR
VIII. PARTEITAG DER SED
10 DDR
VIII. PARTEITAG DER SED
20 DDR
VIII. PARTEITAG DER SED
25 DDR
Sorbische Tanztracht
DDR 10
Schleife
Rejowanska drasta Slepo
Sorbische Tanztracht
DDR 20
Hoyerswerda
Rejowanska drasta Wojerecy
Sorbische Tanztracht
DDR 25
Cottbus
Rejowanska drastwa Chosebuz
JAHRGANG 1971

J –

.

p.s. –

– C

SECRET

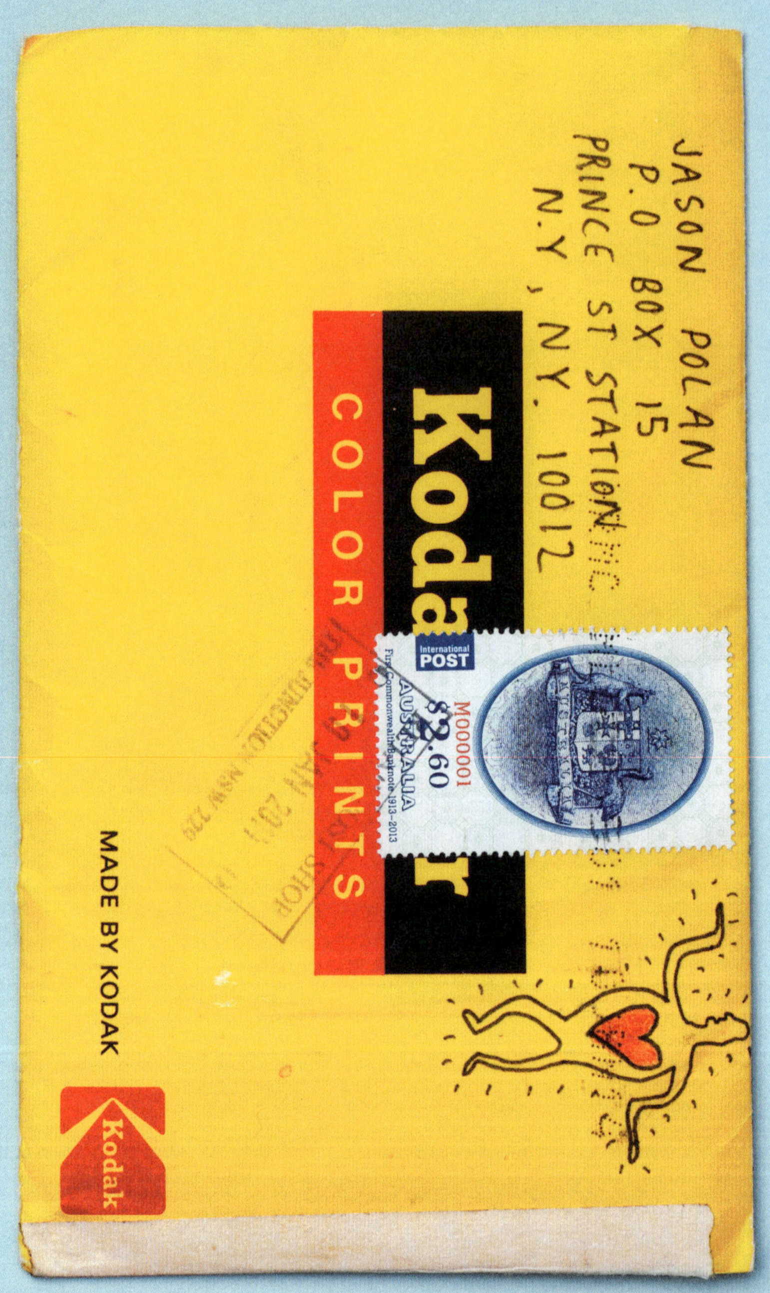
JASON POLAN
P.O BOX 15
PRINCE ST STATION
N.Y, N.Y. 10012
Kodak
COLOR PRINTS
International POST
M000001
$2.60
AUSTRALIA
First Commonwealth Banknote 1913–2013
MADE BY KODAK
Kodak

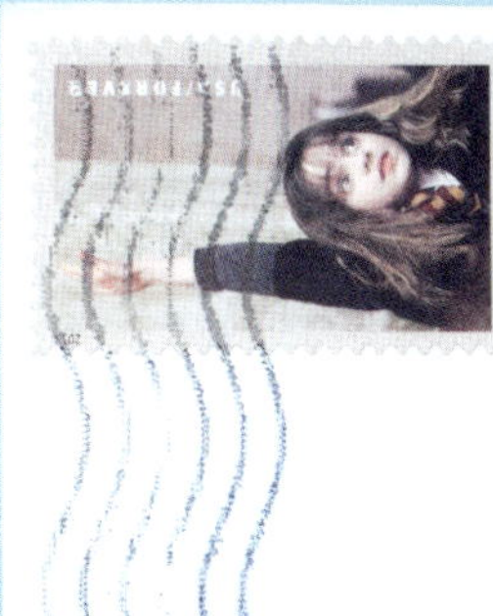
NEW YORK NY 100
04 MAR 2014 PM 13 L

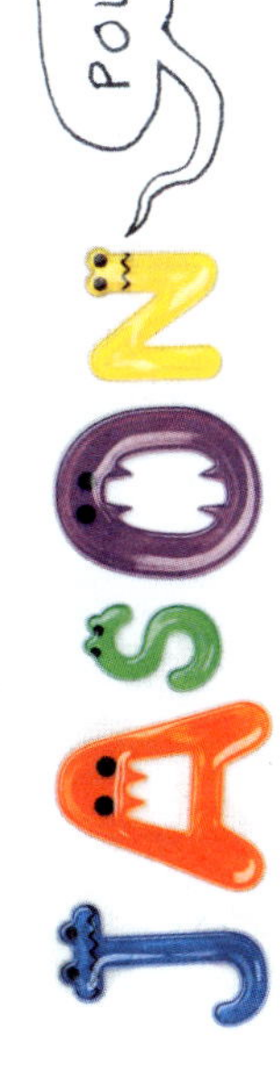
JASON
POLAN
P. O. Box 15.
Prince Street Station
New York, N.Y.
10012

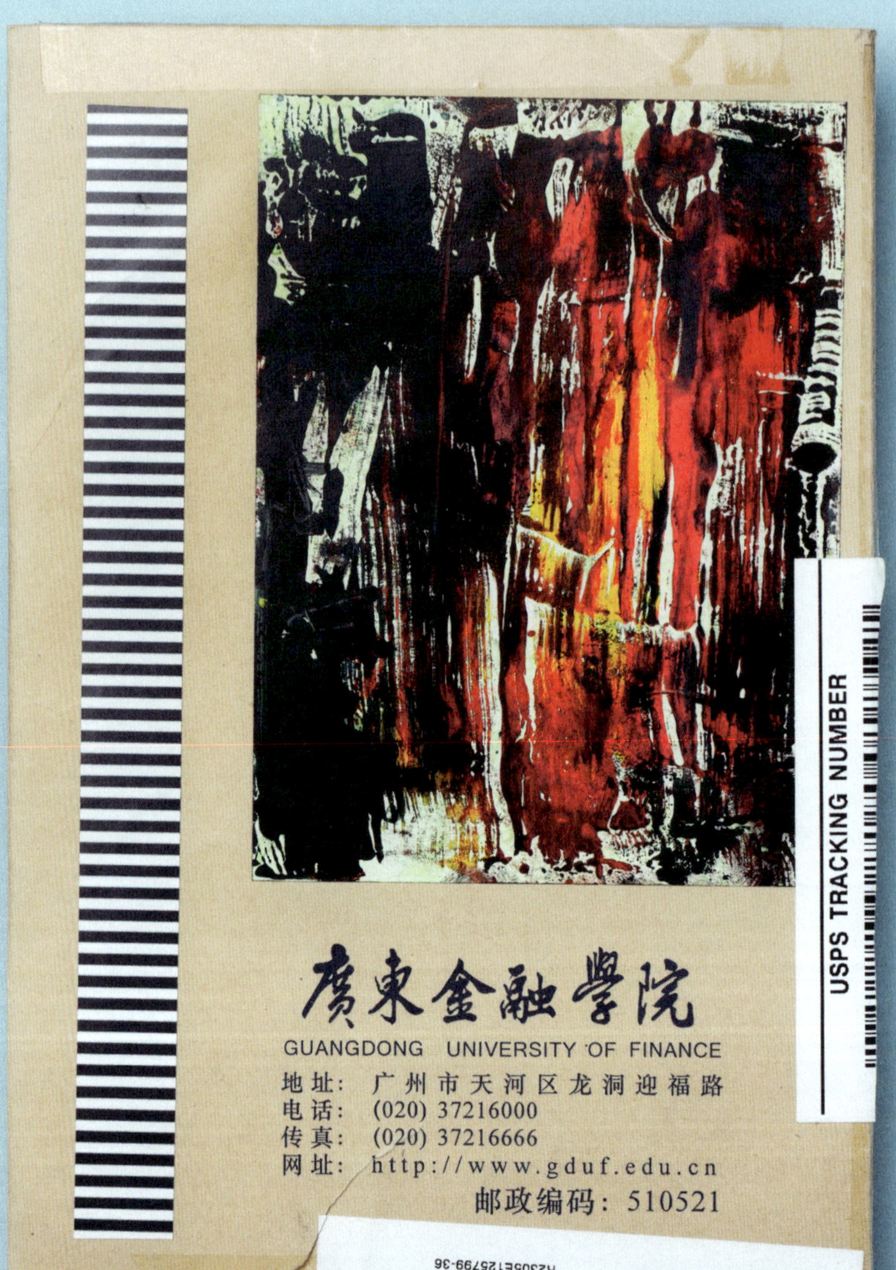
USPS TRACKING NUMBER
廣東金融學院
GUANGDONG UNIVERSITY OF FINANCE
地址：广州市天河区龙洞迎福路
电话：(020) 37216000
传真：(020) 37216666
网址：http://www.gduf.edu.cn
邮政编码：510521

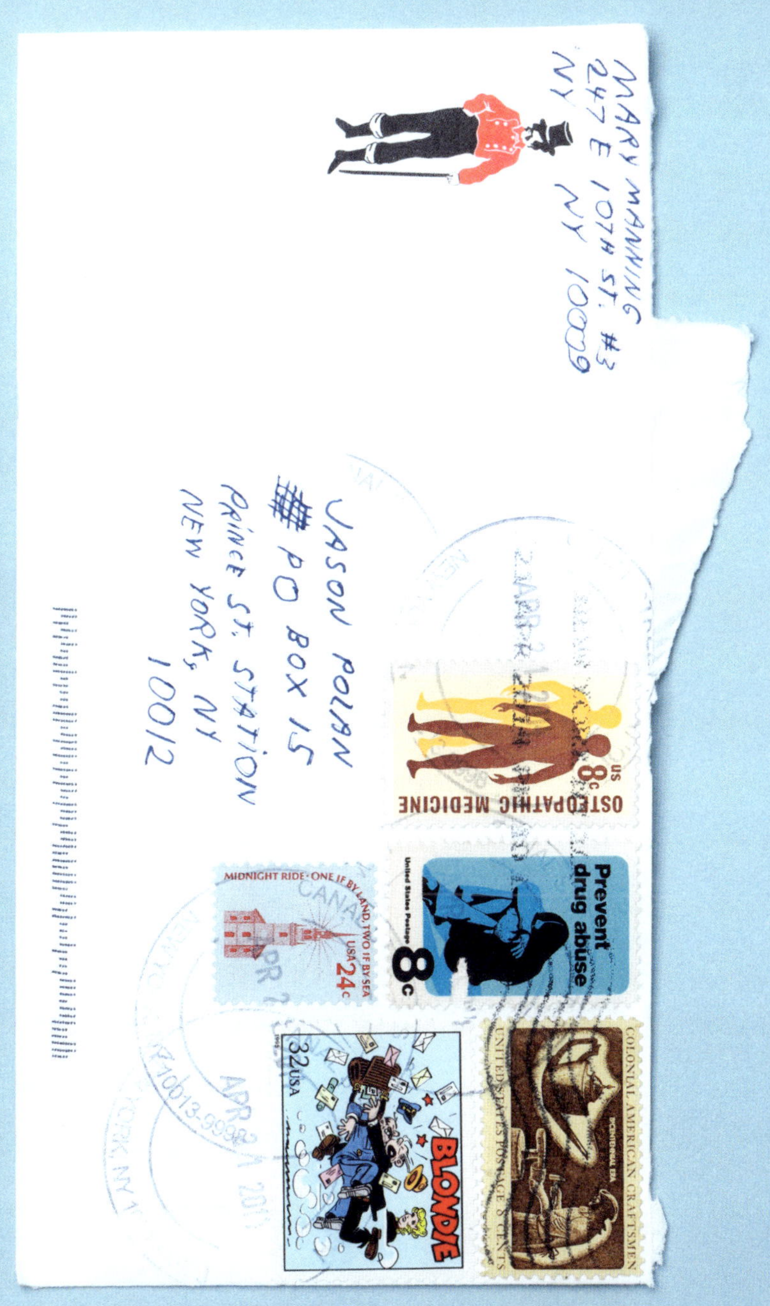
MARY MANNING
247 E 10TH ST. #3
NY NY 10009
JASON POLAN
PO BOX 15
PRINCE ST. STATION
NEW YORK, NY
10012
US 8c
OSTEOPATHIC MEDICINE
Prevent drug abuse
United States Postage 8c
MIDNIGHT RIDE · ONE IF BY LAND, TWO IF BY SEA
USA 24c
COLONIAL AMERICAN CRAFTSMEN
UNITED STATES POSTAGE 8 CENTS
BLONDIE
32USA

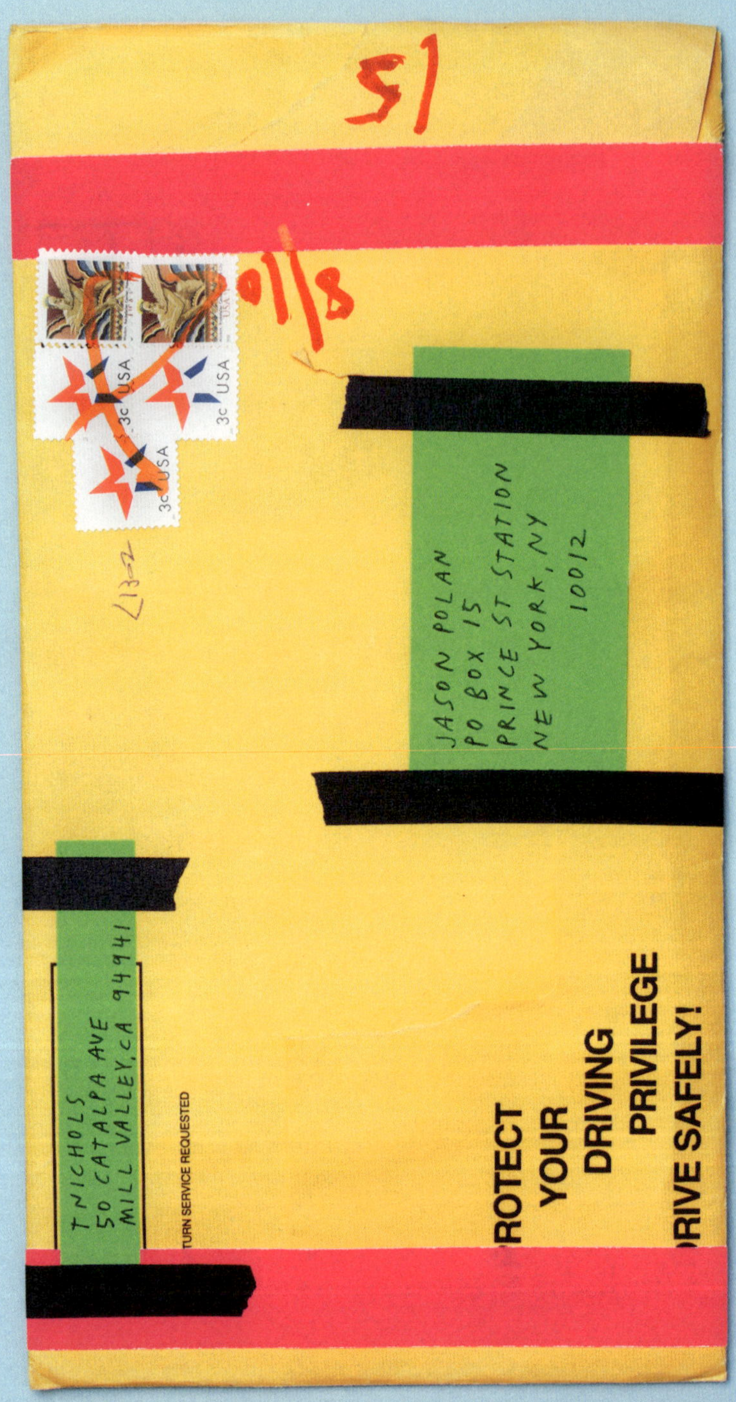
51
JASON POLAN
PO BOX 15
PRINCE ST STATION
NEW YORK, NY
10012
T NICHOLS
50 CATALPA AVE
MILL VALLEY, CA 94941
TURN SERVICE REQUESTED
ROTECT
YOUR
DRIVING
PRIVILEGE
RIVE SAFELY!

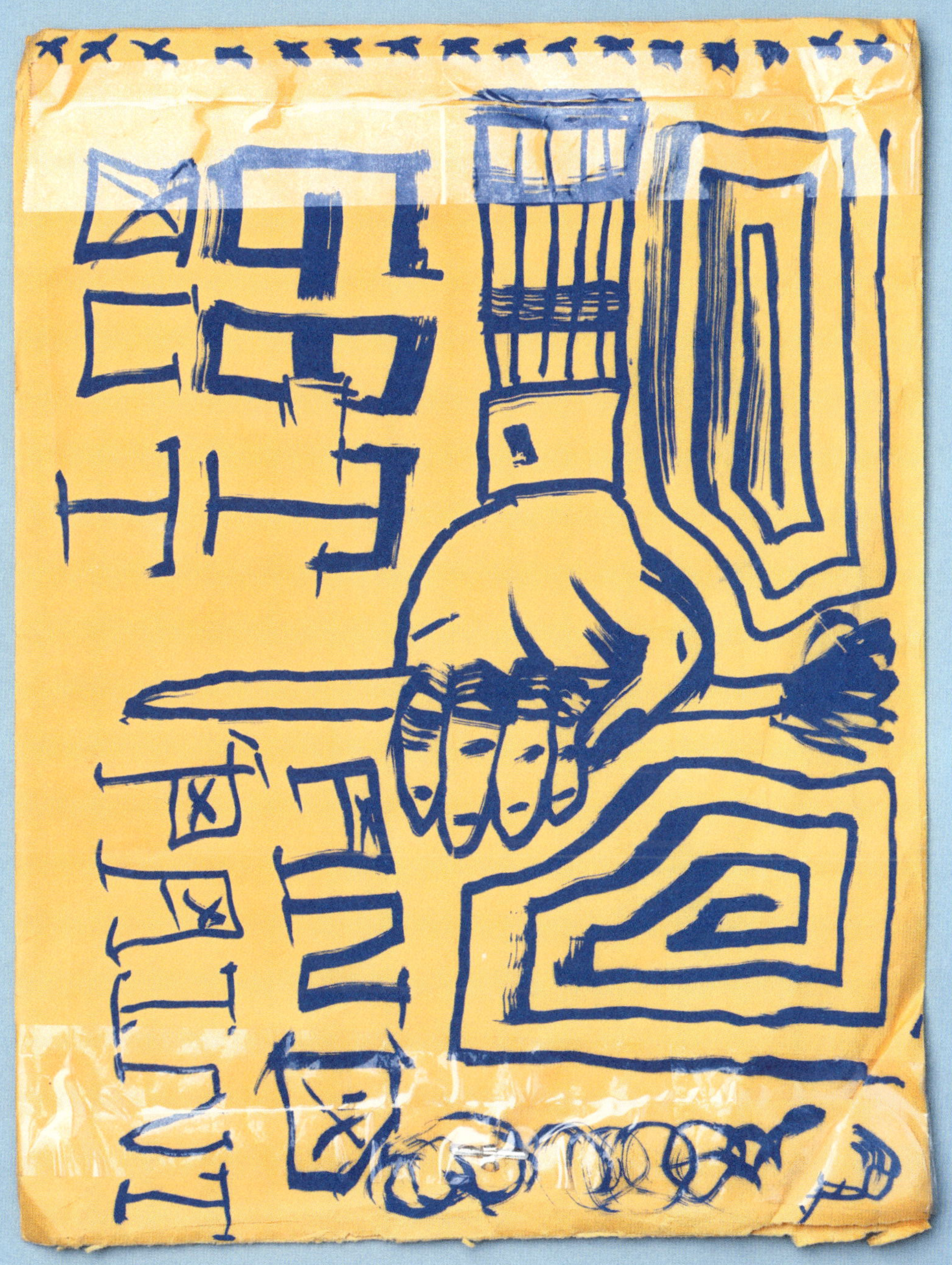

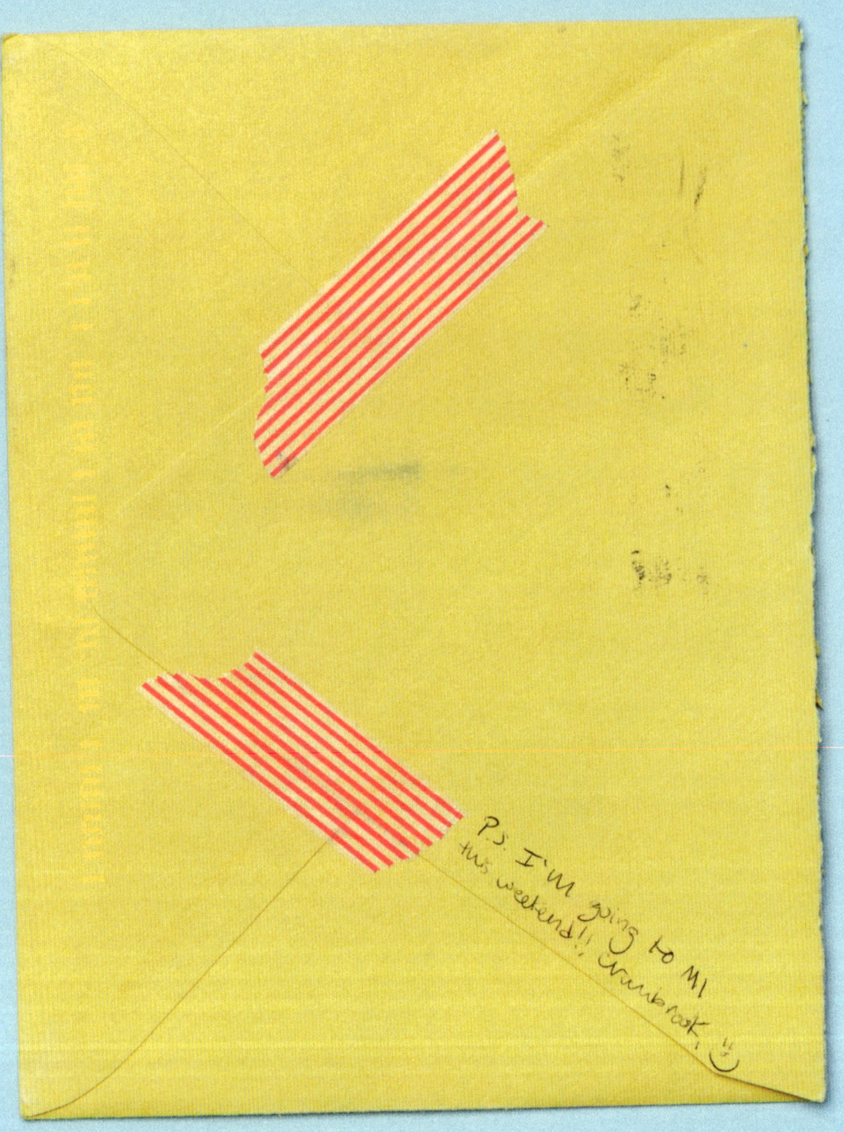
P.S. I'm going to MI
this weekend!! Cranbrook, :)

Hi, hi, hi. I have been thinking about you often and wonder how often you dream you are Spiderman and if Spiderman has been helpful to think about as you deal with cancer ("deal" is the wrong word).

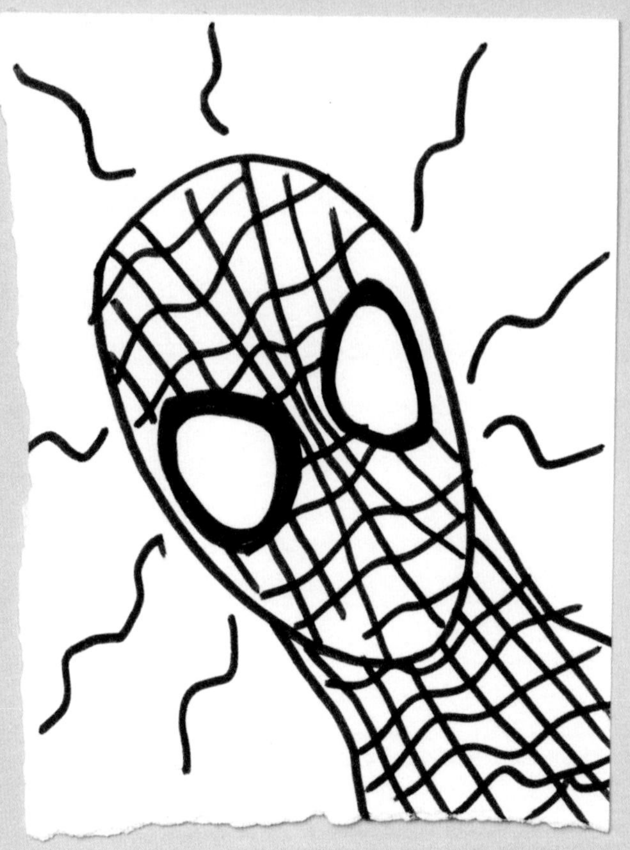

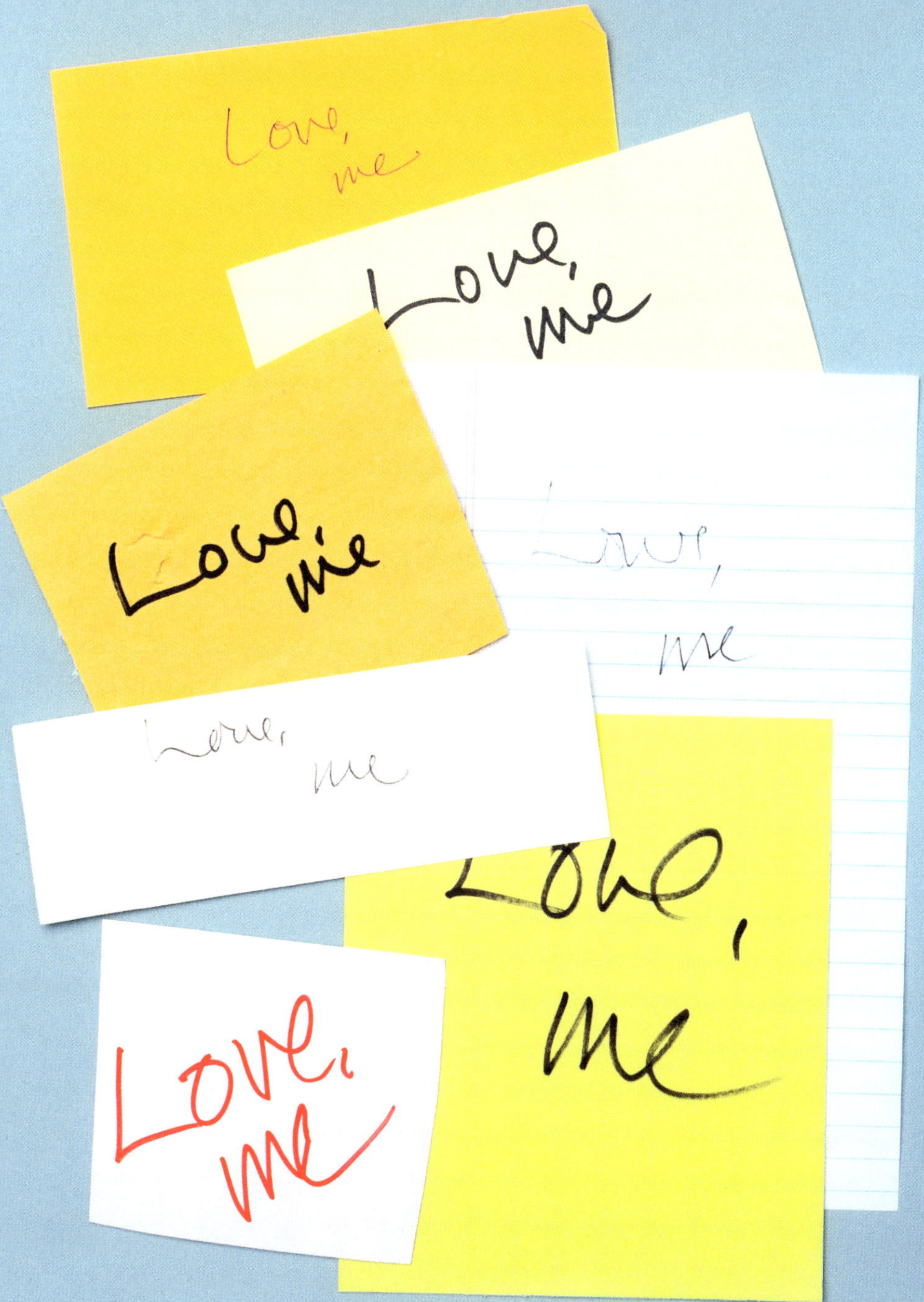

Love,
me

Love,
me

Love,
me

Love,
me

Love,
me

Love,
me

Love,
me

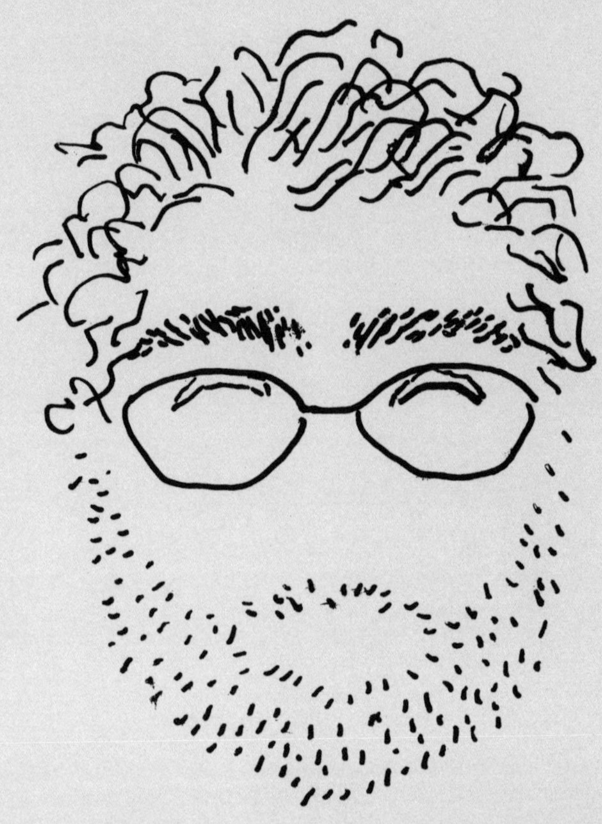

ELEMENTS OF YOUR FACE THAT
I REMEMBER

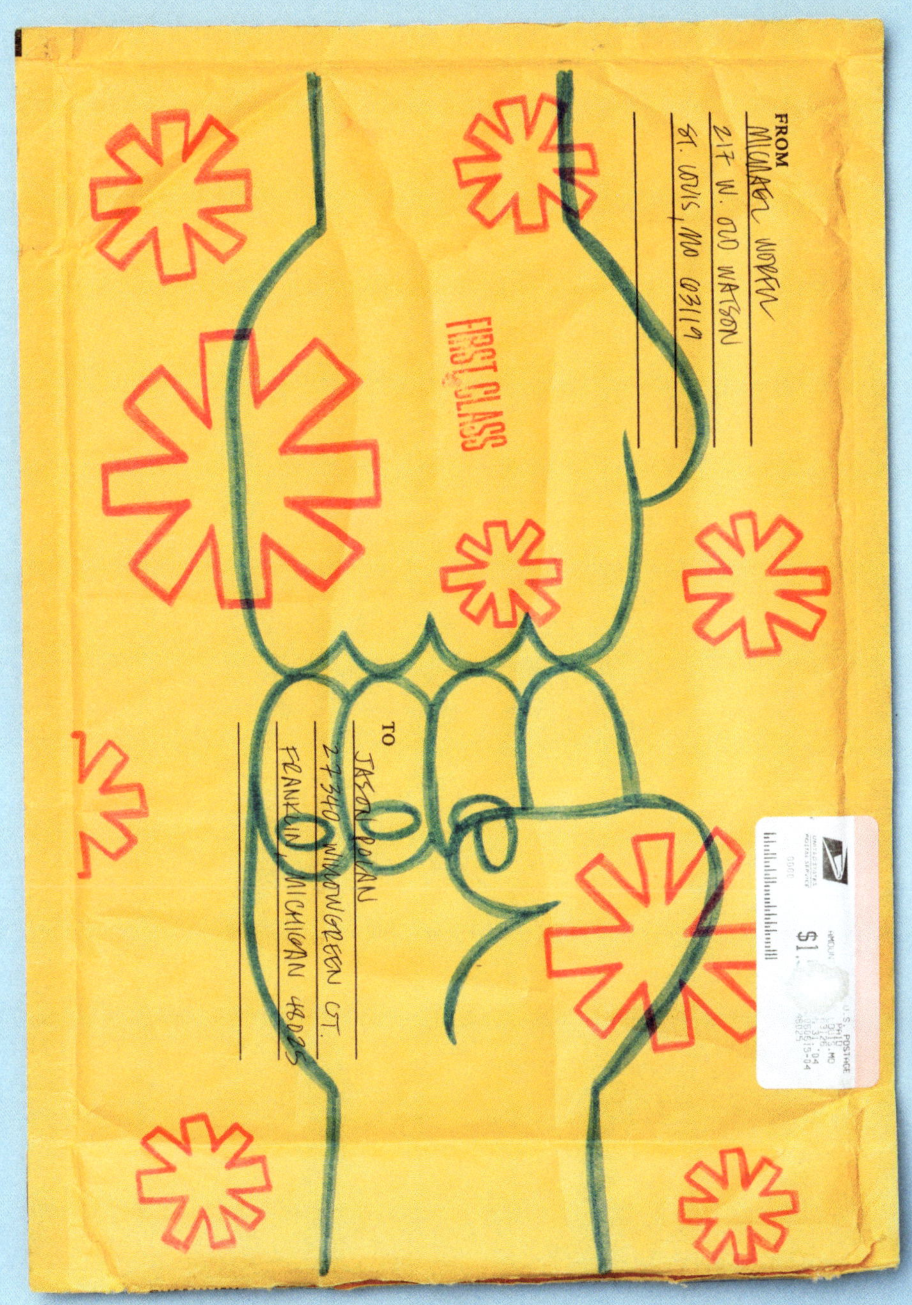
FROM
FIRST CLASS
TO

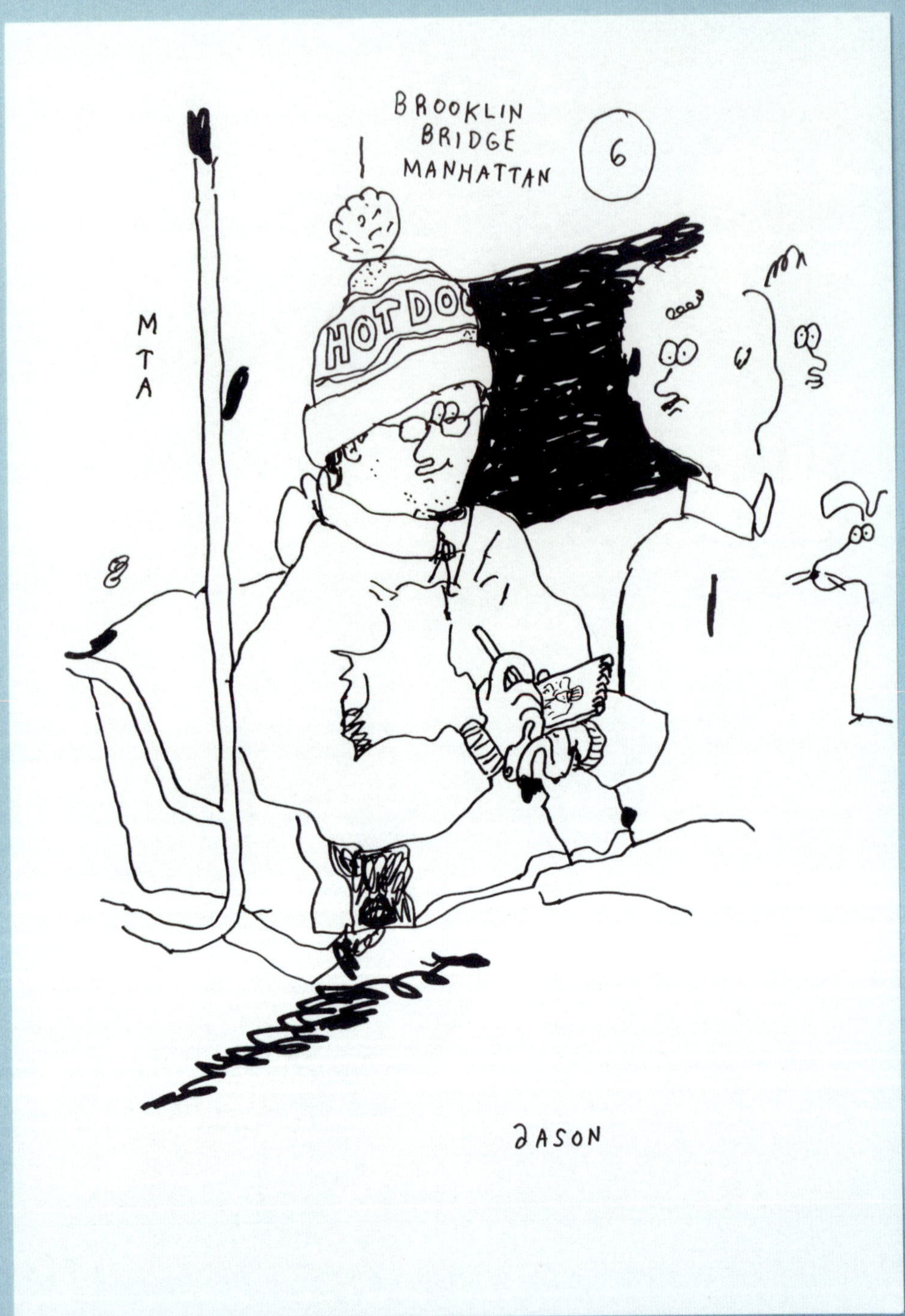
BROOKLIN
BRIDGE
MANHATTAN
6
MTA
HOTDOG
JASON

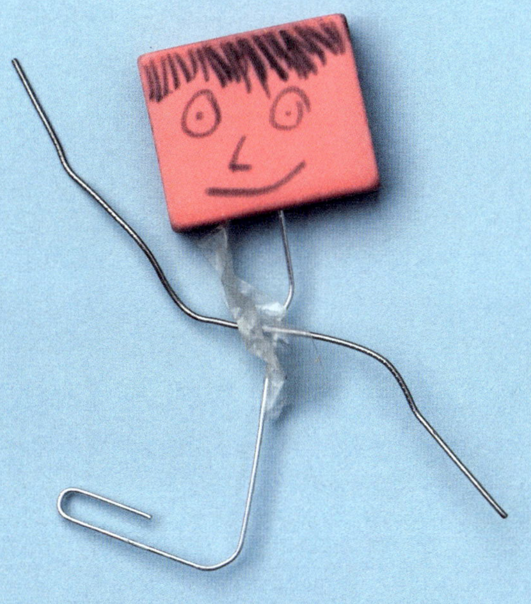

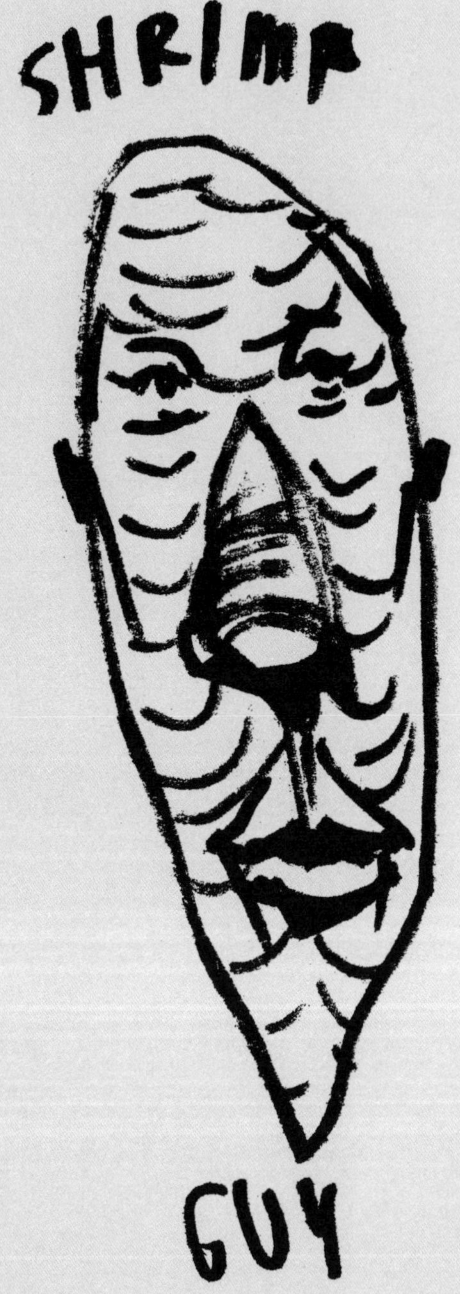
SHRIMP
GUY

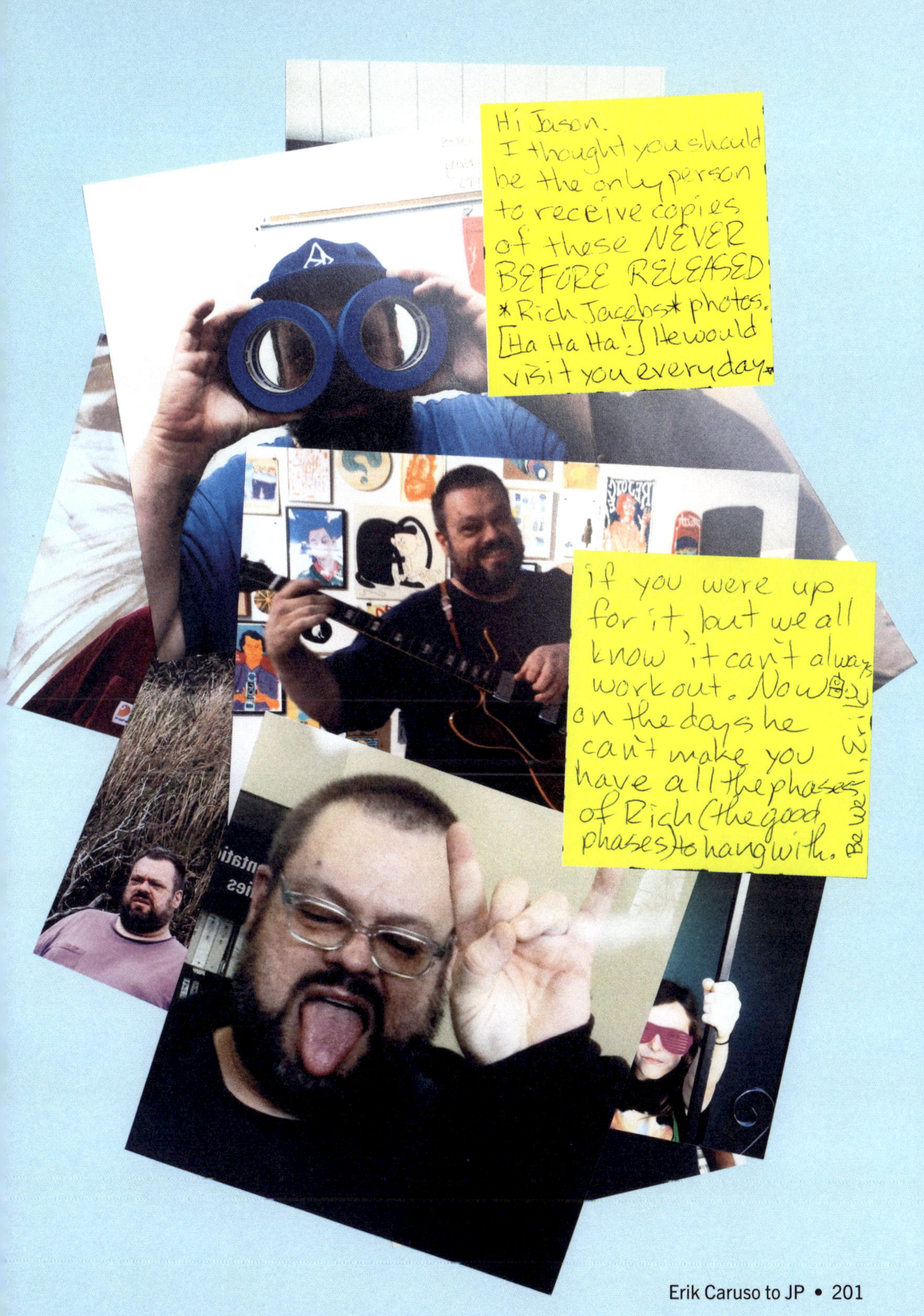
Hi Jason.
I thought you should be the only person to receive copies of these NEVER BEFORE RELEASED *Rich Jacobs* photos. [Ha Ha Ha!] He would visit you everyday*
if you were up for it, but we all know it can't always work out. Now on the days he can't make you have all the phases of Rich (the good phases) to hang with.
Be Well,

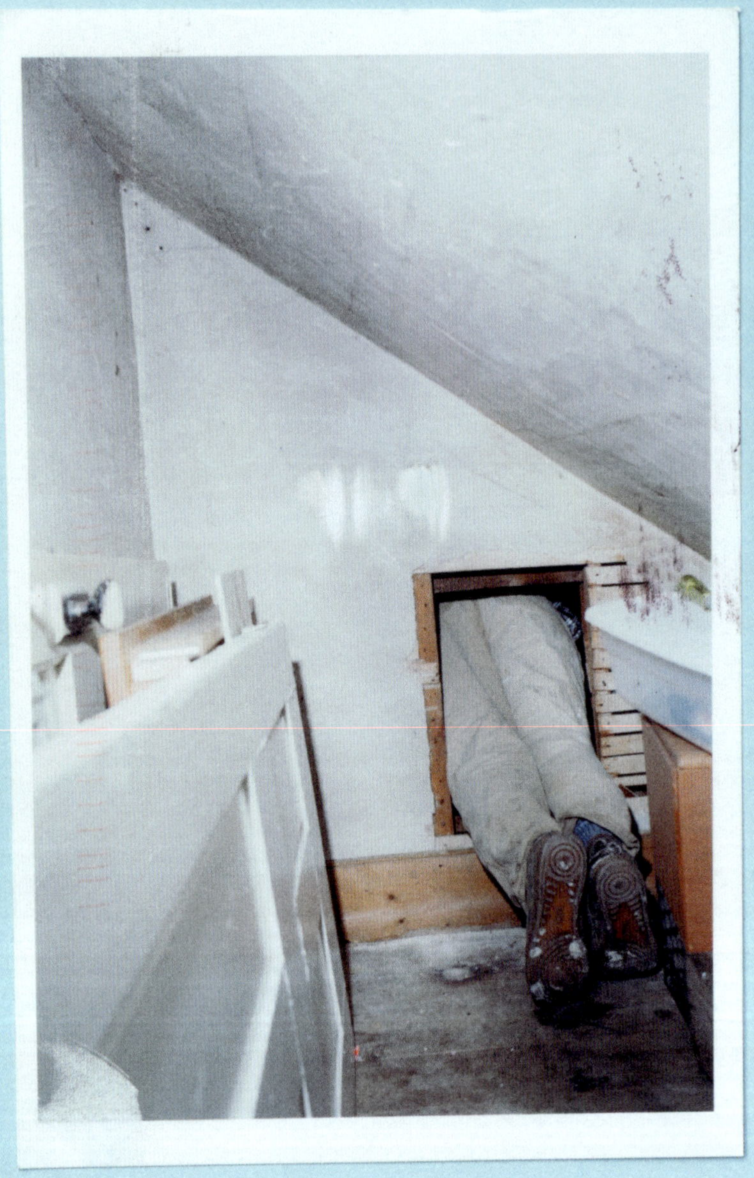

One
thing about time is
it is the thief of itself again —

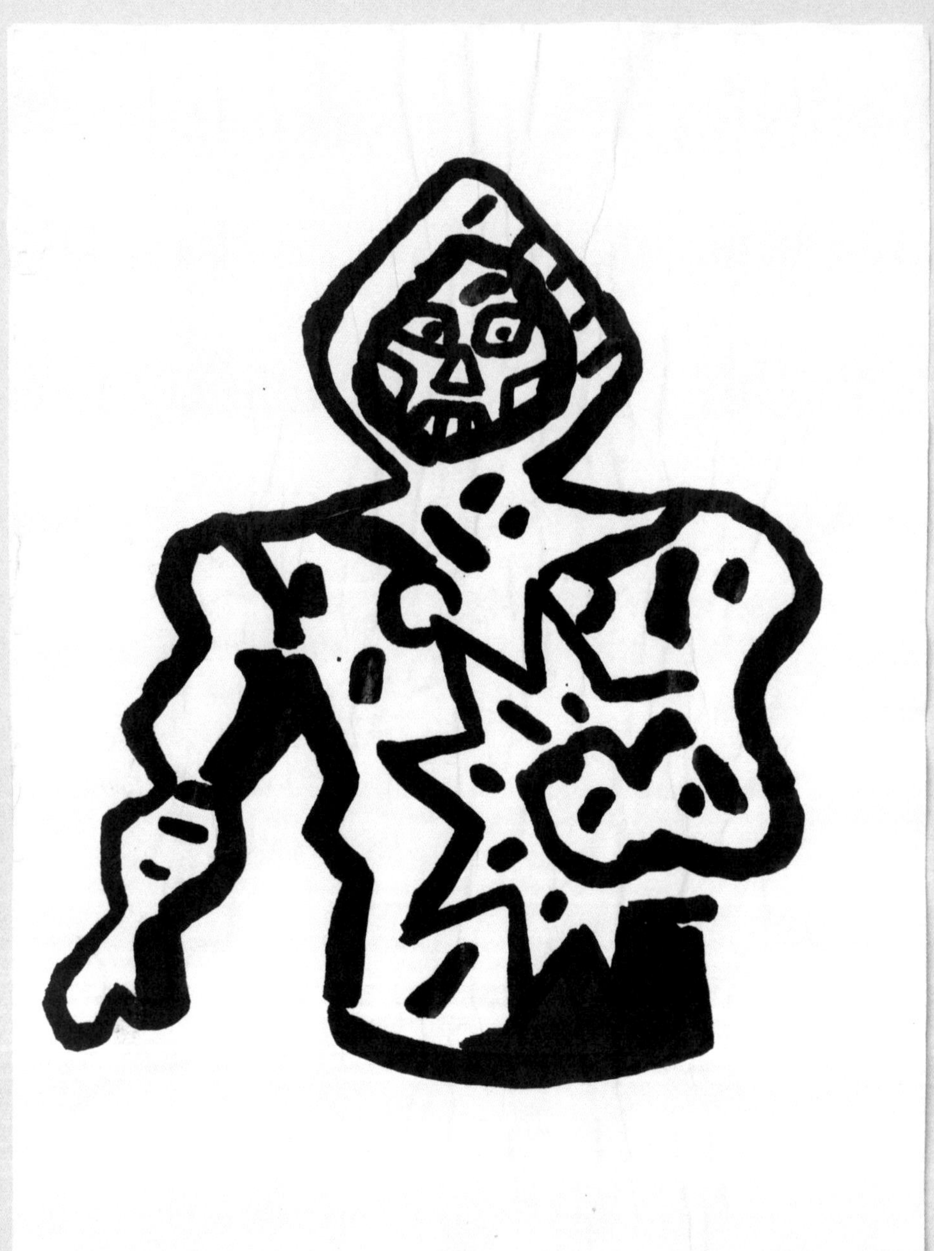

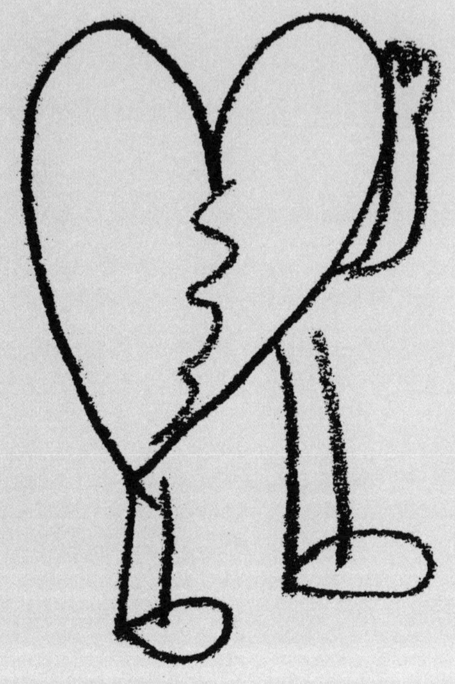

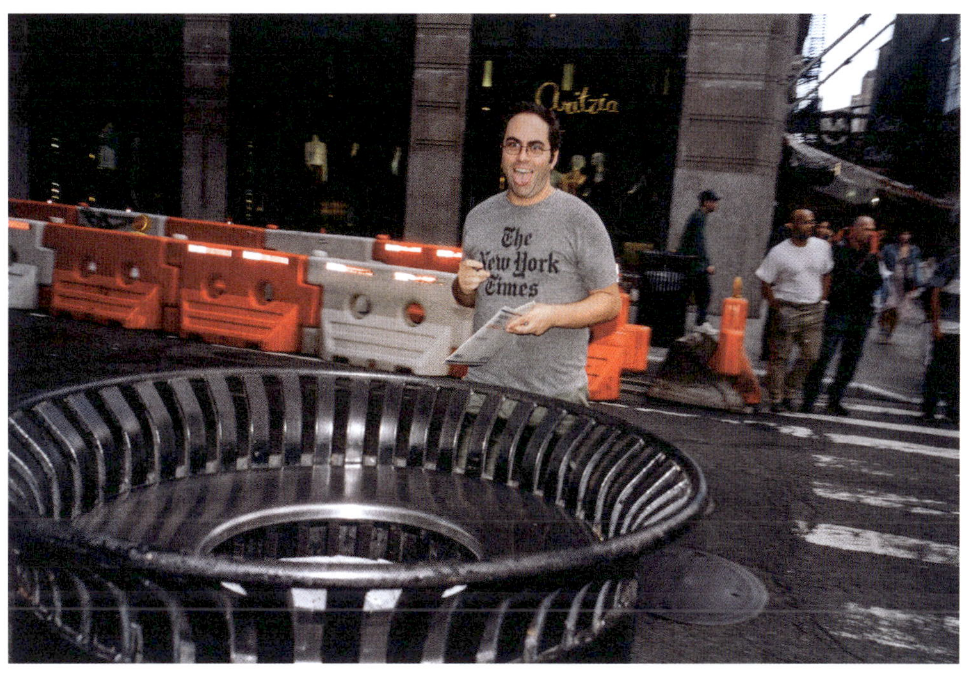

Jason Polan spotted in SoHo on 9/9/17 holding a sketchbook, pen, and USPS envelope.

NOTES

8. JP: *Advertisement for sending someone mail.* The New Yorker *2-16-2015 page 63. Edition size: 1,025,000. Price: $7.99.*

17. Jason sent me this large, sharpied envelope after he came to Chicago on a Warby Parker gig. He'd stuffed it full of his many projects, zines, and ephemera as a thank you for showing him around the library where I worked and spending an afternoon on a long, wandering walk. I'm so grateful it wasn't stolen from my front porch… Jason had a lot of faith in people and USPS. — *Nancy Ford*

21. Ha! Wow, that was so so long ago, a real blast from the past! I wrote Jason at the very baby stages of my career when I cold called (or mailed) any illustrator I admired and envied. He was certainly one of them and I wish I still had the mail he sent in return but it's probably long gone. — *Iris Gottlieb*

26. Jason was a prolific pen pal and a wonderful friend. We met in 2006, a few years after I moved to New York. We used to draw a lot at restaurants nearby his house together.
— *Robin Cameron*

27. Matt [Even] & I had a small chocolate company. (It was really just an excuse to make things and collaborate with friends.) Jason came over on a snowy morning to paint some custom chocolate wrappers, and made this drawing of us with the leftover watercolors. — *Mary Matson*

30. Frankly, I can't remember what's under the post-it, but please don't tell me (and maybe don't look if you haven't already).
— *Eva Rogers*

35. To read a postcard from Jason today is a little like getting it in the mail all over again. He is not here with me, which is why he sent a piece of mail in the first place. The mail brings us together across the miles, across the years, and now across the veil. To act so spontaneously: Tell a friend when you are thinking of them, tell them you love them, make it real with something they can hold and treasure. — *Eva Rogers*

36. On an average Saturday afternoon, my husband Will and I were pal-ing around the city looking for an adventure when Jason posted something to the gram about leaving a 6-toed foot drawing a few books deep on a front table at The Strand (classic Jason). We hopped on citi bikes and Great Race-d our way over. We felt like champions, bought a frame and placed it proudly on our mantle, never telling Jason, knowing he'd come over one day and love the wink-wink.
— *Christina Tosi*

40. When I worked at *The New York Times Magazine*, there were times I'd stay late at the office waiting for the magazine proofs. I recall writing these during that time, practicing my cursive to pass the hours.
— *Stacey Baker*

43. Jason always had a pen in hand and a notebook in the pocket. On gallery walks together, he would bust out his notebook and draw while we shuffled around and talked. It was very casual. He made drawing out in the world normal. We loved David Hockney. I remember we had just missed him at some gallery opening. A few years later Jason sent this to me when he finally got to catch Hockney and wanted to share it with me.
— *Mary Matson*

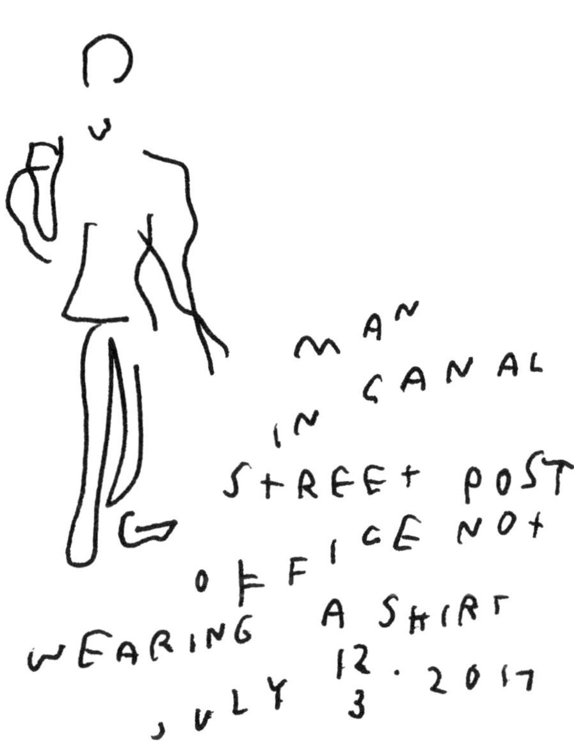
MAN
IN CANAL
STREET POST
OFFICE NOT
WEARING A SHIRT
JULY 12.3 2017

44. I really adored Jason as a friend. We lived in the same neighborhood in NYC for years and years. I probably ran into him on the street out and about more so than most but it was so Jason that way. And my day would change, certainly for the better sometimes, and we'd take an unexpected walk and talk together. Where would I run into him the most? (Besides Prince Street Pizza haha) The post office in Tribeca on Canal Street. I was aware of his love for mail and that was something we shared. Stamps too. I have texts where we share photographs of stamps. The last place I saw and spoke to Jason was inside of that same post office and the last time I was in New York I saw someone had his photo printed and taped to the outside wall. — *Samantha Stoecker (aka Sami Kitty)*

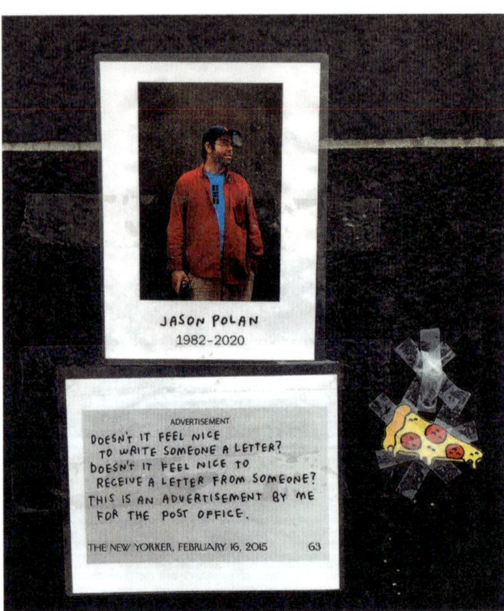

— 01/31/20, outside Canal Street post office
Photo by Gordon Stevenson aka BVF

46. I drew that bat at a time in which Gordon [Stevenson aka BVF] and I were dating and experimenting with silly airbrush art. BVF and I would mail things to Jason back and forth regardless of living so close... Postcards and care packages with fun things like Charlie Brown crayons and baseball cards. Besides his drawings, I also loved Jason's view on life. I too could see a smiley face in a puddle for example and not many people take the time to notice that kind of thing. But he did. And more than that, he would document it. Instagram is such a love hate for me but his Instagram was a real treasure.
— *Samantha Stoecker (aka Sami Kitty)*

50. # 108 from "The Drawing Project"
https://thedrawingproject.blogspot.com

52. I was at my desk at work when Jason called me from a souvenir shop in Florida, where he was on his annual pilgrimage to spring training with his parents. We were talking about a project when he interjected and asked if he should buy a puka shell bracelet. I replied that if he was asking, he had clearly already decided to get it. And then he asked what color he should get. I was not very helpful. About a week later this bracelet showed up on a card that just said "went with purple." — *Lauri London Freedman*

57. Jason and I did some collaborative drawings, including a whole bunch over 3 days in Jen Bekman's old gallery on Spring Street. He would draw something, or I would, and then we'd switch and add to it. He drew the little animal, I added the horizon line, and then he added the jet fires under the feet. (While this was not sent through the mail, I am still including it.) — *Jane Mount*

58. We went to galleries together a lot. It was a great place to catch up and look at work. This is now a souvenir of all the fun we had running around the city. — *Mary Matson*

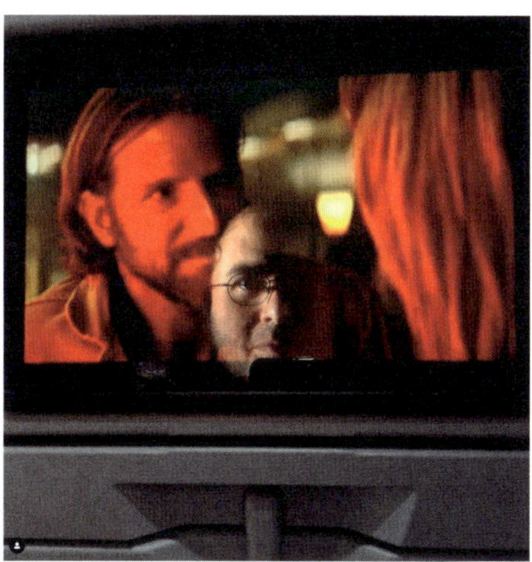

— from JP's Instagram on 03/08/19:
Isn't it weird I was in this movie?!!?

59. I can't say for certain if this drawing is on a Taco Bell napkin, but it would make a good story! — *Nancy Ford*

63. From JP's Instagram on 10/19/19:
I posted a guy at the post office the other day wearing this patch on his uniform and I said I wanted it here on Instagram and someone commented I should look at eBay so I did and found one for $5 including shipping which didn't make sense (didn't seem like the kind of thing I could just buy), so I had one about four days later. About three days after that I got a second one, randomly in the mail, from someone named Caroline [Bjork] *(Caroline, I am sending you something back) which was such an oddly pleasant surprise. Even in a fairly minor seeming thing, sometimes it is hard for me to handle the generosity in the world.*

65. Jason used to put drawings in protective cases. He was obsessed with baseball card-like sleeves, anything that would protect his work. I think this came from his love of comic books and collecting. — *Robin Cameron*

66. This is from a series of prints Jason made with a heart-shaped potato dipped in paint. I bought it for my partner on Valentine's day. — *Andrew Leland*

68. Jason was one of our regular artist friends. He often stopped by Dashwood and just chatted with us or started drawing during the signing events. I think I got close to him after I stopped by Lele Saveri's Newsstand in the Brooklyn subway in 2015. We always said to each other, "We shall work really hard this year, but let's slow down next year." It was a joke since we both knew we would not slow down or become lazy ever... So we used to laugh with each other as workaholic friends. I miss saying that to him. — *Miwa Susuda*

73. # 247 from "The Drawing Project"
https://thedrawingproject.blogspot.com

74. The best thing JP ever sent me was a giant blue hand, which currently lives in my garage. I don't know why he sent this, or how he got USPS to do it. — *Alec Soth*

78. My drawing of "spaghetti" Righetti that I mailed to JP. He had drawn Righetti during one of our drawing sessions in SF and I sent him this in response. While he was known to have Taco Bell Drawing Club in NY, we had our own secret drawing spots in SF/OAK, like at a subpar cafe in the Mission where we drank Italian sodas and drew for hours. There was a Mediterranean spot on Piedmont Ave, a Jimmy John's in a mall in SF, my home, etc. My last memory of Jason was him surprising me at my studio window with falafels. — *James Sterling Pitt*

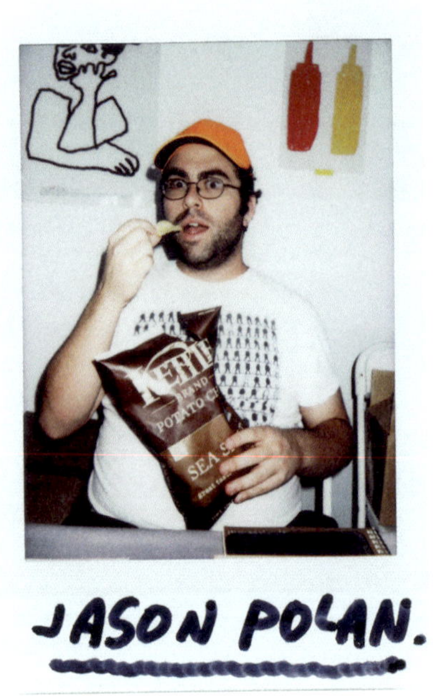

212 • Polaroid by Noah Lyon (signed by JP)

84. I have kept so many things from Jason. Among them, not pictured here, I have a laminated card that reads, simply, "Eva. Hope you are doing something fun. Love, Jason." I'm reminded every day that I really should be doing something fun. — *Eva Rogers*

115. Jason wrote my name for my mailbox, and I loved seeing it every day.
— *Stacey Baker*

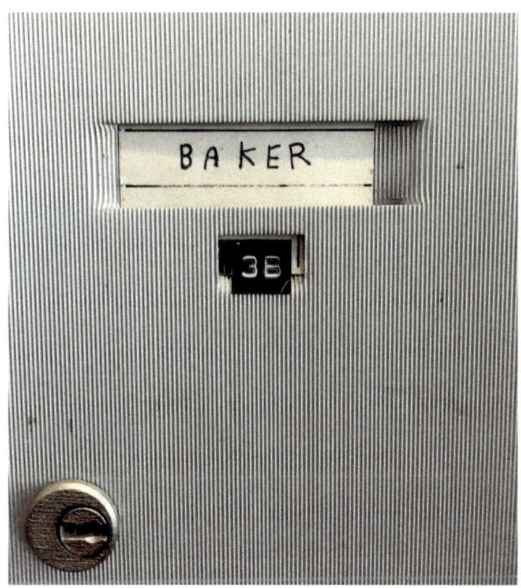

118. My son scribbled out Snoopy's face; the only way my son would draw when he was a toddler was with me, taking turns scribbling. I wanted him to do some art and now he's a towering baseball player, which Jason would have loved. — *Elaine Bleakney*

122. Jason sent me this note with just my name. (He called me by my last.)
— *Jane Mount*

130. # 126 from "The Drawing Project"
https://thedrawingproject.blogspot.com

135. I remember sending this — a cardboard puppet I screened in 2006. It was a pivotal time for me and I'd given up on the idea of being an artist. Jason inspired me to keep going! And validated my work and had such a sincerity that was both serious and playful. It touched me seeing he'd kept it all those years. We finally met in person at a Taco Bell in New York just months before he passed in December of 2019. — *Sean "Purl" Samoheyl*

140. The last thing Jason sent us, in the fall before he died, was this portrait of us as a family, as owls. This is an old family eponym. My grandfather, Oscar, was always The Old Owl. I call my father now The Old Owl. Someday that will be me, I hope. — *Fritz Swanson*

145. When I visited New York, Jason and I would make a drawing at Taco Bell for Stefan [Marx] (or sharpie a face on a tortilla chip).
— *Nancy Ford*

148. The ultimate Jason signature of approval —14th Street TB over a slew of tacos and friends on a random midday afternoon. I remember thinking this is what living life is all about. I keep it in my wallet despite TSA's frequent reminders that it does not double as an acceptable form of ID. — *Christina Tosi*

153. Abstract painting over Wet Paint sign (a small series I think, each different). In his old apartment, Jason had a Wet Paint sign on the wall that stayed there. — *Hans Seeger*

154. This is an (erased) note Jason sent me as a thank you for a giant eraser with an elephant on it I had sent him. — *Hans Seeger*

155. A $13 bill featuring Millard Fillmore, 13th President of the United States, drawn by JP, and letter pressed by Fritz Swanson.
— *Jason Fulford*

162. This must have been a mail trade from a very long time ago. Probably 2006 or so. I still find 9"x12" envelopes filled with things like that from him. I think he had 36 hours in our 24 hour days. — *Derek Erdman*

169. When Jason thought of you he would let you know; he would mark the moment with a drawing, a postcard, a snipping from the world around him that reminded him of you. He was always keeping the wires between us live in this way — between himself and each of his friends. — *Eva Rogers*

170. Jason knew about my fascination for aviation, airlines and planes, and he always sent me photos from airports he traveled to. A few days later I'd have an envelope with a few plane drawings in my mailbox. — *Stefan Marx*

171. Jason and I worked on a project when I was in India where he made me a flip book and it kinda started our mutual elephant romance. I received many over the years but this one felt very special. — *Melanie Flood*

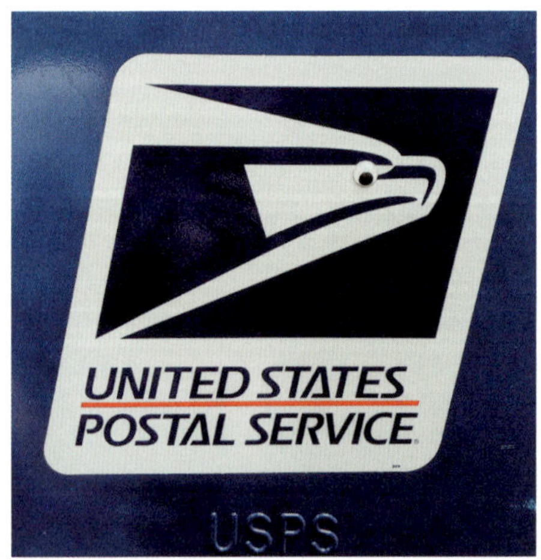

— from JP's Instagram on 06/26/19

---

172. Jason was a kind and generous friend with an appetite for life. He posted this ink drawing in September, 2019. I admired it and he gave it to me. That's how he rolled.
— *Richard McGuire*

173. I had not met Jason. He emailed and asked if we could do a drawing trade. I said sure, and not knowing him, asked what he liked. He emailed back very fast: BATMAN.
—*Tamara Shopsin*

176. Jason was visiting my studio in Brooklyn. I had a pair of Batman 3-D glasses & he really liked them. I tried to give them to him, but he did not want to take them, 'cause I had told him earlier that my son liked them. Later I wrote a letter and sent him these homemade Batman glasses I made.
— *Marcel Dzama*

181. Even tho we saw each other all the time (I lived across the street from the Blick he went to everyday) we sent each other mail constantly — I often sent him scraps and garbage and sketches my kids left around.
— *Peter Meehan*

190. My first interaction with Jason was purchasing via email (for like $10) a life-sized portrait of me based on my given height and (maybe?) a photo, which arrived rolled in a tube days later. We got together to look at art anytime we were both in the same city. He was the very best version of the art world.
— *Tucker Nichols*

199. [Submission to a contest Jason proposed to a middle school class: *Make a 1-minute Art Piece*] My art is called Lil' Larry. I have one older brother and one older sister. I like to play tennis, baseball, soccer, football and basketball. I am in sixth grade. I hope I win! — *Lawrence Chan*

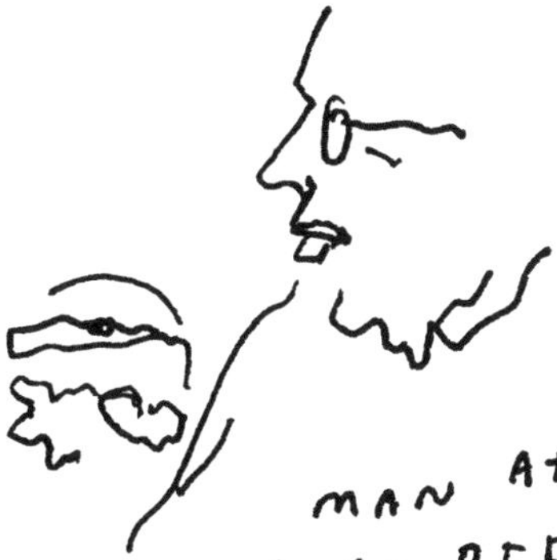

MAN AT THE
POST OFFICE
(SUPERVISOR)
WITH A FISH
TANK!
SOMETIMES HE
PLAYS MUSIC
FOR IT
70TH STREET
12.7.2019

I WAS
RUSHING
A LITTLE
TOO MUCH.

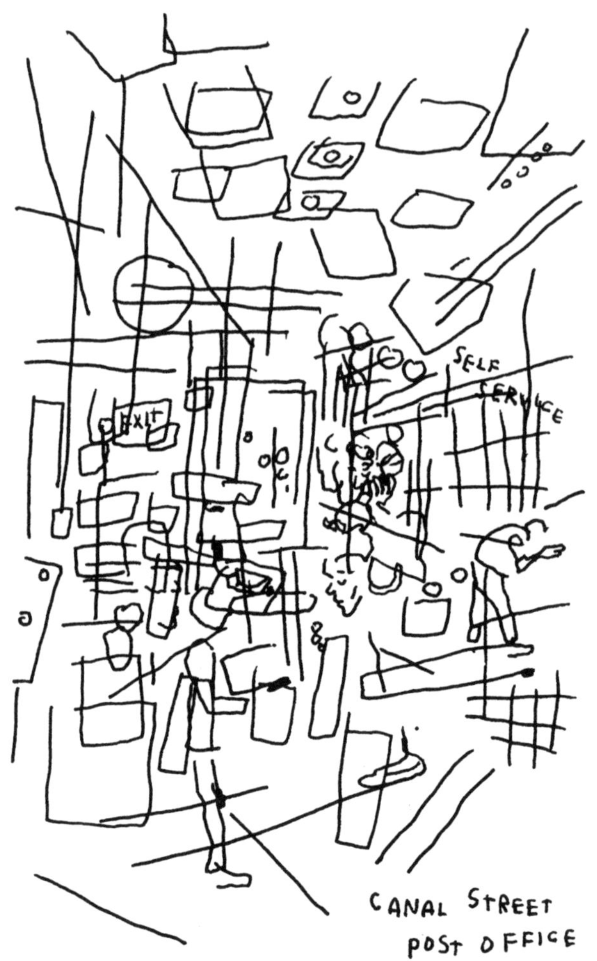
EXIT
SELF SERVICE
CANAL STREET
POST OFFICE

207. Early Dec '19 Jason texted "what's your mailing address you ding dong," about a mystery trade he'd proposed, but I was in the chaos of moving apartments and I got the numbers wrong. Our friendship was so sweet in that era and we talked about probably being cousins as I sent off a crate of Biscoff cookies and Bic pens (a joke that I can't imagine landed) without attribution. I also made Jason a big yellow book of food-on-the-street pics that was delivered to my apartment a few days after he died — same day I discovered the address error. I was devastated. Did all the legwork I could think of to try to recover an envelope, but in the end I just talked myself into believing that he never got the chance to send it. That 'ding dong' text came Dec 3. On the 8th he sent a photo from a gallery where I was showing some work, but I was out of town. He wished me a good trip and said to hurry home. That was the last time I heard from Jason. — *Daniel Arnold*

221. Note found in an envelope from "DJ" that said: *Three Gifts for Jason*.

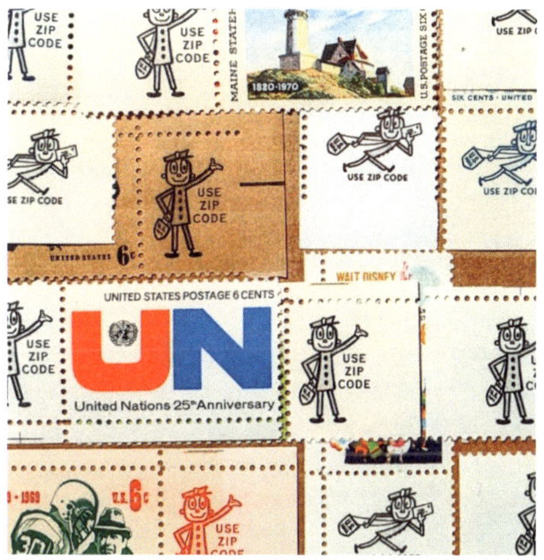

— from JP's Instagram on 01/18/19:
Mr. Zip forever

[In 1963, to encourage the use of the new five digit ZIP (Zone Improvement Plan) Code for improved mail processing, Postmaster General J. Edward Day introduced "Mr. ZIP."]

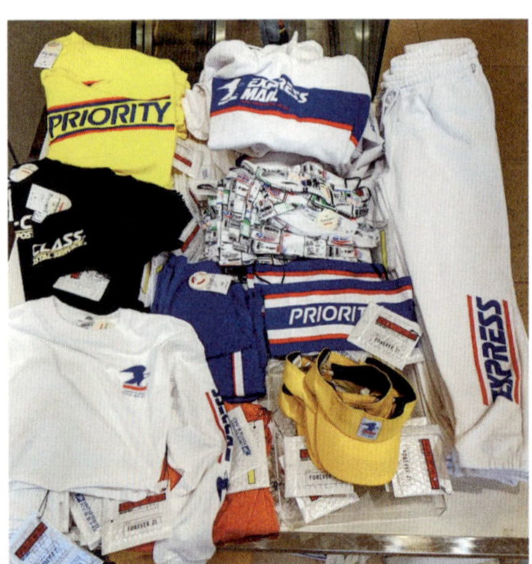

— from JP's Instagram on 03/27/19:
I don't mean to be throwing negative vibes all over but this is such a crazy missed opportunity. They are cut really weird and some of it looks cool but all just feels confusing to me I FEEL LIKE I AM 103 LOOKING AT THIS STUFF.

Thank you
thank you
thank you

14-CARROT NOTE

ACKNOWLEDGMENTS

A big thank you to Jason Polan's friends who helped organize the hundreds of boxes he left behind in Michigan. And to everyone who contributed to this book for sharing these mementos and trusting us with them.

Regarding the mail that Jason saved, we have attempted to contact everyone who appears in the book. If you see something of yours here, and we did not find you, please reach out to Printed Matter.

Thank you to Lauri London Freedman, who instigated this project and helped in countless ways to shepherd it into being.

To Lesley Martin and Keith Gray at Printed Matter for their input and guidance.

To Tamara Shopsin, my second pair of eyes.

And to Jane Polan for her support and continuing efforts to keep Jason's spirit alive.

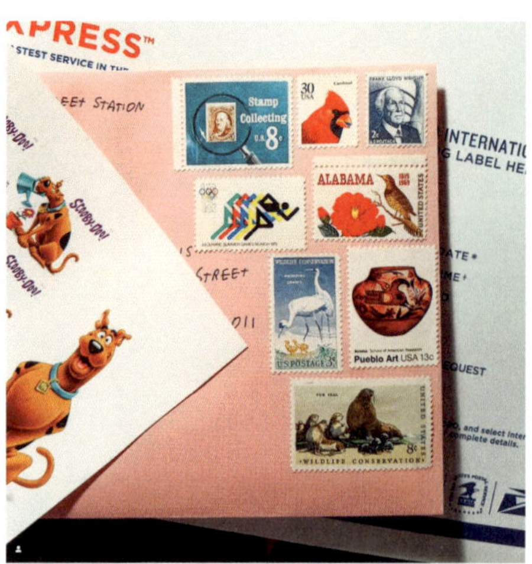

— from JP's Instagram on 01/15/19:
Reminder: the price to send a letter (buy a first class stamp) is going up on the 27th. It is 50¢ now and will be 55¢. Buy some forever stamps! Mail people stuff! Also, as I was licking these I was thinking about how people under the age of 30 or so have maybe never tasted the back of a stamp. I don't think this is such a big deal, anything to really dwell on, but I was thinking about it.

JASON POLAN was an American artist celebrated for his observational sketches of everyday life in New York City. A graduate of the University of Michigan with degrees in Art & Design and Anthropology, Jason moved to New York in 2004, where he became known for his *Every Person in New York* project—a series of over 50,000 quick, real-time drawings of city residents published in two volumes (2015 and 2021). His work appeared in *The New Yorker*, *Esquire*, *McSweeney's*, and *The New York Times*, and his books and zines have been collected by the Metropolitan Museum of Art, the Whitney Museum of American Art, American Museum of Natural History, University of Michigan, Columbia University, and Yale University.

A near-complete set of Jason's books and zines are in the collection of Museum of Modern Art, New York, where he also drew every piece of art on view twice and published these drawings under the title *The Every Piece of Art in the Museum of Modern Art Book* (2005 and 2009). This project was further immortalized in the 2015 exhibition *Messing with MoMA: Critical Interventions at the Museum of Modern Art, 1939–Now*.

The founder of the Taco Bell Drawing Club, Jason built community with the same sincerity that defined his art. In his short but prolific career, he produced a remarkable body of work, guided by a steadfast belief that inclusivity and an unwavering commitment to kindness through art are essential to a better world.

1. a nurse holding a Big Gulp and wearing cherry-red glasses

2. An orange traffic barrier named "Pizziotti"

3. One hundred and eleven tiny saffron blossoms in a glass bottle embossed with the number 100

p.s. How did you get the Po Box number '15'? Are you 100 years old or something?

PS. THIS IS MY FIRST FAN LETTER TO ANYONE EVER, SO YEAH... IF IT LOOKS STRANGE OR WHATEVER WE CAN BLAME THAT I'M JUST A ROOKIE AT THIS!

PS - My apologies if this envelope smells like cat food.

FRAGILE
FRAGILE

DO NOT BEND